MOUNT ATHOS

Essays on Religion, Sw

REV. DAVID WILLIAM PARRY

Edited by Daniele-Hadi Irandoost

ALSO BY DAVID WILLIAM PARRY

Caliban's Redemption

The Grammar of Witchcraft

Cover Art: Haralampi G. Oroschakoff, "Prorok", 1988, Pigment, Paint on Canvas, 220 x 120 cm, Private Collection.

Mount Athos Inside Me: Essays on Religion, Swedenborg and Arts
Rev. David William Parry
Edited by Daniele-Hadi Irandoost
978-0-6484996-7-1

Thema Classification:
QRA (Religion), QRYC (Belief Systems), Q (Philosophy & Religion), ATD (Theatre), AGA (Art History)

MANTICORE PRESS
WWW.MANTICORE.PRESS

Contents

Map of the Peninsula

List of Mount Athos Monasteries

1. Great Lavra. DOS in 963, the feast day of July 5, the day of prep. Athanasius of Athos.
2. Vatopedi. DOS in 972, the feast day of March 25, the day of the Annunciation.
3. Iver. DOS in 976, the feast day of August 15, the day of the Assumption.
4. Hilandar (Serbian). DOS in 1197, the feast day of November 21, the day of the Presentation in the Temple.
5. Dionysiou (St Dionysius). DOS in 1375, the feast day of June 24, the day of the Nativity of St John the Baptist.
6. Kutlumush. DOS at the end of the thirteenth century, the feast day of August 6, the day of the Transfiguration.
7. Pantocrator (Almighty). DOS in 1363, the feast day of August 6, the day of the Transfiguration.
8. Ksiropotam. DOS in the tenth century, the feast day of March 9, the day of the Forty Martyrs of Sebaste, and September 14, the day of the Exaltation of the Cross.
9. Zograf (Bulgarian). DOS in the tenth century, the feast day of April 23, the day of St George.
10. Docheiariou. DOS in the tenth century, the feast day of November 8, the day of the Archangel Michael, and October 14, in honour of BM Skoroposlushnitsa.
11. Caracalla. DOS at the end of the tenth century, the feast day of June 29, the day ann. Peter and Paul.
12. Filofei. DOS in 990, the feast day of March 25, the day of the Annunciation, and August 24 day prep. Cosmas the Aetolian.

13. Simonos. DOS in 1257, the feast day of December 25, the day of the Nativity of Christ, July 22, the day of St Mary Magdalene.

14. St Paul. DOS in the tenth century, the feast day of February 2, the day of Candlemas, July 10 and August 28, the day of St Paul Ksiropotamskogo.

15. Stavronikita. DOS in 1541, the feast day of December 6, the day of St Nicholas.

16. Xenophon (St Xenophon). DOS in the eleventh century, the feast day of April 23, the St George.

17. Gregoriou (St Gregory's). DOS in 1345, the feast day of December 6, the day of St Nicholas.

18. Esphigmenou. DOS in the eleventh century, the feast day of the Assumption day.

19. St Panteleimon (Russian). DOS at the beginning of the tenth century, the feast day of July 27, the day of St Panteleimon.

20. Konstamonitou. DOS in the eleventh century, the feast day of December 27, the day of St Great Martyr Stephen.

A Preface by Bernard Hoose

IN DAVID PARRY'S VIEW, THE HUMAN CONDITION CAN BE understood as a scientific problem that demands analysis, as an act of defiant creativity, or as a dazzling mystery. Now Mount Athos, it seems to me, has a great deal to do with the last mentioned of those three, and not merely because it has been home to a number of Orthodox monasteries for many years. It has become, in many ways, representative of mountains in general and the role they have played in human attempts to relate to mystery. In examining images of Mount Athos in English literature, it seems to me, Parry confronts this very issue. Too often, in their own writings, clerics and theologians have become obsessed with definitions and neat descriptions. The concept of mystery thus necessarily disappears from their pages, even though the writers themselves may well insist that mystery is at the core of their religion. Creative writers, on the other hand, are much freer to use metaphors that open doors and point in certain directions while, at the same time, somehow succeeding in allowing the mysterious to remain mysterious. Having said this, we should, of course, be careful about where we draw our lines. Not all holders of office in organized religions are obsessed with definitions, and some have been among the more remarkable creative writers in English and in other languages. The point has been made, however, and it is an important one. That alone makes a venture such as David Parry's truly worthwhile.

Even a cursory glance at the history of spirituality and religion reveals that, for thousands of years, deserts and mountains have been regarded as special places. That is most certainly the case within the Judeo-Christian tradition. As far as deserts are concerned, at least a part of the explanation lies, no doubt, in the fact that they have a tendency to be deserted places. There is a long history of people retreating to such spots in order to escape from distractions and to be alone with God. Something similar can be said about mountains, but the recorded history of the relationship between these great rocks and God displays other features as well. That much becomes evident when we examine, for instance, the story of the Israelites' wanderings in the wilderness after their escape from Egypt. They had already been in the desert for three months when God spoke to Moses on Mount Sinai. Moses, moreover, had experienced an earlier theophany at Mount Horeb (which, incidentally, many scholars take to be simply Sinai called by a different name). Some centuries later, Gregory of Nyssa wrote his Life of Moses in Greek. In it he makes it abundantly clear that he is not one of those clerics who try to escape from the idea—or awareness—that mystery is where we live and flourish. But there is more to be said. If, the human condition is mystery, to paraphrase Parry, the ground of our being—what we usually call 'God'—must inevitably be mystery, and Gregory is well aware of this. Now Moses, he notes, enters into the darkness on the mountain and there he sees God. Gregory confronts this statement with the declaration in the first letter of St John that no one has ever seen God, but sees no contradiction. When Moses announces that he has seen God in the darkness, says Gregory, he is saying he now sees that the divine is beyond all knowledge and understanding. Darkness, it seems, indicates the invisibility of God, but, more than that, it indicates our inability to understand what God is. Incidentally, some later writers indicated the same impossibility using the metaphor of light rather than darkness – too much light making it impossible for us to see (in the various senses of the verb 'to see').

The theme of darkness is also found, however, in the writings of a man who has been identified by a few names over the centuries but is now usually referred to as Pseudo Dionysius. It is thought by numerous researchers that he was probably a Syrian monk. He too wrote in Greek, and in a piece of work entitled Mystical Theology, he discusses the notion of mystics finding themselves in the darkness of unknowing. In this darkness, he says, although their reasoning powers are inactive, they are united to the wholly unknowable. While knowing nothing, they come to know what is beyond knowing. This, of course, is very mysterious, but a statement about the same sort of thing by a fourteenth-century Englishman is helpful here. The anonymous author of the Cloud of Unknowing was well acquainted with the writings of Pseudo Dionysius, whom he referred to as St Denys, but, in his own presentation of things, he described things rather differently, saying that there is a cloud of unknowing between us and God. There is not merely ignorance, if you like, but an inability to know. Or rather, there is an inability to know through reason. We cannot think God. Like Dionysius, however, the author of The Cloud acknowledges that there is another kind of knowing. It is certain that nobody can think God, but God can be grasped by love. In other words, we can have a relationship with God. We can know the unknowable.

We have moved somewhat, it may seem, from the mountain of Moses and Gregory. In doing so, however, we have identified a connecting thread, or perhaps rather an important line of influence between Eastern Christianity and England – an interesting thought, given the connections that Parry sees between English literature and Eastern Orthodoxy. But let us move on to other mountains – again eastern ones, of course. Moses is not the only Old Testament luminary associated with high places. Another such is the prophet Elijah, who, we are told in three of the gospels, spoke with Jesus, along with Moses, on Mount Tabor. Some centuries before this event, however, two other mountains had played prominent roles in the life of this prophet. They were Mount Carmel and Mount Horeb. For our purposes, it would seem that the latter has the greater importance, because it was there that Elijah experienced a theophany. The location of Horeb, however, is unknown. Carmel, on the other hand, is locatable, and, in the thirteenth century, a group of Christian hermits lived there, inspired, says tradition, by the prophet who had made the mountain famous. They made Carmel their home, and there they dedicated their time to prayer. This, however, was during the time of the Crusades, and violent circumstances eventually made the place no longer suited to the purposes of the hermits. They therefore moved west and adopted a way of life not very different from that of the then newly formed Franciscan and Dominican friars. Among the earliest houses they founded were two in England – one at Hulne, near Newcastle, and another at Aylesford in Kent. Because of their association with the mountain, they came to be called Carmelites, although, in England, they were known for a long time as the White Friars – the Franciscans being called the Grey Friars and the Dominicans the Black Friars.

It was not English White Friars, however, who wrote the most influential literature about Carmel. In the sixteenth century a Spanish Carmelite who is regarded as one of the major poets in the Castilian tongue wrote a mystical piece called Ascent of Mount Carmel. He was Juan de la Cruz, or, as he is better known in English speaking circles, St John of the Cross. This piece of work starts out as a commentary on John's poem On a Dark Night, but goes beyond that to become a treatise on achieving union with God. The Franciscan Saint Bonaventure had earlier written a piece of work entitled simply The Journey of the Mind to God. The notion of climbing a mountain, however, emphasizes the ascetical features of what John has to say about such a journey. The notions of the dark night of the senses and the dark night of the soul, which John develops in this and other works, were, however, prefigured to some extent in Gregory's Life of Moses, where, we are told that God is not contemplated through the senses or any of the usual faculties of the mind. Indeed, we have to rein in these wayward aspects of ourselves. Only then, thus purified, can we attack the mountain. True knowledge of God, he says, is a steep mountain that is difficult to climb. Now John was surely influenced either directly or indirectly by Gregory. I say that the influence may have been indirect because Dionysius and Gregory had already had a very noticeable impact upon other mystical writers with whose works John was no doubt acquainted. As for the impact of John himself upon others, we find in the world of English literature that his influence is most clearly seen, perhaps, in some of the work of

T. S. Eliot – although, perhaps in his case, 'Anglo-American' may be a better label. A much wider sphere of influence is surely indicated, however, in the many references to those 'dark nights' in the writings of others in the English-speaking world, although it may not always be clear that those who have made use of those 'nights' have fully understood what John means when he uses those expressions. In short, the Eastern mystical tradition may have travelled to England by more than one route.

The last mountain to which I shall refer has no name and, according to some biblical scholars, may have been merely a product of the imagination of St Matthew. That, however, does not reduce its importance. What I am referring to is the location of the Sermon on the Mount. This part of Matthew's gospel, say those biblical scholars, does not have the structure of a sermon. They are inclined to think, rather, that the evangelist has gathered together a number of sayings of Jesus, delivered perhaps in various places on various occasions— perhaps more than once—and presented them in the form of a single discourse. The fact that Jesus is presented as speaking on a piece of high ground is important, not as a historical fact (which it may well not be), but because it indicates a link to or comparison with Moses the lawgiver, who received the Ten Commandments on a mountain. Jesus, however, is not merely a new Moses, and not even a new lawgiver whose law replaces that of Moses. He is much more than that. As a former university colleague Tom Deidun put it, Matthew is indicating that Jesus is the law.

A statement like this last one leads us into another aspect of mystery, where Jesus somehow reveals God, and mention of mystery brings us back to that central point about how creative writers deal with that concept. The Sermon on the Mount certainly figures in English literature, but what we are concerned with here is that Mount Athos can in some way take the place of that mount (real or metaphorical), along with the other mountains listed above and what they represent. Looked at in this way, Parry's adventure appears more than worthwhile. He is not unhappy, we know, when others describe him as a pagan. That said, however, he is well versed in Christian theology. It is worth mentioning, moreover, that mystics are often inclined to play down the importance of the differences among religions. Again, in line with some of my earlier comments, I suspect Parry feels that free creative writers find it easier to deal with mystery in general, and perhaps, therefore, the mystery of Athos in particular, than many of those strict adherents of religion who may turn their attention to it. And, of course, let us not forget that Parry is himself a creative writer. So what does English literature make of Athos? And what does Parry make of that? Turn the page, dear reader, and see.

Dr Bernard Hoose
Emeritus Lecturer in Moral Theology (Heythrop College)
Tonbridge 2012

"While the laughter of joy is in full harmony with our deeper life, the laughter of amusement should be kept apart from it. The danger is too great of thus learning to look at solemn things in a spirit of mockery, and to seek in them opportunities for exercising wit."

– *Lewis Carroll*

Opening Poem by Caliban

Don't Love a Poet

At least we can return home at sundown.
At least we will eat our victuals this evening.
At least we will kiss our loved ones asleep.
At the very least, we can feel safe as houses.

Although, as globalisation invades our bodies,
Removing History, Truth and Liberty,
Don't love a poet.
A wordsmith whose eyes simply see
An artificial empathy in bubbling thoughts.
Synthetically produced, of course,
In staccato café's bereft of every critique.

Yet, at least we can return home at sundown.
At least we will eat our victuals this evening.

At least we will kiss our loved ones asleep.
At the very least, we can feel safe as houses.

While refugee's pour past Georgian rooms,
And hotel suits and Embassy parlours.
Oh, don't love a poet.
A penniless heart indignant at regional foods
Grotesquely served by malnourished children.
Crying hellfire through their mumming lips,
Which conceal diaspora's in a house licked clean.

We, however, can return home at sundown.
At least we will eat our victuals this evening.
At least we will kiss our loved ones asleep.
At the very least, we can feel safe as houses.

Aside stable bricks and enduring mortar,
Peopled by negligent drunkards with skittish lags.
So, don't love a poet.
A desperate tongue writhing in frustration –
At existential news from exhausted neighbours,
Compelled to stand and listen to curses
From faraway advocates feigning innocent coins.

After all, we can return home at sundown
And we will eat our victuals this evening.
At least we will kiss our loved ones asleep.
At the very least, we can feel safe as houses.

"What are men to rocks and mountains?"

– *Jane Austen*

A Cautionary Preamble

ESSAYISTS GOUGE LANGUAGE. A SKILL DEMANDED BY THE meticulous linguistic chiselling of our vocation. When, therefore, the Swedish scientist, theologian, philosopher, author and practising mystic Emanuel Swedenborg (1688-1772), hints that multiplex aesthetic data may be untangled into an approachable discourse, his suggestion proves extremely alluring.[1] Albeit pre-empted, as he clearly was, by the sixteenth-century polymath Giordano Bruno (1548-1600), while thereafter (arguably), by devotees of transrealist literature across twenty-first-century Eurasia. Not as merely wordplay, of course, characteristic of phenomenological debates undertaken by contemporary philosophers, but as a clear-sighted examination of the rich communicative layering in-built into any Personalist interaction with the world around us – as well as between ourselves. More than simply pioneering "Gestalt," after all, these gifted individuals "intuited" the tacit desire to find alphabetical closure concerning the self-imposed delusions of our "Western" past. A position my mentor, Sir George Trevelyan (1906-1996), would have greeted wholeheartedly.[2] Similarly inspired, my own openly arcane attitude towards Mount Athos remains indebted to these giants, along with additional spirit guides, including; HRH Charles, the Prince of Wales, Eileen Caddy, Neil Watson, my muse from The Gambia Assan Badjie, Ambassador Fakhraddin Gurbanov and Rev. Elder. Wanda Floyd. Moreover, allied to these heartfelt thanks, Mr Glyn Paflin deserves my deepest gratitude for offering incessant encouragement throughout the composition of this project. As for that matter, does Rev. Dr Robert McTeigue S.J., for his supportive reading of this text; together with Mr Jack Gale for introducing me to "psychic questing" as a qualitative step above mundane attempts to grasp atmosphere, authorial intention, and location. Mountains are never, when all said and done, only high-raised geographical peaks. Rather, they are rocky Apostles evoking realities beyond themselves; at the same time as insisting on alpinism both internally and externally. Indeed, they are mineral saints reflecting superconscious worlds, as well as subtle realms, exceeding the landscape they physically occupy. In this telling fashion, these huge, stony, protagonists equally uplift those who look at them from afar, while demanding reverence from the truly rugged few dwelling thereon. Twin actors, some would say, in a sacred drama promising redemption to frail human flesh. Mutual performers, others might supplement, who participate in the religious rigours necessary to refine multidimensional Consciousness. Still, these granite Landlords refuse to offer the slightest earthly luxury to their hardened tenants. Contrarily, as the marbled ancestors of humankind made adamantine through beatifying pressures, they insist on an honesty of purpose and a vitality of heart.

Undoubtedly, this contended, such craggy thespians demonstrably provoke great literature. Especially among people who live in places where there is neither a grand symbolic zenith, nor sunken mythic nadir (of terrain) to ponder upon. Confessed so, this decidedly British book reached its birth. Called forth, as it was, from the surrounding luminiferous ether through strangely significant chance and wilfully probing circumstance. In other words, from those liminal spaces where hidden intelligences dwell! So, weirdly synchronous with other related projects, I recall Mr Vladimir Weidemann (an Estonian colleague), inviting me to speak at a conference being held in Salzburg during the summer of 2011: an international gathering entitled, the World Public Forum: Dialogue of Civilizations. Instinctively, I agreed with this captivating concept, not to mention the enticing fact I have always been in love with Austria. With each and every one of the freezing vapours, rising like majestic Valkyries from the pinnacles of its splendid vertiginous peaks! And with the hale, blond-haired, and hardy people, whose ancestors interbred with my own to nurture noble bonds of an everlasting fealty. Thus, somewhat gleefully, I immediately accepted his kind offer. As a thoughtful aside, my scholarly associate suddenly rejoined, "What do you want to speak about?" Avowedly put on the spot, I found myself unsteadily replying, "Oh, I don't know, something like images of Mount Athos in English Literature?" To date, the latent origins of my desperate response remain obscure, even though I knew our collective cogitation would be focused around the enriching cultural contribution made by this gritty and exceptionally complex conundrum in European life.

At this stage, it needs to be noted that the World Public Forum (WPF) serves as a deliberative aggregation of individuals, regional bodies and non-governmental organisations (NGOs) with eyes awake to contemporary secular sterility, along with its coupling to the political despotism increasingly displayed by an ignorantly enforced globalisation. Accordingly, each participant strives to find a productive interconnection within this planetary network of councillors, academics, faith-based groups, state institutions, representatives of Culture and the Arts, civil-society organisations, and the media. Linked, as these groups are, with business interests from contradistinct backgrounds who, mindful of their differing positions, hold fast to the tested and tried principle of respectful cooperation between diverse nodes of activity. Incontestably, one of the agreed objectives developed through the WPF is discovered in its aim to galvanise a "worldwide community," so-called, into a vivacious defence of inherited, traditional, as well as received, aerobicised, cultural values. Certainly, by adding a consultative faculty to its everyday functioning, the WPF equally attempts to create an open space for honest and frank discussion among specialists from around our Earth: causing some "globalists" external to this project to raise tentative—although unconsciously ironic—objections to the entire enterprise. Insiders, meanwhile, find themselves given a rarefied freedom of expression to defend real diversity on ground-level terms. Hoping to subdue, in the process, the fractious and false fundamentalisms plaguing many of the world's religious communities, whilst simultaneously silencing calls to violent extremism through bringing together representatives of divergent beliefs in a confirmedly inter-confessional encounter! This may be why proportionalist models of moral concurrence officiate as the affective medium of palliative negotiation between everybody concerned.

By the same token, my unquenchable and well-attested enthusiasm for English Theatre undoubtedly initiated this unexpected spiritual and textual crusade. A bona fide quest, dare I suggest, that ended up uncovering previously imperceptible literary panoramas obscured behind my uneasy preconceptions of mainstream Christian narrative. A standpoint partially explaining my locus as the sole member of our British contingent contributing to debates on these lyrical themes – to say nothing of my contorted position among respected Orthodox clergymen, Conservative politicians, and professionally niched scholars. All creating an almost oppositional stance, which became a source of severe uncertainty for me. Somehow, it felt awkward. On the verge of genuinely puzzling! My background, at the end of the day, was Quaganry,[3] revolutionary Expressionist stagecraft, Libertarian political theorising and, last, but never least, deeply experimental poetry. Not iconography, the enduring value of Byzantine civilisation, or speaking about the need to preserve inherited European Identities. Admittedly, no one commented on this potential thorn in my side and, overall, I sensed my brief talk stretched the parameters of our roundtable wrangling by delivering a different dimension to our continuing debate. Either way, everyone slowly came to understand that Mount Athos, as an enduring spiritual powerhouse, could not be left in the limited hands of an expert few.

Another prompt, the above noted, to this prose pilgrimage, was my private obsession with the intricate ritual of Christian Orthodoxy. Not being in this tradition myself, I nevertheless recognised the liturgical adornments of Eucharistic vestment, portable lights, incense, and choral chants, as aesthetic structures allowing participation in the transcendently beautiful. In some mysterious way, the sorrows of our world seemed to be subsumed in these ornamented metaphors. Many a man, they testify, bitterly regrets the time he has seen ruby "red" when intoxicated in a tavern. Likewise, these bejewelled analogies divulge that the sapphire "blues" of domestic vacuity often haunt long-term relationships through a dangerously numbing drudgery. In a manner reminiscent of oriental alter-pieces, such opulence affirms that our misdemeanours invariably lead to diamond thunderbolts of faith, accompanied by golden acts of heroism. Hence, in an uncharacteristically exotic manner uncannily close to passionate Quagan temperaments, Swedenborg moodily exclaims: "Man knows that love is, but not what it is."[4] This, quite patently, is a prismatic denunciation, reminding us that our human condition must be understood from three radically contrasting angles. As a scientific problem demanding diagnosis: an act of defiantly creative self-expression, or a dazzling mystery within which truly courageous souls choose to battle. Positioning intelligently appears to be our single choice in these affairs – and little more. With such apperceptions maturing in our minds, it may be British theatricals who offer the most insightful comment on spiritual intercourse, as opposed to English clerics. Undeniably, when all is finally done and said, performers are avidly aware that Truth, Compassion and Beauty are never captured by a system of ideas and that lexical accuracy cannot present the only indicative technique wherein the religiously enlightened may measure their ascent into higher states of Being.

In climbing this type of Rainbow Bridge, Christian Orthodoxy fares better than most "organised" denominations, because it grasps the enormity behind naked testimonies declaring there are no creeds in the New Testament. Even though, this argued, a concern for "sound doctrine" is occasionally expressed therein – as in 1 Tim. 6.3. Furthermore, Orthodoxy is delightfully cognisant that the earliest "articles" of faith in Christian communities were evidentially so fluid they proved insufficient as tests for any ideological norm. Assuredly, during the second half of the second century, and for most of the third century, various Christian "confessions" espoused a number of ideas in an undogmatic and extremely flexible way. It was not until rival formulae and creeds emerged from the great councils of the Church in the fourth and fifth centuries that a religious "configuration," so to speak, requiring the assent of believers, emerged as a stringent series of definitional tenets. The "Athanasian" Creed[5] (probably fifth century) tightly expresses such perceptibly didactic concepts, when it makes eternal salvation dependent upon an abstract and doctrinally exact codification of the Holy Trinity. For those who eventually became seen as Easterners, possibly learning by their repeated failure to achieve any advance on the Chalcedonian Formula,[6] there was little inclination to add extensively to such early, classical, codas. Others, who finally became viewed as Westerners, felt no such inhibitions, and perpetually developed both religious equations and epicyclical appendices in a number of directions – all the way up to the Reformation. Unabashedly continuing this bewildering praxis in the Church of the Counter-Reformation through to present times! Instances of this process, if any were specifically needed, being easily discovered in the proclamation of the Immaculate Conception in 1854, Papal Infallibility in 1870, and the Assumption of the Blessed Virgin Mary in 1950. This is probably why those adhering to Roman Catholicism estimate there have been twenty-one Councils in number – the last of which was the Second Vatican Council (closing in 1965), whereas Easterners reckon on seven General Councils, the last of which was in 787 AD, as concluding the list.

Yet, with hindsight, even the Athanasian Creed does not say "we assent to One God in Trinity," but more inclusively "we worship One God in Trinity," a position reflective of the Easterners' concept of "sobornost" as a living unity of conduct, faith, and worship, more than the word-tournaments of Westerners. All besides revealing astutely distrustful attitudes on the part of Orthodoxy—in a style reminiscent of Hamlet[7]—regarding every contrived and regulated linguistic array! A wise decision by Easterners, considering the sobering effects of historical criticism on subsequent Western theologists, many of whom have been forced to re-examine the role of accidental, or specific circumstance, in the formation of religious dogmas. Easterners, this observed, have always stood their ground in claiming the essentials of belief do not rest in predetermined semantics, but in supernatural realities outside of transitional, time-bound, mental apprehension. As such, they felt it was existential striving and experiential theology that must take precedence in any Personalist descriptive enterprise: even though, this does not imply that notions of religious commonality are irrelevant, evanescent, or unintelligible, to them. Preferentially, this acknowledged, a continual and inescapable cluster of Christian practices and "living doctrines," scarcely affected by functional, or denominational, variation, were envisaged as the only way to proceed in these doughty matters. Roughly summarised, as this is, in doctrines of the Incarnation, Atonement, and the use of Sacraments like Baptism and the Eucharist. Clearly, these are some of the countable "mutualities" whereon all those involved in ecumenical endeavours may stand in surety!

Eastern Christianity, that detected, tends to go further by stating the concept of "Orthodoxy" is found in a divinising spiritual quality making whoever, or whatever, "Orthodox." Dissimilar then, to analogous terms like "Anglican," or "Methodist," it is regularly applied to the whole body of persons, buildings, and cultures, perceived to share this beatifying attribute. In such usage, the term "Orthodox" seems to be formed from two Greek words, meaning "straight," or "correct," as well as "opinion," or "thought." An "Orthodox Christian," therefore, is a "right-thinking" or "correctly-minded" person, whereas an "Orthodox practice" is one common to "Orthodox people." Accepted so, these referential frames of interpretation regarding "Christendom" infer a superior and inherited religious orientation by which to live in relation to the Saviour: a claim with far-reaching ripples! Undoubtedly, as a consequence, the earliest recorded uses of the word "Orthodox" are found through a condemnation of "unorthodox" Christians i.e. those of Monophysite, or Nestorian, Confessions. Anyhow, such theocratic rulings hide a number of time-worn issues, since it is usually assumed that when the word "Eastern" is prefixed to a term, this stands in direct contrast to "Western" Christianity – almost invariably defined as "Roman Catholicism." Paralleling this, Church politics frequently prove guilty of semantic conjuring tricks and sleight-of-hand lexicography, whereby phrases everybody knows on a "gut" level are bizarrely reinterpreted to fit an ideological agenda. Roman Catholicism, for instance, moulds language to present itself as locked in legal battle with illegitimate Protestant assemblies across Europe, meanwhile casting Orthodoxy as simply exotic, or antique. On top of this, an overly persistent theme in various historical documents appears to be that Orthodoxy was irrelevant, marginal, and schismatic: an institution setting itself up as an unholy rival to the original (Western) Church. Nevertheless, in spite of rabid misrepresentation and falsifiable aspersions, a Universal Church clearly recognisable to Orthodox practitioners held its hegemony before the eleventh century, and it is simply inaccurate to call this church "Roman Catholic" in the modern sense. Indisputably, with this critique in mind, Eastern divisions in the Ancient Roman Empire can be roughly marked out by a great geographical square: the sides running east from near contemporary Belgrade, through Bucharest and Sebastopol, to Batum (present day Batumi); south from Batum in the Gulf of Aqaba; west through Alexandria to Benghazi; thence northwards through Corfu and Albania, back to Belgrade. However, geopolitical imperatives on their own never narrate the entire story of a religious sensibility.

Secondary to such reflections is the incontestable evidence supporting Greek as the lingua franca spoken everywhere within this square, despite Orthodoxy itself resisting linguistic labelling, due to the fact "no tongue prevailed." Unfairly, documentation and folk-wisdom notwithstanding, Westerners continued to speak of a "Greek Orthodox" Church: delineating it as those convocations in communion with the Ecumenical Patriarch (of Constantinople). Understandably, for the Orthodox themselves, the "mind of all others like-minded" was not reducible to either Hellenistic expressive utterance, or topographical features, but antithetically, demonstrative of a flourishing Christian culture wherein "no Bishop can command all others:" binding custom, along with religious edict – envisioned as gifted to later generations by sanctified ancestors. Contrasting to untutored Western invective, so shamefully inscribed, the "Feast of Orthodoxy" on the first Sunday in Lent commemorates the recovery, in 842 AD, of a renewed freedom to venerate the sacred images (icons, which the Council of 787 AD had defended and meticulously outlined) and must not be misapprehended as wilful, recalcitrant, or stubbornly sectarian. Instead, blessings are invoked on the champions of Orthodoxy, anathemas pronounced on its foes, and healthy communal diversity celebrated, because it is feverishly felt that this divinising tradition must be maintained for posterity at all costs.

As hand in glove to this process, Orthodox scholars recount that as a Council, Nicaea I gave to the Church its universal creed and asserted the divinity of Christ's person against Arius (256-336 AD), although Constantinople I, in actuality, completed the formulation of dogmas against those who denied the individual Divinity of the Holy Spirit. What is more, Constantinople contended the fullness of Christ's manhood against Apollinaris of Laodicea (died 390 AD), thereby securing a vital facet of traditionalist observance. Recollecting further, Eastern scribes talk of the Cyrillian factor at Ephesus condemning Nestorius (386-450 AD) by announcing the unity of Christ's person in his two natures – so that Mary is rightfully styled "Mother of God," or *Theotokos*. In addition, it is remembered with pride that Constantinople II tried to reconcile those who had rejected the formula of Chalcedon by posthumously condemning certain opinions of Origen Adamantius (185-254 AD), while (significantly for Orthodox believers), Constantinople III claimed there were two distinct centres of "activity and will" in the One Christ. Therein allowing Nicaea II to state the Incarnation makes it lawful to depict the manhood of God Incarnate, along with the figures of those whom God indwells without incurring accusations of blasphemy. Be that as it may, this characteristically Orthodox celebration of Deity in our material sphere has been common since 250 AD, until, that is, the puritan reaction across Asia Minor in the mid-eighth century.

Pioneering the vast expansion of Orthodoxy, both outside and within the boundaries of the Empire, were two Byzantine Greek brothers, St Cyril (828-869 AD) and St Methodius (815-882 AD). Each born in the city of Thessalonica, they became Christian missionaries among the Slavic peoples of the Great Moravia and Pannonia, where they strode like giants. Through their hallowed work, these sanctified siblings guided the entire cultural progress of all Slavs, for which reason they received the well-deserved title *Apostles to the Slavs*. Atop this, they are credited with devising the Glagolitic alphabet, the first script used to transcribe Old Church Slavonic: one of the accounts entailing why these Holy Men are venerated with the epithet "equal-to-apostles." Unarguably, by modifying the Greek alphabet into new and accessible symbols suitable for the diverse lands towards the East, they facilitated learning, the spread of *Scripture*, common literacy and hands-on service books for peoples thirsting to reach a greater spiritual calibre. Thereafter, ecclesial Slavonic became (and remains), the liturgical language of the Serbian, Bulgarian and Russian Churches. Ultimately, this recognised, it needs to be recalled that Orthodoxy is no more co-terminus with Slavonic than with Greek speech; a linguistic fact occasionally hiding the secret of this tradition's cultural strength through continual adaptation. This may additionally outline why modern mission churches dependent on support from outside their territories, such as in Yakutsk, Finland, China, Hungary and Japan, find the religious choices offered by Orthodoxy so conducive to broader Church development.

Organisationally, within national churches, the Bishops and their dioceses see themselves as mirroring a supernatural Order, whereby they are bonded together according to the dictates of Grace: represented to one another by celestial affiliations, and steered by the best insights of human sense, within themselves. In a fashion reminiscent of the Anglican Communion, especially in England, the Bishop of a capital city, styled Patriarch or Metropolitan, may trace his pedigree all the way back to "the peace of the church" under Constantine. Commentators argue, moreover, that the Church, following provisional divisions found within the Empire, still enthrones the Bishop of each chief city, in every province, to speak to, and for, all Orthodox believers within it – after the manner of a procurator. Over time, these customs were regularised at the great councils, albeit with the wider dominance of Alexandria, Rome and Antioch acknowledged; due to their de facto preeminence. The later inclusion of Constantinople, that agreed, and eventually Moscow, being won by the diplomatic assertion of a factual shift in cultural power. Jerusalem, for its part, gained patriarchal status on purely honorific grounds: remaining representative, nonetheless, of an "organic" pattern of inclusion that has been pursued ever since.

This model of Church organisation, together with Latin rigour and a Greek willingness to adopt the use of liturgy and Scripture in the native vernacular languages of indigenous converts, along with a Turkish insistence on treating their Christian subjects as a separate people (administering and taxing them through their Bishops), has had a long-term and "double" result. It effectively identified each ethnic group with their respective Church through four hundred years of shared servitude and, more significantly, it made it hard for these subject peoples to differentiate between Christianity and nationality. Looking back, from 1453, or thereabouts, till the nineteenth century, the south-east and north-west of the square in the Eastern Empire had been at the mercy of the Turks; thereby strengthening Orthodox solidarity. Elsewhere, the stultifying rule of the Tartars was experienced in Russia from 1240 to 1418. An experience made worse, from 1721 to 1917, when the Russian Church went through a series of cramping strictures imposed by the (Germanic) St Petersburg bureaucracy – until this, itself, fell beneath the even more fearful tyranny of Communism: working, as it did, to deliberately destroy organised religion unlike earlier tyrants who had only oppressed inadvertently, or sporadically, these metaphysical outlets. All factors, of course, further differentiating Orthodox religious witness. To keep such an innocent and ageless faith vital, therefore, in the face of dissonant diversity, political degradation, linguistic upheaval, spiritual defilement, and physical martyrdom, has more often than not been the glorious hallmark of this most noble tradition.

For a believer, loyalty to Orthodoxy is fidelity to Christ, the Master of the Apostles. Himself the living revelation of His Father. Freedom within Orthodox tradition is thus the after-effect of realising it is the Holy Spirit, the Gift of Christ from his Father, who comforts the faithful and restores within the Church Triumphant an image of God according to the likeness of the true Trinity; who empowers these convictions. Orthodox believers thenceforth upheld every impetus towards monasticism: especially in the third and fourth centuries, as well as the role it played in developing techniques of depth worship. This was, and is, an escape into liberation: the type of liberty discovered in sophisticated states of beatified awareness. Said so, this is probably why every Bishop in Orthodoxy must be a monk and the monasteries continue to be the chief centres of spiritual direction. Datum contextualising why the most learned of men amongst the Desert Fathers, Evagrius (349-399 AD), transparently bequeathed teachings later evolved by Simeon the New Theologian (949-1022 AD) at Constantinople in the tenth century. Also, a habituation shedding light on those meditational rubrics explored by St Gregory Palamas (1296-1359) on Mount Athos itself in the fourteenth century, not to forget those contemplative skills exemplified by St Seraphim of Sarov (1754-1833) in Russia during the eighteenth century. Each discipline continuing to be handed down to new, eager, religious specialists. Unquestionably then, these Orthodox titans persist in persuading us that solitary prayer is a matter of turning from a world that passes away with each moment, whilst common prayer, along with the Blessed Sacraments, remain the materials permitting us to ideate a transfigured Earth beyond the apocalypse. In this, the "ordinary" Orthodox believer stands radically indebted to these previous metaphysical explorers for their transformative ministrations.

Unreservedly, worthwhile exceptions to every type of worldly rejection (even with this adjured), always overshadow such stark rules. Hence, the presence of Holy Mount Athos in English Letters remains a monument to its own ubiety. An unsettling observation that, along with my avid admiration of Swedenborg as the "godfather of Quagans," has enabled me to understand Literature as anything apart from the "poor relation" to either Theology or Philosophy! So, shepherded by his axiom, "All religion relates to life, and the life of religion is to do good," I came to understand each of these descriptive disciplines as "appropriations" around something supremely valuable; something Quagan. Providing, as they do, comprehensible resemblances between signs and the supernal objects they designate. On top of this, by extending Swedenborg's reasoning into purely literary undertakings, reciprocity could be suddenly unearthed between deep and surface structures of symbolic grammar. The engineered use of metaphors in Philosophy, for example, and their evocative application in Literature, unexpectedly becoming apparent! This is because, slightly paraphrasing Swedenborg, a lifelong pursuit of Philosophy reveals that the central question inside every syntactical search arrives back at the issue of "individuation," or what it means to realise oneself as a finite person-in-process. Correlated, of course, with this probing, are projected theological "solutions" derived from indescribable Theophanous experience and, as I will argue, preternaturally layered visionary literature. If agreed, readers discover on one side of this calculation there lies a clinical dissection of our Quagan predicament, whereas on the other side a healing and cathartic Mystery shines with suggestive radiance. All making sense of Swedenborg's sustained rebuttal of reductive vocabularies as completely inadequate to the subtle task of depicting our staggeringly intricate world. Upholding, as he continued to do in practice and theory, that "imagistic" language partakes in the reality it signifies. A viewpoint encompassing, with hindsight, why some of the writers examined in these pages have consciously taken a number of conceptual liberties with their originating source: overlaying, in lieu of disclosing, a series of primary themes in the style of a painter, or sculptor! Textual technologies of this sort, somewhat contrariwise, usually having a habit of undermining the recorded mysticism encountered on the slopes of Mount Athos overall. Even though, like a Zazen Dojo, this sorcerous location plays with empirical phrases and logic, while resisting these pedestrian vehicles of expression in the pursuit of an enlarged heart-consciousness: using, one could say, the literary arts to tease out inbuilt impressions confirming a raw intersubjectivity outside of Global Text.

Call me a Gnostic then, and have done with it. My position stands its ground by claiming works of imagination can trace paths into Glory as effectively as any graph, professorial tract, or documented historical almanack. Maybe even more so! I merely ask acceptance of this imperfect, but honest, examination of Poetry, Prose, Creative Imagination and Drama with an extremely clear eye towards the Absolute. Arguably, a defining feature of English Literature at its very best! My one caveat is that, at no point, does this study claim to be definitive. Frankly, following initial research, echoes of Christian Orthodoxy unnervingly seem to resonate in many a secluded narrators' nook and connotational cranny. Most feasibly in deliberately unnamed magical mountains playing a central part in the recounting of morality tales! A well-known literary device, which will continue to beleaguer serious critics in the years ahead! Slight indulgence, therefore, I humbly beg in one matter alone; having included a selective essay on travel writers in this volume. Beyond doubt, the second Conference on Holy Mount Athos in Weimar 2012 effectively demanded this necessary inclusion, although it defies inherited notions of literary propriety. In defence, I should stress that deformation of this nature is required, because the peninsula itself conjures literary sensibilities in its visitors. Lone rocks stirring unexpected acts of penmanship in the unwary: massed pebbles insisting upon a contemplative response from even the most hard-nosed and practically-minded of honoured, venerable, guests.

Without reservation (all of the aforementioned stated), my final words of gratitude must go to the various correspondents whose generous help and courteous demeanour have enabled this volume to reach tangibility. Specifically, Tom Rowsell, Paul Obertelli, Ron McVan, Carl Jung, Mick Brooks and Dr Tamara Dragadze, along with the exceptionally patient Dr Graham Speake, Hon Secretary for our indigenous Friends of Mount Athos! To conclude, I will also always remain indebted to Manticore Press for grasping the speculative implications of an almost unheard Orthodox (but not Byzantine) tongue reverberating behind so much of British authorship and for saying that my exploratory addresses at both Conferences should be expanded into a full manuscript. What is more, my American colleagues (particularly Curtis Childs of the Swedenborg Foundation) were enthusiastically won over by my unstoppable need to "analyse" Mount Athos from a Quagan-Swedenborgian perspective – as a means by which I could unravel the "problem" of this immortal cultural force in the fullness of its magnificence. Their confidence in climbing this initial, unsteady, piste—let me promise them—will never be forgotten.

SELECTED ENDNOTES

1. Mukhtar Shakhanov, the Nobel Prize winning poet, discussed this with me when I first visited him in Almaty, Kazakhstan.

2. Sir George Trevelyan IV Baronet (1906-1996) was a British educational pioneer and a founding father of the New Age movement.

3. With hindsight, I have been some sort of Quaker-inspired Pagan (Quagan) most of my adult life. However, I have never seen why we always need to abandon comparative Poetry, Myth, and the Arts, as largely irrelevant in our human quest for Esoteric Truth. Moreover, contemporary (warm) Quagans integrate Quaganry with modern philosophy, as well as the current state of agreed scientific knowledge. All of which has produced a wide variety of private beliefs under this broad theological classification. For example, "classical" Quaganry held that a human's relationship with the Absolute was transpersonal. The only possible type of "intervention" being through Divine Providence for the good of all humankind. Yet, some recent Quagans have modified this standpoint, thereby upholding humanity's relationship with all-encompassing Deity as (ultimately) internal. Put differently, the Primal Substance (Logos) transcends personal/impersonal duality and easily moves beyond such empirical notions. Thus, following their lead in these matters I, for one, have tended to use "synonymous" metaphysical terms interchangeably with Quaganry such as Paganism, Gnosticism, Personalism and Hylozoism to express my religious concerns. Applied so, Hylozoism is best seen as a doctrine defending deep-seated intuitions regarding all matter as intrinsically alive. This may equally include views contending that "inanimate" matter across our Universe has latent powers of abiogenesis; a widely-accepted position in the scientific community nowadays. As for Paganism, this concept (in its contemporary usage) mostly denotes an Odalist who seeks to revive the indigenous religious beliefs and practices of ancient European peoples – and not merely someone who denies the God of Judaism, Christianity, or Islam.

4. Despite being personally obsessed with Emanuel Swedenborg, I have tried to restrict all of my quotes to readily accessible manuscripts.

5. Although not written by Athanasius (300-373 AD), but attributed to him in the seventh century, the Athanasian Creed states: "And the Catholic faith is this: that we worship our God in trinity and trinity in unity; neither confounding the persons, nor dividing the substance." Possibly, the fact it stresses those failing to accept these systems of belief will be excluded from salvation helped

it to attain equal importance with the Nicene and Apostles' Creed as time went by. The Chalcedonian Formula was adopted at the Council of Chalcedon in 451 AD in Asia Minor and is accepted by the following Christian denominations: Eastern Orthodoxy, the Roman Catholic Communion, and many present-day Protestant Christian churches. Interestingly, it is the first Council not recognised by any of the Oriental Orthodox churches who may be classified as non-Chalcedonian. The Formula defines that Christ is "acknowledged in two natures," which "come together into one person and hypostasis." Furthermore, this formal definition of "two natures" in Christ was understood by the critics of the council at the time, and is understood by many historians and theologians today, to side with Western and Antiochene Christology, as well as diverging from the teaching of Cyril of Alexandria, who always upheld that Christ is "one." Yet, a modern analysis of the sources behind the creed (by A. de Halleux, in Revue Théologique de Louvain 7, 1976, for instance) along with a deeper reading of the proceedings, or acts, of the council manifestly shows the bishops considered Cyril a great authority on these matters and that even the language of "two natures" derives from him.

6. In any case, skilled seers such as Swedenborg always remained cautious of theorising without direct experience.

7. Hamlet's infamous outburst being "There are more things in Heaven and Earth, Horatio, than are dreamt of in your philosophy."

"Thousands of tired, nerve-shaken, over-civilized people are beginning to find out that going to the mountains is going home; that wildness is a necessity."

– *John Muir*

PROBLEM I.
Religion: What's the Point?

W AY BACK WHENCE, SCHOOLTEACHERS TOLD ME ROCK and water were opposites and light couldn't bend. Each declaration sounding false even to my childhood ears. Yet, circuitously referring to the doctrine of correspondences, Exodus 17 tells us the Prophet Moses struck a rock at Horeb with his staff to release its imprisoned liquids. Proving, thereby, the sentient benevolence of our Cosmos and the nature of paradox; along, it needs saying, with interconnections between fundamentally different levels of existence. Truths, it must also be confessed, that have always resonated within me. So, extending this particular viewpoint further, it may be more accurately commented that light not only twists under the dictates of gravity, it analogously corresponds with wisdom. After all, insightful knowledge enlightens the mind as radiance brightens the eye. What is more, warmth clearly correlates to love, because loving dispositions actually fire our brains as heat does the body. Correlations explaining why Scripture incessantly outlines metaphysical affinities at such considerable length. A textual recognition meaning that inside its laws and histories, every minute detail describes interpersonal bonds between God and humanity; each nexus being the true subject of the Word. Hence, as a Swedenborgian-inspired Quagan priest, I am fully aware that most apparent contradictions remain, nonetheless, a continuity. Ergo, looking back through this decades-long interweaving of these religious influences, I have hatched, matched, and dispatched with the best of them, tied myself to countless trees in acts of protest, prostrated myself in front of various Bulldozers to defend Anglo-Saxon burial sites and introduced both ancient, as well as Surrealist "magical" theatre into our British auditoria – as attempts to recover our "map" of indigenous immaterialist domains. Stated thus, I have consciously interwoven my Swedenborgian convictions into a living weave with my religious roots, in order to openly speculate on the surprisingly weighty topic of legitimate "starting points" for religious inquiry. Investigations leading to a fortressing of my present slant wherein imaginal cartographies of our human spiritual condition eventually gift us with a sense of primary emplacement and archetypal measurement in our private and collective cultural lives.

Thuswise, it is quickly intuited that one of the Big Ideas behind Swedenborgianism is spiritual Ecology. Oddly enough, a Quagan position earmarking Swedenborg as an agent of our Ancestral Religion and not merely a naturalist who enjoyed visionary escapades. Furthermore, a stance erecting metaphysical scaffolding around Quaganry through shared environmental misgivings, at the same time as actively staving off the bewildering distain flamboyantly declared by some religionists regarding Great Nature Herself. Admittedly, this recalled, existential questions like "what's the point of anything?" still hold water. However, we Quagans are simultaneously mindful of the fact that without a healthy biosphere there will be no one left alive to ask these questions.[1] So, playing "devil's advocate" for a moment, let's take this pessimistic line of reasoning further. Indeed, why get up in the morning to struggle with a world of urban strangers masquerading as neighbours? Why work increasingly longer hours for wages losing their purchasing power? Why keep in contact with family spread across continents, let alone different cities? Received wisdom maintains, somewhat curiously, that even amidst the palpable natural marvels surrounding us, vast numbers of people confront grinding ennui, acute loneliness, and a paralysing alienation inside themselves. Drugs corrupt our sons and daughters. Crime of every description runs rampant in our towns, whilst random shootings are rife. Despair tempts the vulnerable into suicidal actions, and brute violence poisons our collective municipal expression. Each of these social phenomena, if acknowledged, helping to explain why sizable numbers of citizens retreat into the trivial as a means to escape apparent absurdity. And all against the wider global backdrop of starvation through warfare or climate change, polluted water supplies, curable diseases made malignant through a lack of affordable healthcare, advanced decrepitude due to scarce, or unsuitable, shelter, crippling political inequality, and debt-based slavery. So, what's the proverbial point? Particularly, if our only guiding light is the type of scientific inquiry seeking to discover "how" things work for commercial gain? Well, needless to say, these estrangements from our Sources of Being are not the entire story. Moreover, such kibbling conditions have never stifled justifiable questions concerning our human place and purpose within a Sentient Continuum. Neither, for that matter, has this jaundiced set of views ever diminished the glittering significance of a new birth, Beauty in the arts, the delights of sex, the miracle of love, or the profundity of a human death. Thence my initial response to the question of religion's "point" is that it awakens us from the anxieties of narrow immediacy into a view of Being *sub specie aeternitatis*: or in other words, from the perspective of Eternity. Unquestionably, religion (when practised correctly) allows us to stand back from ourselves, while simultaneously inducing a vital objectivity in our affairs. Professed so, it is right and proper that religious questioning arises, provided the actual frameworks of human existence are fully acknowledged – as theological inquiry searches for ways to expound transcendent lucidity.

At this juncture, another "point" of religion starts to emerge. Especially, if we follow the lead of outstanding intellectuals such as Emanuel Swedenborg when he argues that theological investigation exceeds wizened academic reasoning due to its focused examination on our "Ultimate Concern."[2] Put differently, Swedenborg is contending that instead of endless linguistic abstractions characteristic of Anglo-American philosophical debate, religious activities like prayer, symbolic ritual, and meditation, permit us to elucidate our fundamental orientation as human beings; at least to ourselves. Extrapolating his position, it is fair to say our very participation in these spiritual activities broadens our conscious awareness as bio-chemical organisms into modalities of experience above undigested dogma, or merely inherited traditions. Hinting, as this does, that these techniques can take us into subtle territories wherein the structural patterns of our world are equally discernible inside our own bodies and minds. In this sense, may I suggest, we find ourselves to be vehicles of the One Life pervading all things: aspects of Nature's Soul. Thus, using an enhanced Swedenborgian vocabulary, it is fully legitimate to describe a "Homo Maximus," or allude to an "Absolute God," since we may grasp such supernal verities upon undertaking these exercises on a regular basis. Thenceforth, as a Quagan, I tend to discuss angels and spirits. Symbols, dare I suggest, of this "Being-Itself." Yet, I am not referring to signs in the dry and dusty sense of the schoolmen, but rather to living Presences somewhere between imaginative semiosis and archetypal Myth – which keep their Eternal Court as localisations of Divine Immanence. Some of my sisters and brothers, no doubt, are polytheists in the commonly accepted meaning of this word, believing, as they do, in many different divinities from various heavenly tribes. Others would contend, these entities are actually Figurative Ideals within the Universal Unconscious. Either way, such sacred personages allow us to engage with the realities they signify. And what's the point of that? Well, only direct involvement in Quagan ceremonial can answer this more mysterious issue.

Nonetheless, a few observations may be proposed. To begin with, this form of Personalism allows people to find meaningful connections within themselves to their fellow human beings, as well as the Family-of-Life generally. Responsive hylozoic processes, so to speak, that every one of us embodies, in a reactive weave binding all things together. For instance, I need ancestral ground to stand on, a virile exchange of fluids, substances, and airs, with my surrounding environment; all accompanied by freshened atmospheres to breathe – let alone recognisable companionship and unending cultural interactions for a qualitatively rich life. Furthermore, by taking the concept of "person" as a primary theological identifier, a necessary religious humanism (opposed to reductive Materialism) evolves as a corrective to the often-dehumanising effects of postmodernity. Initially introduced by the theologist Friedrich Schleiermacher in 1799, and then applied by Ludwig Feuerbach in 1841, "Personalism" may be understood, therefore, as an intelligently cautious notion rejecting dangerous appeals to impersonal principles as the best, or only, way to grasp human conditionality. This may also be one of the reasons why the poet Walt Whitman published a somewhat reactionary essay on "Personalism" in 1868, whilst novelists like Kafka and Dostoyevsky regularly adopted this position in their literary works. As an addendum, it might be important to stress this epithet is frequently applied to those who feel uneasy with the designation "Existentialist" (like Pope John Paul II), due to the remissive implications often associated with its usage. Having said that, Personalism is easily reconcilable with a wide variety of spiritual positions, and on close inspection, there are sufficiently common themes among Personalist writers to enable its discourse to shed a powerfully revealing luminescence on elative religious experiences throughout the ages.

Okay, but why Quaganry? Given that, for me at least, the central point of religion is to embrace our environment as the "lost twin" or "other Self" of our own souls? A claim I have championed across the years through pagan rituals designed to promote a more sophisticated relationship with the elements, or the "Old Ones", even though more recently within the context of specifically Heathen rites encouraging bonds of fidelity towards wood and stone. Described so, an extra reservoir of explanatory power regarding the "point" of religion is discovered in its call to fellowship with non-human and human Friends. Its moral demand that community be established between people of like mind, as well as those of dissimilar opinions – whenever it is possible. In order to flesh this out, let me share two testimonial anecdotes. For my part, I find Quaker-Pagan worship very advanced. Undistractedly, I sit in the Silence of our Meeting waiting on the Universe. Others occasionally talk to their God in Hebrew, while locals Muslims once prepared breakfast snacks to celebrate Eid al-Adha (Tabaski) with us. Never forgetting that some of the more mature ladies in our Meeting were selling home-made crab apple jelly (which is spicy and delicious) to raise funds for charity. Goodwill was in the air, everyone's tradition remained intact, and our correlative humanity was truly affirmed. Consequently, I have come to love my Sunday mornings, since they clearly demonstrate intercultural peace is possible: albeit in microcosm. Atop this, I continue to recall voicing my first flagrantly "Swedenborgian" prayer at our Meeting after being absent for nearly a decade. Strangely, I became nervous (even though I am used to public speaking), because sensing my Friends' theological agitations, I nonetheless knew they were solidly behind me. In some weird way or other, it felt as if I was prompted to pray aloud amid a Silence I find increasingly addictive. Intuitively, I should add, I recognised taking the steps required to initiate a sort of "homecoming." Experiences when appropriated together, making me recall why even a die-hard atheist like Bertrand Russell (1872-1970) could see valid reasons behind becoming a Quaker: whilst, simultaneously, I tried to resist the mental picture of a witch now comfortably worshipping amongst the Puritans.[3]

It is here, possibly, that we come to the greatest "point" of collective religious practice. When not twisted out of all recognition by ideology, or the angry demands of genuine injustice, religion creates social institutions with the sole purpose of spreading goodwill throughout Society. Undisputedly, churches, synagogues, and mosques, can become beacons of Light once this ethical stance is articulated and expressed. Besides, it is something of a "judgement" on most organised religions that a refusal to preserve this moral position tends to see them empty. At the end of the day, people vote with their feet and few want their families exposed to the hatred of sectarian minds in a place of worship, unless they themselves are already fanatics. Thusly, from its inception, the Religious Society of Friends has actively avoided creeds and hierarchies to seek inspirations above inscribed letters. A vision enclasped by approximately half a million adult members attending Quaker Meetings in 2013, owing, perhaps, to the unprecedented preaching of our Founder, George Fox (1624-1691), when he declared: "Be patterns, be examples in all countries, places, islands, nations wherever you come; that your carriage and life may preach among all sorts of people, and to them; then you will come to walk cheerfully over the world, answering that of God in everyone; whereby in them you may be a blessing, and make the witness of God in them to bless you".[4] In order to achieve this goal around 49 per cent of Friends (worldwide) still practice "programmed worship" – that is, largely traditional worship with a prepared message from the Bible, frequently coordinated by a pastor, whereas roughly 11 per cent of Friends practice the far more experimental "waiting worship" (also known as "unprogrammed worship"), as previously described. Interestingly, some Meetings of both styles have Recorded Ministers who have been recognised for their gift of vocal ministry. Evidently explaining why some commentators contend alternating crystalline Silence with the aesthetics of the Word can create a veritable laboratory for liberated spirituality.

In the past, Quakers were known for their plain dress, refusal to participate in war, and an unwillingness to swear oaths: accompanied by a heartfelt opposition to slavery and a perceived need to champion women's suffrage. Beyond doubt, Friends have always been at the forefront of innovative and progressive social change. Likewise, our neighbours noticed we had a steely ethical disposition, forged through interior fires burning deep inside ourselves whereupon we crafted the virtuous armour demanded by industrious service to our fellows. Curiously, even our detractors started to speak of a "Beloved Community" behind the banks and financial institutions founded by Religious Friends. For example, Barclays and Lloyds were established by Quakers; in addition to manufacturing companies like Clarks, Cadbury, Rowntree, and Fry's.[5] Each developed to fund philanthropic efforts such as reforming prisons, advancing social equality, and raising the frame-expectations of common folk beyond the mundane. So, what is the point of all this religious zeal? Little, I suppose, apart from honestly trying to make the human world a slightly better place to live in – for our families, our neighbours, and ourselves.

Rounding off, the shofar (warning) horn of our postmodern period must be something along the lines of, "Has the greatest atheist in Athens anything in common with its most devout citizen?" Or, phrased alternatively, what has the scepticism of Richard Dawkins to do with the pious ministrations of Pope Francis? Obviously, there is no easy, or quick, answer to this question if we are equitable to both sides. But, theological formulations like this make me disagree with Camus when he propounded the Myth of Sisyphus as the spiritual narrative of our period. Rather, to my mind, the Myth of our era is the combat betwixt Hercules and Antaeus; a fight between Heaven and Earth. But, I digress. As public perceptions appear to wan before unprecedented pressures, the temptation for many people is to pull back from the lifeline offered by religionists. Besides this, even "detoxing the soul," or qualitative psycho-soul development, is sometimes wantonly criticised nowadays as the reserve of New Age utopians, overly sensitive "wafty" (romantic) candles, or those needy people who lack personal direction. Naytheless, for me, none of these objections adequately reflect the "point" of religion once understood in its most significant configuration. Surely, when all is championed and trumped, its gift is discovered through allowing us to stand back from a given situation and see wider panoramas: to focus on matters of our personal and collective "Ultimate Concern," as well as to achieve its message of unconditional goodwill among all humankind; irrespective of ethnic origin, political convictions, and ironically, the particular creed of a specific indigenous culture. Values, achieved through meditation and sacramental ritual, which then access an authentic Quagan meaning in our private lives: including a clarifying orientation before the saving Absolute. And that's the point!

SELECTED ENDNOTES

1. This section is based on a talk I first delivered in the British House of Lords, which was hosted by Lord John Laird and convened by Dr Roger Prentis on 29 October 2014. Other panellists included Lama Gelongma Zangmo (Kagyu Samye Dzong Tibetan Buddhist Meditation Centre) and Rev. Rana Youab Khan (Diocese of London).

2. The phrase "Ultimate Concern" was originally used by the theologist Paul Tillich to designate that which is above all profane and ordinary realities: the sacred, numinous or holy. Undoubtedly, the perception of its reality is felt as so overwhelming and valuable that everything else seems insignificant – a conception of faith more explicitly defined in his work, *Dynamics of Faith*.

3. A standpoint vindicated through personal conversations and visits to The Westminster Meeting House at 52, St Martin's Lane in Covent Garden, London WC1. Interestingly, Bertrand Russell and the American-born Quaker activist Alys Pearsall Smith (1867-1951) married in this meeting house in 1894. An occasion Russell relates in his autobiography when their wedding guests seemed moved to preach about the Miracle at Cana and inadvertently offended his bride's teetotal sensibility. Indeed, the artist Richard Morris Smith made a drawing of their wedding and a photograph of the drawing was donated to the National Portrait Gallery in 1999.

4. As George Fox memorably stated in *The Works of George Fox* (1831).

5. Fascinatingly, Roman Catholic institutions like Banca Monte dei Paschi di Siena S.p.A., may prove to be the working models behind commerce perceived as potentially salvific. Certainly, I had these unfamiliar incongruities in mind when I delivered my talk *The Soul of Business* to The Royal Society of Arts in April 2019.

"Great things are done when men and mountains meet."

– William Blake

Problem II.
The Enigma of Athos

I T IS EASY TO FORGET THAT WE BRITISH ARE AN ISLAND PEOPLE. Adventurers, who nevertheless have allowed notions of national identity, as well as inherited cultural parameters, to slowly weaken with the passing of careless years! Time, it needs to be said, and strangers in our midst, have more than taken their toll; alongside an almost wilful neglect of our own tribal interests. Still, bounded as we are by sapphire and icy Atlantic seas, this realisation always returns to us as a point of convergence. An awareness remembered with the impact of an uncomfortable burden. It makes us feel isolated and in the very same moment essentially distinct. Pushing to the back of our consciousness that this "Sceptred Isle," to quote William Shakespeare (1564-1616) in King Richard II, is analogous to other, strangely similar, lands. As a case in point, Japan instantly springs to mind for the purposes of direct comparison, on both a literary and political level. We are, as our mutual ancestors will have it, two small, proud, Kingdoms at the very edge of a great and mighty continent, whereon most of the major artistic and scientific advances have taken place. Innovations eventually trickling to our respectively emerald shores! Be it there or here, however, once such progressions find root in island soil the necessary genius of geographical restriction transmutes these materials into something unique. This may be why Japan looks with fear, as well as admiration at mainland China, as do we British at the Continent of Europe.

Unsurprisingly then, sites of the European Sacred have had a noteworthy effect on English literature. Despite the fact that in periods past, perceived exoticisms within Continental society had become a cause for moral concern. Our innate puritanical tendencies, deemed as vital to island survival, only capable of understanding more ancient and sophisticated cultures as either centres of decadence, or in the evocative terms of faraway fairy tale. And Byzantium was just such a place. It was remote from the North in every sense of the word, while known for its opulent and elaborate customs. Additionally, its gem-encrusted spirituality was held with a deep suspicion. It could not be condemned as entirely Pagan, but neither was it seen as honestly Christian. Accordingly, with a frigid modality usually confusing to non-islanders, even its glittering sanctuaries of gentle prayer were viewed as threatening; wellsprings of potential glamour, full of dangerous, or archaic, ideas. Anxieties, dare one imply, fuelled by the persistence of distant and indistinct memories that our forebears had themselves once been Orthodox. Meaning, in real terms, that one manifestation of our Ancestral Faith had suffered a number of terrible betrayals, stretching back to the origins of misty Albion itself: a nearly unforgivable ethical error and tantamount to the committal of a Clan sin. So unsettled, some insightful scholars came to conclude that either we had freed ourselves from the poisonous religious promiscuities plaguing Mediterranean peoples, or, much more disturbingly, holiness had deserted British affairs of state and the educated classes in general. Other pundits chorusing that our previously blessed condition had retreated into the heart of this nation; to the monks and the common folk, who alone had remained faithful to their ageless devotions. Echoing, quite possibly, half-digested memories that the Norman Barons had done little apart from spreading civil war across an island wherein the saints had fallen very deeply asleep. Thus confused, angered and riddled with guilt, British eyes looked towards those territories sharing parallel experiences to our own, as theoretical sources of spiritual remedy.

In this, rightly or wrongly, the Mani was felt to offer sturdy family resemblances to British popular tradition. Despite their bloodthirsty vendettas, unstoppable Palio Maniatiko dances and the entrance to dark Hades being located in an ominous cave near Cape Tainaron, this southernmost tip of the Peloponnese was the abode of people recognisable to us. Distant unacknowledged cousins, as it were! At least, such appears to be the thinking of Henry Herbert, the third Earl of Carnarvon (1800-1849), when he toured there in 1839. Probably, to his mind, it came as little surprise that Hercules had brought up Cerberus from the depths of dank judgment onto this hard, dry, even though candid, landscape. The fortified villages of the Maniots, as lineal descendants of Ancient Sparta, demonstrating the obvious bodily rigour of its inhabitants! Had they not, when all said and done, resisted the Ottomans to a man, and even fought with the armies of William II (1056-1100)? Didn't surviving these demanding, and searingly hot fields, amid rich oil-producing Koroneiki olive groves, connote our hardy British sense of natural paradox? The firm psychology of indigenous Mani youth mirrored in the simple, although deliciously sustaining foods, banqueted on every household table? Clearly, the Mani was an enticing home away from home! Without paying undue attention, thenceforth, the Earl must have noticed huge baskets of freshly baked bread, jugs of sweet wine, and unending supplies of Spanakopita and Tiropita pancakes; served to the most casual of acquaintances. Habits of hospitality, albeit with different cuisine, cherished by rural gentlemen from our green and pleasant land throughout the ages! Eavesdropping accidentally, he may additionally have overheard conversations between mature Maniot matrons recounting the eldritch lore involved in cleaning their house-towers at Eastertide and Christmas, while older men worried about the temptation to smile in front of evil-eyed foreigners – who might count their teeth to intentionally cause sickness and death. All, facets of a society, it was felt, demonstrating disturbingly common ground.

Now, an argument might be made that we British feel slightly intimidated by Italian high culture, as well as French manners and etiquette. Also, even though far less exotic than Byzantium, these extremely pleasant countries have, nevertheless, risen to a stunning cultural preeminence! But, the Greeks, who once did likewise, have always been identified by us as kith! We can sit back and relax with them. They are felt to be long-lost relatives, somehow or other, abiding in a disgracefully sun-saddled neck of the reasonably distant woods! Impressions vaguely documented by a number of British travel writers and possibly shared by Dr John Covel (1638-1722), when he toured the peninsula in 1677. Sensations, which could equally be the actual origin of ironies penned by Edward Lear (1812-1888), regarding monastic life on Mount Athos itself! Undeniably, a letter to Lady Waldegrave records the satirist's remark: "So I am looking forward to escaping from the hustlefusledom and perhaps may settle down as a monk on Mount Athos eventually."[1] A statement that is manifestly "nonsense," since Lear could only see superstition, coupled with a severe form of evasion from worldly responsibilities within its monastic institutions. This gentle jape reflecting the middle-class intellectual prejudices of his specific age!

In a manner similar, perhaps, to the innately impulsive and restless critic Peter Levi (1931-2000), the most neoteric visitor to the Blessed Mount in the last few years. A man who studied, as I went on to do, at Heythrop College, London, and, at one stage, had been a Jesuit priest; receiving theological training at this University. Besides his gadfly about Oxford town's reputation, Levi, as a Professor of Poetry and accomplished biographer, eventually came to treasure his stay among the Holy Men of Athos. In fact, he eventually stated that monks across the world attract fewer suspicions these days than in the past, due to the evidence that conflicting Church passions had cooled. Somewhat contrarily, his evocative book, *The Frontiers of Paradise: A Study of Monks and Monasteries*, demonstrated an unabated enthusiasm for the monastic life, which stands previous British apprehensions on their head. Levi even chides Henry VIII over the dissolution of the Monasteries and remarks on the intellectual and cultural contributions to our Society made by men called to continual prayer through realised vocation.

Or a seeker like Bruce Chatwin (1940-1989), who explored Afghanistan in the 1970s, searching for traces of Greek culture in this sadly overlooked region, only to be struck dumb, years later, by the presence of this sacred peninsula. So much so, that his friends intriguingly reported Chatwin as making arrangements for his own Baptism on Holy Mount Athos just prior to his untimely passing. Undoubtedly, this commented, around 1980, he had tragically contracted HIV[2] and died in Nice at the age of 48. Compassionately, a memorial service was held in the Greek Orthodox Church of St Sophia in West London. Happening, coincidentally, on the same turbulent day that a fatwa was pronounced on Salman Rushdie (born 1947), a close friend of Chatwin's who attended the service, and obliging the legendary travel writer Paul Theroux (born 1941)—a one-time associate coequally attending the service—to comment on these absolving events in a piece for *Granta*.[3] Finally at peace with the Orthodox Church, Chatwin's ashes were scattered near a Byzantine chapel above Kardamyli in the Peloponnese.

Or, for that matter, authors like the literary rambler Sir Patrick Leigh Fermor (1915-2011), a soldier known to have celebrated his twenty-first birthday on Blessed Mount Athos with the Russian monks. Undoubtedly, from an early age, Sir Patrick, or Paddy as he is universally known, admired the fact that these holy men lived a Spartan life of prayer, practically unchanged for a thousand years. Moreover, he respected their determination to embrace the challenging conditions of this Greek peninsula as one of their principal teachers in the religious life. As such, he too seems to have perceived Holy Athos as a teacher of life-lessons. Accordingly, after the rocky inevitability of many years together, Leigh Fermor married, in 1968, the Honourable Joan Elizabeth Rayner, daughter of the Viscount Monsell I. Following which, she companioned him on many of his travels until her death in Kardamyli in June 2003, aged 91. Assuredly, learning to appreciate Nature's rhythm after the manner of the Athonites, they lived part of the year in their house within an olive grove near Kardamyli on the Mani Peninsula, southern Peloponnese, and part of the year in Worcestershire, England: like their neighbours, learning to embrace good things as gifts of the Spirit.

Or again, like fully trained British archaeological visitors to the Holy Mountain such as Frederick William Hasluck (1878-1920), who worked at the British School in Athens. For his part, Hasluck published a book on Mount Athos and its monasteries inside of which he tells readers that he confronted his own preconceived repugnance of monasticism in general, along with "Greek" monasticism as non-productive and especially "parasitic," in particular. Curiously, it was a quarrel with one of the Fathers that defused this potentially explosive situation and deconstructed his rancour towards the sanctity of these cloisters. Undoubtedly, this Quagan battle with a member of one of the communities led to a wider recognition of their spiritual authenticity. The world being as it is, however, Hasluck's new accord with the Fathers, as well as his professional work on Mount Athos, was cut short by a combination of factors: one being his allegedly becoming the career-target of Alan John Bayard Wace, an erstwhile colleague in Athens, who appears to have regarded Hasluck as a potential rival. Sadly, apocryphal wisdom has it that Wace, upon returning to London, prepared the ground for his attack by becoming a member of the managing committee, thereby gaining the post of Director of the School. Thence, upon ascending to this position, apparently, he speedily asked London to sack Hasluck, and, somewhat astonishingly, they did. So dismissed, Hasluck and his wife nonetheless stayed in Athens; eventually working at the British Legation to assist with the United Kingdom's wartime intelligence operations!

Monasticism aside, the Maniots, as a sort of spiritual kindred, continued to raise uncomfortable conundrums for us British folk concerning the enduring, if roundabout, connection between a vibrant ethnicity and innate organic culture. Along with the subtle continuum joining hedonistic lifestyle choices to sincere religious exertion! As Matthew Arnold (1822-1888) stated in the preface to his groundbreaking tome *Culture and Anarchy* in 1869, human culture, spiritual or material, is best seen as "the disinterested endeavour after man's perfection." Speculative claims, which do not mean, as contemporary critics need to note, the false nirvana of suppressed desires, numbed passions and blunted horizons: aided and abetted by a palpable psychological suppression. On the contrary, rabid political correctness, both then and now, simply spurred this renowned social critic of Victorian England to go further and contend that culture, at its height, meant to "know the best that has been said and thought in the world." Dual concepts celebrating real diversity, as well as sounding a clarion call, in the hearts of Maniot and Briton alike!

Geographically, of course, this sandy puzzle is like many another peninsula and a common enough mountainous area in Macedonia, northern Greece. Accordingly, Robert Draper's recent article, *Called to the Holy Mountain*, published in the August 2012 edition of *National Geographic*, mechanically scribes:

> The holy peninsula of Mount Athos reaches 31 miles out into the Aegean Sea like an appendage struggling to dislocate itself from the secular corpus of northeastern Greece. For the past thousand years or so, a community of Eastern Orthodox monks has dwelled here, purposefully removed from everything except God. They live only to become one with Jesus Christ. Their enclave—crashing waves, dense chestnut forests, the spectre of snowy-veined Mount Athos, 6,670 feet high—is the very essence of isolation.

Observations, it must be said, managing to avoid any mention of the blisteringly pleasurable temptations presented by these living elements to the *"Athletae Dei,"* or athletes of God, abiding there. The Greek Islands, alongside this peninsula in particular, known for their dangerously sensual, although unashamedly, Edenic, delights! Undoubtedly then, the seductively glittering waters surging around the end of the peninsula, still known for their unpredictability, offer threatening, even though kaleidoscopically Pagan distractions to this day. Ever cautious in pragmatic details of this agitated type, it became known that Xerxes I (518-465 BC) commanded a channel to be excavated across the isthmus, thereafter giving safe passage to his invasion fleet in 483 BC. Sharp grey gravel, treacherously sparkling surf, and belligerent bark serving as triple witnesses to the nervous plans of Emperors and Bottlenose Dolphins, on this initially polytheistic bridge to the Sanctified!

Precisely because physically incarcerated, Mount Athos is practically accessible only by boat to this day. As such, there are two large ferries, cleverly named the *Axion Estin* and *Agios Panteleimon,* that (weather permitting) travel on a daily basis between Ouranoupoli and Dafni. Stopping, when appropriate, at some of the monasteries on the west coast and serving travellers from across the globe with a cheap means of transportation. What is more, there is a smaller speed boat, Agia Anna, which tries not to splice the mainbrace as it sails the very same route, although without unspecified or unscheduled pauses. Conversely, travelling by a newly regularised ferry, both to and from Ierissos, access to those monasteries bordering the eastern coast is made much easier. Never forgetting, of course, that the daily number of visitors entering Mount Athos is carefully restricted, and everyone is required to obtain a special entrance permit; valid for a limited span only. Orthodox Christians patently taking a favoured precedence in the issuance procedure. At the end of the day, that recognised, Mount Athos has always been greater than the mere sum of its manifest quantities, the fame of its guests, or the incessant demands of History. As age-worn intuitions by knowledgeable hermits and gifted, sensitised, spaemen, endlessly testify. So, maybe it is at this point of inquiry that our profound bonding with this alternative seat of Mars starts to clarify.

For the monks, without doubt, the mountain is an arena. Not of flesh and bone made implacable by indigence, but for purified soul and beatific purpose. Hosting, as the peninsula does, twenty Orthodox monasteries under the political sovereignty of the Greek State, this autonomous region of Greece may productively be understood as a metaphysical wrestling ground: a reason, possibly, why Monastics alone are permitted to establish any type of permanency in these sacerdotal gymnasia. Currently, there are said to be 1,400 Athonites: or as some call them Hagiorites, flexing their devotions among the robustly coloured boulders. Numbers easily exceeding those of the initial community in 963 AD, when St Athanasius (920-1003)—not to be confused with St Athanasius the Great who lived in the fourth century—founded the Great Lavra: a sanctuary which is still the largest, not to forget the most prominent, of all 20 monasteries. A distinction achieved, in large proportion, because of its nearly permanent protection under the Emperors of the Eastern Roman Empire! Yet, in spite of these shields, through the unfolding centuries its wealth became tantamount to legendary. Cynics contending this explained one of the reasons behind the Fourth Crusade (in the thirteenth century) bringing transparently avaricious Roman Catholic overlords in its "protective" wake. Forcing the monks, in their turn, to appeal directly to Pope Innocent III (1161-1216) for his overarching patronage! Until, that is, the Byzantine Empire was more or less fully restored in the fourteenth century, and ecclesiastical "independence" was achieved. Unfortunately, if further proof were needed with respect to the perpetual economic plundering of Mount Athos, Catalan mercenaries continuously raided its otherwise peaceful confines decade, after decade, after decade, after decade!

On a more uplifting note, the first historically commemorated hermits attempting to heal the Soul of its greedy weaknesses were Peter the Athonite and Euthymios of Salonica; each of which date from the ninth century, and both of whom remain influential in the historical development of this curative location as a clinic for mortal ailments. As custom has it, Peter was said to be sailing past Mount Athos when he found his ship had become weirdly immobile in the sea and incapable of forward movement: while off of sandy Karavostási as gleeful Maniots still recount. A site nowadays called, rather predictably, the "Bay of the Standing Ship." Immediately realising this was a celestial sign that his journey was over, Peter promptly climbed the rugged ravine in front of him and settled in a dreary cave to embrace, without a second thought, the medicinal battle of asceticism. Much to the astonishment, it needs to be emphasised, of the ship's crew watching him; who quickly found they were able to set sail anew. From his side, this event marked the commencement of fifty years in pious solitude for Peter, and resulted in his eventual canonisation by Orthodox authorities. Atop of these marvels, it is mentioned that on one propitious occasion, a hunter accidentally encountered Peter at prayer and, being spiritually awoken by the holy man's piety, vowed to pursue the ascetic life himself. A year, or so, later, locals tell us, when the converted forager arrived with a small group of converts eager to take up their own meditations they found that the saint had already passed over. Only his scattered bones (strewn throughout the cave) were left as a memorial to his ministrations. Undeterred, the little group collected the holy recluse's remains as healing relics; ultimately handing them to the monks of Klementos as a token of their brotherly respects. A monastery, native folklorists explain, that used to stand where Iver is currently situated. Incidentally, as a cross-selection of these amateur, but highly informed, historians have verbally annotated, this story appears to confirm that, by 840 AD, when Peter the Athonite arrived on the mountain, it was still largely uninhabited, even though by the time of his death, fifty years later, the Monastery of Klementos had itself been built.

As for young Euthymios, indigenous scribes recount he had already taken up his healing activities on the Holy Mount by then. Despite, that is, if judged by our modern standards, presenting supporters of monasticism with a far more problematic exemplification of saintliness than Peter. Born near Ankara in 823 AD, Euthymios, somewhat caddishly, abandoned wife and child to live out his vocation as a hermit! By 862 AD, the story continues, he had become the effective head of a small, but prestigious, community on Holy Athos. So, elevated and empowered, Euthymios proceeded to establish numerous settlements throughout the peninsula. Anecdotally, John Kolovos (eighth century)—a strange epithet typically meaning "the Dwarf"—arriving somewhere around this time, is said to have founded the Monastery of Kolovou, in 875, together with Euthymios. One early account placing the monastery close to the village of Ierissos—well outside of the present-day border—whilst others situate it at *Meglia Vigla*, inside the recognised boundaries of this Holy enclave. The only surety in such matters, all things considered, especially in these orally recorded tales, being that Kolovou lasted for a whole century before becoming subsumed, in the tenth century, into the Great Larva itself.

Proponents of these righteous institutions must be cognisant, nonetheless, that, by definition, monasticism is an acquired taste within the wider Christian Community taken as a whole. It is a rarefied charism, to say the least. An exceptional act of service! Not to avow, a debatable lifestyle choice, even if understood as an honoured form of spiritual witness by an informed majority. Admittedly, from the disciplines of the Desert Fathers onwards, some of whom settled on Mount Athos during the seventh century, deliberately arid forms of religiosity retained all the hallmarks of the wilderness; embodying, as these practices do, a constant mindfulness towards profoundly non-material goals. From the Greek term, *monachos,* therefore, typically interpreted as "solitary," a monk is a person who uses exterior hardship to strengthen elative internal qualities. Living singularly among the wastes, in order to substantiate these aims, or in the virtuous vicinity of other holy hermits! Such a man may be a total recluse, as far as this is possible, who voluntarily decides to leave the secular world of momentary indulgences behind him, or a man who has chosen to dedicate his life to the selfless assistance of all other creatures on this Earth. But be it this way, or that, a Christian monastic treads an antique path once trodden through Egyptian sands, long before our Civilisation twinkled in anyone's eyes. Representing a form of ceaseless rubric best explained by Swedenborg's comment, "The deeper we look, the more wondrous are the things we run into." By which the sanguine Swede meant to firmly defend an individual's personal spiritual practice.

Digressing slightly further, in Greek languages, the word "monk" can be applied to women, while in modern English it can only be used for men. The word "nun," by gender convention, recognised as a more appropriate term for the fairer sex. Interestingly, this minor linguistic distraction obscures one of the most distinctive features in traditional Christian monasticism. Sexuality itself, rather surprisingly, being considered as integral to these mystical transformations! Experientially tested as they have been, these prayerful cogitations promise spiritual emancipation without a crushing denial of femininity, or masculinity per se. So described, the life of a Christian eremite is that of a person travelling backwards to a lost paradise: a half-forgotten unmapped location existing before the binary curses of limitation and despair. Monks gradually, through Divine Grace, trying to recover the scattered virtues and perfections of Adam; the archetypal ancestor of all humankind. Thusly, they walk a path intended to recover their own divinity. Buddhist Monastics, by contrast, are loners purging themselves of all earthly desires! Hindu holy men, upon comparison, seem better understood as solitaries attempting to overcome this earthly sphere in order to find release from all material bondage. Still, unlike these parallel religious pioneers, a Christian monk aims at restoring his full capacities as a child of God.

Faiths of equal Abrahamic descent, likewise, speak of similar ascetic rubrics, despite in reality, focusing on the demands of ritual purity. In Judaism, for instance, cleansing and continence were undertaken by the Community at Qumran in the first century BC, as safeguards to their "untainted" psyches. Essene brotherhoods, throughout this period, testifying to the importance of undefiled and flawless lineal rites! Many of which form a weird continuum, it should be noted, with kosher prohibitions among the Jews into modern times. In addition to holding sway in some Hebraic neighbourhoods as active symbols of Semitic selfhood! Furthermore, in Islam, as another emergent faith from the very same desert wilds, hygiene restrictions remain vital to morning and evening ceremonial observance for both the ordinary householder, as much as an appointed Mullah. Nonetheless, these superficial semblances to monasticism are hardly surprising when recalling the shared origin of such cultic regulations; coupled with the evidence that there is nothing more basic than the need to purify oneself before an alter raised to the Most High in the midst of scorching, debilitating, and purgative, wastelands.

At this point, it is advisable to remember the monks of Mount Athos follow a ritual tradition dissimilar to mainstream Western Christianity. Their heritage having alternative ordinances probably forged from the fires of growing schism (between Church East and West) throughout the twelfth century. This may be one of the reasons why, in Orthodoxy, the process of becoming an anchorite is intentionally delayed. Internalised monastic vows considered to categorically entail a lifelong, and unbreakable, commitment to stillness, tranquillity and repose: along with endless repetitions of the "Jesus Prayer" as a subjective, transformative, science. Arguably, the earliest written reference to this "Prayer of the Heart" originates in a text from the *Philokalia*, by Abba Philemon, who lived around 600 AD. Although, St Diadocho (c. 400-486 AD) describes repetitive prayer procedures for achieving inner peace in a slightly earlier timeframe! Writing, as he does, in terms comparable to St John Cassian (c. 360-435 AD), who, himself, mentions an inherited Biblical prayer formula used in Egypt, "O God, make speed to save me: O Lord make haste to help me." Nonetheless, the now classic, devotional incantation, "Lord Jesus Christ, Son of God, have mercy on me, a sinner" finally found open, unadulterated, citation, in the work of St Hesychios the Priest (c. eighth century), calling instantly to mind mystical attitudes treasured by an unknown monk in fourteenth-century England who authored *The Cloud of Unknowing*.

Since that period, practitioners of this prayer technique have been prudently advised, by various authors, to undertake these hallowed repetitions in complete stillness. One needs to "empty" one's mind of all concepts upon closing the eyes, tyros are told. This contemplative process coequally accompanied by an individual intensification of personal consciousness regarding God's immanent presence in the world. Enhancing, as this cryptically does, sensations of one's own place and purpose in Creation! Inexplicably, all things considered, the bodily signs of such gnarly interior exercises didn't identify a contemplative "movement" within the Eastern Church until the fourteenth century, despite having embodied a thoroughly Orthodox regimen from the first occasion of their formal, institutional, establishment. Visible allegiance to this type of profession being alluded to as "Tonsure" – a term referring to the ritual cutting of a monk's hair during his dedication to the recondite oracles of solitude. A ceremony, in itself, once considered to be a sacred mystery analogous to funerals, blessing, and exorcisms. Extra devotional steps were nevertheless required (after finishing a novitiate) before a monk finally received his habit. Even though it is translucently clear that nothing is considered more important to the fulfilment of a vocation than the spiritual urgency surrounding these repeated interior litanies.

Combative as human nature intrinsically is, however, the monasteries have occasionally witnessed open dissension around their innocent ranks. Maybe particularly regarding these complex methodologies of depth prayer and their theological implications! Competing interpretations of which, sadly, managed to produce conceptual struggles that aggressively orbited the peninsula as a whole! Issues, moreover, very quickly entangled with other, much less hermetic affairs, like the material distribution of chattels, goods, properties, and Church authority! Hence, carefully disguised legal assaults and subsequent counterattacks on the ethereal subject of Hesychasm were preserved by clerical secretaries, who came to loosely define these psychic procedures as a "retreat" to the inner planes through ceasing to register physical sensations altogether and achieving, thereby, an experiential knowledge of the Numinous. But definitions of this sort did not always reflect the real issues under scrutiny. Charges of Gnosticism, perhaps understandably, were then thrown down like a gauntlet by ecclesiastical opponents of such unarguably subversive stratagems. Although, it went without saying that the monks themselves claimed arcane protocols of this type were unreservedly based on Christ's injunction, as read in the Gospel of St Matthew, to "go into your closet to pray;" a Scripture plain for all to digest. Nevertheless, required as they were to safeguard their financially precious bequests, these schools of repetition searched for, and discovered, a robust defence in the writings of St Gregory Palamas. A writer respected by friend and foe alike, as someone who understood the differing sides of this debate well before he became Archbishop of Thessaloniki.

The Holy Bible, of course, comparably tells its readers not to look for firm foundations in this world. An injunction regrettably ignored by Prince and Potentate likewise when the eventual political collapse of Byzantium was seen to cause seismic social upheavals in the fifteenth century. Advancing, at the same moment, opportunities for the newly established Ottoman Empire to dominate life on Holy Mount Athos! For the most part, Islamic authorities left the monasteries to their own affairs, even though they heavily taxed the incumbent Fathers. Consequently, as their fortunes withered, the unfurling seasons witnessed a lengthy period of decline for the monks. Regenerative forces only starting to stir in the nineteenth century with the timely arrival of newcomers from other Orthodox countries such as Romania, Russia, Serbia and Bulgaria: escorted as these settlers were by hefty financial donations designed to assist the work of the sanctuaries. It took the outbreak of the First Balkan War in 1912, that evidenced, to compel the Ottomans to finally withdraw from the peninsula. What is more, it necessitated a brief, but bloody, conflict between Russia and Greece, over the matter of sovereignty, to see the Mount formally coming under Greek jurisdiction at the end of World War I. Nowadays, in political reality, this region is mostly self-governed, consisting of a capital city and an administrative centre, Karves, acting as the home to representative Governors of the Greek State.

Outside of the monastery complexes, there are roughly 12 sketae, or smaller communities of monks, as well as solitary hermitages throughout the entire peninsula. Pilgrims are, metaphorically, embraced with "shovels of Caviar," while other lay visitors are encouraged to spend their time on Athos reflectively. Prudence is, nonetheless, advised when stepping inside this combatant's ring, and it seems to be felt that females (of every species) should be forbidden access for this reason. Something of an ironic prohibition, considering that the Blessed Virgin Mary herself, is said to be the guardian of these cloistered confines, along with engendering practical difficulties when it comes to the demand for fresh egg yolk used in icon painting. Indisputably, difficult times have seen a relaxation of this rule, as when shelter was given to women and girl refugees during the Greek Civil War. Yet, apart from periods characterised by extreme political conditions, this ban continues to operate; giving unintended offence to present day "liberal" sensibilities. Stated so, critics of this prohibition have pointed out that if the word "woman" was to be replaced by "black" or "Jew" the moral affront given by such a policy would quickly become apparent. Maybe so! But, when all is tallied and totalled, neither the vocabulary of contemporary human rights, nor the juridical assertions of capitalist private ownership, appears commensurate to a full understanding of this ban. The most workable rationale discovered in safeguarding the ruminations of the monks in their fight against those wicked powers limiting human expansion, along with their right to religious privacy.[4]

With comments like these in mind, folktales of the *Theotokos*, the very Mother of God, being blown off course whence sailing to Cyprus, and her setting foot on a Pagan Athos, take on a new radiance. Forced, as the story goes, to anchor near the port of Klement (close to the monastery of Iver), the Virgin walked ashore, blessed the natural beauties surrounding her, and asked her Son for these lands to be her enclosure. It is lovingly recounted that a celestial voice was then heard to reply, "Let this place be your inheritance and your garden, a paradise and a haven of salvation for those seeking to be saved." Indelibly, from that moment to this, the mountain has been consecrated as the Blessed Virgin's personal greenhouse, as well as an enigmatic precinct out of bounds to all other women. As Draper wryly states in his attempt to interpret these symbolic narrations on a practical basis:

> Each monk forms an abiding bond with his cell's elder, or monastery's abbot, who becomes a spiritual father. The retirement or death of these eminences can be difficult for the younger monks. Conversely, a young man's decision to return to the world may also be wrenching. "Last year one left," recalls an elder. "He didn't ask for my opinion," he adds, his voice betraying a fatherly hurt, "so it's just as well that he's gone."

Monks, all things considered, are still men. If truth be told, proudly so! Chastity is thus felt to be slightly more secured by this "all male" environment of pastoral pugilists. And as such, some commentators have openly mentioned that the extra pressure posed by the presence of women on Holy Athos would be too great a burden for the majority to bear. Henceforth, stories of sexual naivety, and recovered innocence, are all the more explanatory in this ethical context. So, women entering Mount Athos, it could be argued, present the problem of an extra temptation, which, as our Western civilisation becomes more liberalised, simply weaves further ties to earthly flesh and bodily desire.

Logically, even with this confessed, a greater danger is posed to these chivalric communities by the repeated outbreaks of wildfires on the Holy Mount. In August 1990, and in March 2004, flames all but gutted a large section of the Serbian monastery Chilandari. A fact recently confirmed by Serbian representatives at the International Conference on Holy Mount Athos held in Weimar. Beyond doubt, the secluded locations of the monasteries, often situated on top of small hills, compounds a problem posited by the lack of suitable firefighting equipment. The damage inflicted through such accidental events being, without exaggeration, genuinely devastating. Primary problems increased, some would rejoin, by the babble of languages spoken across the peninsula. Greek supersedes any other tongue, without qualification. Nonetheless, more peregrine forms of parlance are predominantly heard in some of the monasteries. Russian is the de facto lingua franca of St Panteleimon, pundits declare. In Chilandari it is, defiantly, Serbian. The monastery of Zographou boasts of the music in Bulgarian gutturals, whilst in the Sketae of Lacu and Prodromou it is impassioned Romanian – which thunders across the cloisters. Observed so, the majority of monks understand rudimentary English, along with innumerable phrases from other European languages!

Conceivably, the most pugnacious practice of the monks presently living on Holy Athos is that their lives are timed according to the "Byzantine calendar"[5]: a distinctive custom seemingly not much more than charming at first sight, but one which quickly starts to speak volumes upon closer reflection. Differences of this kind tending to conceal the hidden, even though manifestly continuous, influence of Byzantine culture on Western European affairs. For the Fathers, as a community, it is principally a matter of religious testimony. Christians are called, they are quick to stress, in the Epistle to the Ephesians 5.16, to "Redeem time because these days are evil," or in other words, to the fervent and unending prayer they each practice. The monks of Athos, however, have taken this sacred admonition to a stage above ordinary deponents. Debatably drawing on the Spartan habit of tenacity abounding throughout the region, their daily activities vociferously proclaim that exalted religious entreaties are the only way to make a full use of every mortal moment. In the kitchens preparing breakfast, as in the noontide heat, or during the evening when taking minted tea, they grapple to express their realisation that time is temporary, not abiding. Besides this, every unhallowed minute that disappears is apparently lost forever. Only those times eternalised through our contact with the Unknowable, they contend, will endure in any meaningful way. To support such views, the more learned Fathers will point to St Gregory of Nyssa (335-395 AD) who, in his *De Octavo*, PG XLIV 609A, talks of time as "sullied" and "dirty." The reason being, for Gregory, that all of Creation, since the Fall in Eden, is soiled with Sin. Thence originates the well-known impediment to measuring time with pinpoint astronomical accuracy, according to this weighty scholar, and explains our constant relapse into reductive images of mundane imperfection.

Exigently, perhaps, a few ground rules need to be drawn with respect to the function of sacred literature, theological reasoning and the proactive application of image, symbol and sign by an author. Indubitably, essays aspiring to express metaphysical axioms aim at surpassing the fractured limitations of pedestrian duration! In a manner reminiscent of the half-light of an autumn equinox awaiting the silvery illumination promised by the brilliance of a full Harvest Moon, these text types avowedly stretch beyond the linguistically attainable. They writhe and struggle with semantic conventions in an attempt to articulate the Absolute. To irradiate our worldly minds with the uncreated shimmering of a superior understanding: an enterprise we need to thank the masters of this genre for even attempting to engage with. Maybe this is why their semantic machinery seems above peer when searching for previously unsuspected depths in communications. Neither necessarily at war with the Holy, or Greek Archetypes, nor continuing Byzantine cultural influences, these personalists, for want of a better epithet, argue that the original objective of their studies was to hold a metaphorical spyglass against Scripture: to unwrap the interplaying weave of syntax with emotions and thoughts. Indeed, slightly reworking Swedenborg's lines, "Man, when he is re-born, passes through the ages as he who is born; and the preceding state is always as an egg in respect to the subsequent one, thus he is continually conceived and born: and this not only when he lives in the world, but also when he comes into another life to eternity: and still when he cannot be further perfected, then to be as an egg to those things which remain to be manifested, which are indefinite," I would stress that if we really wish to ascertain the meaning of a lexical item, it becomes vital to survey the "practical" consequences conceivably resulting from that notional bundle: plus start an investigation of the linguistic consequences constituting the entire meaning of that term. Swedenborg himself, hinting that teleological signatures, suspended indices, as well as prophetic marks, chaperoned by a writer's advocacy of a specific theory, frequently reveal a great deal more about the impact of a work than a fully outlined explanation!

This is why Quagan approaches to "storytelling" tend to accent its protean character – because no single prosaic source for these narrations can be skirmished into identification. Something the shapeshifting god Proteus would have wholeheartedly approved of! Therefore, "consecrated" inscription, or momentous glyph, become immediately recognised as nephews to the mythic. Be it a Pagan Greek folktale, or, without any intended disrespect, an Orthodox Byzantine homily. Such tales, moreover, valued as encapsulations of Being are easily seen as invaluable lexical varnishes, formed from the passionate remnants of previously energised articulations. Making the probability of deeply nourishing collective recollection realisable through the continual recitation of local fable and universal allegory alike! In this sense, we write our greater Identity and are written by it; whether understood as soap opera, or read as saga. We weave our daydreams around the larger than suburban realities embodied by Monks, Fishwives, Priests, Knights, Thieves, Holy Mountains, Vendettas, Farmers, Kitchens, Seraphic Messengers and Journeymen. As Maniots, Monastics, or Britannic authors, we distil our pictographs in the same manner as drinking wine and finding love. Passing inherited verse, as well as oral wisdom, from generation to generation as a means of entertainment, education, cultural preservation and ethical instruction. Private anecdotes designed to build an instinctive cooperation with our fellows, as well as a mutually enriching context.

Literature, be it Biblical, Mythic or otherwise, is an attempt to store the old secure ways of behaving, whilst reconstructing worth in the visceral bonds between everything created. Through human stories, *sub specie aeternitatis*, the mores and metaphysical glosses held dear by our forebears can be revived anew. In ancient Greek mythology, as a case in point, Athos, rather instructively, was the name of one of the rebellious giants who challenged the gods in the Gigantomachia.[6] It was recounted that he threw a huge rock at the god Poseidon, which fell into the warm erotic waters of the Aegean Sea to become the Mount we know of today. Fascinatingly, a variant recounting of this story, tells how Poseidon used the mountain to bury the defeated giant, thereby restoring Order and Law to the area. Homer, as the undisputed master of Hellenic letters, mentions Mount Athos as a place touched by powers celestial in his *Iliad* (Book 14: 222), where we may musingly read:

So spake she, and ox-eyed, queenly Hera smiled, and smiling laid the zone in her bosom. She then went to her house, the daughter of Zeus, Aphrodite, but Hera darted down and left the peak of Olympus; on Pieria she stepped and lovely Emathia, and sped over the snowy mountains of the Thracian horsemen, even over their topmost peaks, nor grazed she the ground with her feet; and from Athos she stepped upon the billowy sea, and so came to Lemnos, the city of godlike Thoas. There she met Sleep, the brother of Death; and she clasped him by the hand, and spake and addressed him: "Sleep, lord of all gods and of all men, if ever thou didst hearken to word of mine, so do thou even now obey, and I will owe thee thanks all my days. Lull me to sleep the bright eyes of Zeus beneath his brows, so soon as I shall have lain me by his side in love. And gifts will I give thee, a fair throne, ever imperishable, wrought of gold, that Hephaestus, mine own son, the god of the two strong arms, shall fashion thee with skill, and beneath it shall he set a foot-stool for the feet, whereon thou mayest rest thy shining feet when thou quaffest thy wine.

Now, this atmospheric unification of humankind with the Holy Summit is second to none! Writing in a similar vein, the historian Herodotus (484-425 BC), when corroborating these notations, informs his readers that this belligerent peninsula, once called Akte or Acte, was, undoubtedly, populated by restless Pelasgians from the Island of Lemnos. Elaborating correspondingly received details, the chronicler mentions that they actually founded five cities: Sane, Cleanae (Kleonai), Thyssos (Thyssus), Olophyxos (Olophyxis) and Acrothoi (Akrothoon) in his attempts to meld man with Nature. From his side, venerable Strabo (63 BC-24 AD) talks about the noble city of Dion (Dium) in this vicinity, and concludes that Acrothoi was near to the mountain's crest (*Geography*, V11-33:1). He adds, it was documented that Eretria established colonies on Acte and, at least, one other city was built in the Classical period, by the name of Acanthus (Akanthos). Some of these cities even minting their own coins as a defiant tribute to their own power! Also, following Alexander the Great's (356-323 BC) death, the celebrated architect Dinocrates (Deinokrates, fourth century BC) drew designs for the entire mountain to be carved into a statue of this colossal conqueror. Though, in later ages, the union of people with the peninsula became strangely cloaked, due to a sudden lack of suggestive texts: historical, legendary or otherwise. Potentially, this is why it continues to be believed that when the Christians took up residence on Athos they found little except surreal ruins.

Pondered so, the lore, geography, and history of Mount Athos presents sympathetic commentators with a linguistic archaeology of pivotal events and previous peoples. In this regard, the enigma of Athos must surely remind Britons of the Matter of Britain. On one hand, it is myth. Substantially, on the other hand, it is history. Producing in their turn, twin streams of text involving already famous archetypal Cavaliers, who usually find themselves accompanied by symbolically armed retainers! Every one of which has metaphorically fallen into suspended animation in remote dwelling places. Caves on high mountaintops, remote islands, or supernatural retreats, serving as stylised landscapes for the realities of our Collective Unconscious! Almost invariably, that stated, folktales gathered by the Brothers Grimm concerning Charlemagne (742-814) and Frederick Barbarossa (1122-1190) are representative of these cultural memes; helping to explain the ancestry of many preserved derivatives, along with their subsequent adaptations. Intriguingly, the presence of a hero is nearly always concealed, until some herdsman, or other, wanders into the aforementioned prototypical location, looking, maybe, for a lost animal, only to suddenly see this legendary figure. Complimenting their inherited charm, such stories mention minute details like the warrior having grown a long beard; illustrative of the time he has slept on top of the mountain etc. Notably, in the Brothers Grimm version, the hero tends to speak with the herdsman. Their carefully scripted conversation inevitably involving the hero inquiring, "Do the eagles (or ravens) still circle the mountaintop?" The herdsman, or some unnamed voice, replying, "Yes, they still circle the mountaintop." At which point the visitor is dismissed because the warrior's time has not yet come. The merely mortal herdsman, conversely, finds himself preternaturally changed by these astonishing events. Either, he ages rapidly as a result of this confrontation, or he leaves the hollow with his hair shocked white. Sometimes, in the narrative, he dies following his recitation of the tale.

Thusly, as arenas of Recurrence, Rebirth and Restoration, Holy Mountains are normally at their most glorified towards the peak. Mythographers, wryly suggesting, this is because the summit is customarily indicative of a promised Nirvanic state, or the peak, itself, being related to august outpourings from "on high." It could then be reasonably argued that there is a Matter of Mount Athos, in a category parallel to that of Britain, France, or Rome: each of these perennial localities having developed a sheath of axiological layers fusing the fate-laden activities of Art, Life and Existence. The very topographies wherein historical figures move, breathe, and have their Being, transformed by the dominion of metaphysics and viscous terrains of subconscious, imagistic, thought. Several mythic strategies can, therefore, be ascertained throughout these bodies of literature. Together with the Matter of France, concerned as it is with the legends of Charlemagne, and the Matter of Rome, which included symbolic material derived from, or inspired by, classical mythology, Christian Mount Athos can take its place as an embodiment of Byzantine Civilisation: edifying, as this does, our human condition. In innumerable ways, after all, the peninsula is reminiscent of Mount Sinai in Judaism, and Mount Hara Berezaiti in Zoroastrianism. Even its ancient name distinguishes Athos as a place where the claustrophobic and numbing restrictions of contemporary society come to an abrupt end. Anyone journeying into its charged atmosphere discovering, on the level of full awareness or not, transition, as well as freedom, from their burdens. It is a location where the contours of the Miraculous have etched their presence upon the lowly. So, in a manner strikingly dissimilar to the medieval Matter of benighted Britain and the bloodcurdling themes sculpting the "Matter of Rome," not to neglect tales of the Paladins of Charlemagne (and their wars with Moor and Saracen) constituting the "Matter of France," the Matter of Athos is continuously told through Byzantine icon and hesychastic prayer as the longest-serving Christian amphitheatre in the world. It is a place where the Uncreated Light forever shines upon the woes of our world.

It is increasingly unwise, when this is acknowledged, to relinquish these intersubjective "residues." Especially in an epoch characterised by radical political absurdity and its attendant social atomism! Unrepentantly, within such a sterile period, Art's relationship with

Life neither reflects psychological dysfunction, nor the desperate need to find any conceivable pigeonhole (of orientation) to settle the nerves, but instead, surprisingly, shows the bare bones of a sacred quest. The need to ascend interior mountains as a latter-day wanderer (*homo viator*) oneself! Looking for the gods as an urban Knight Errant searching for his, or her, Blessed Grail! Mature literary critics, so apprehending this situation, have tried to detect an underlying motif centred on notions of "mountaineer" as Hero. The Quagan desire, that is, to find more exalted and better ways of living, than merely becoming content to sink into our empirical selves. Passions, like these, fusing Life and Art into "something" more than the workaday. To undertake this goal of the Angels may, of course, be impossible, although the very task of Literature is to ask, "What if it is not?" Literature overall, and English Literature in particular, not simply being the remembrance of evils past, but the documented capacity to look morally diminishing scenarios in the face with a steely fortitude! King Arthur, thus arisen, reappears as the chief exemplar in our own, individual, Matter of Britain; less illustrious characters in this corpus (debatably including) conspicuous opponents—Brutus of Britain, distant rivals, Old King Cole and uncle Gogmagog—as supporting role models preparing their Squires for a future resurrection day.

Ancestry is the secret. This may be why a variety of genealogies were devised for a number of Welsh princes in the ninth century to personify this "Royal" attribute among the Celts! Unfairly, the monk Nennius (ninth century AD) tends to be blamed, by historians of Literature, for unleashing plans to picture these largely inadequate men into the weave of immortal Anglo-Saxon Myth. Still, their stories achieved a wider currency than expected because their inventor, whoever this actually was, linked King Brutus to the diaspora of Heroes from Greece after the Trojan War. Positing, in his textual wake, the raw material, which later mythographers such as Geoffrey of Monmouth (1100-1155) and Michael Drayton (1563-1631) could refine! Associated so, the ethnic settlement of Britain proved a literary heir to the heroic age of Greek literature! Just as Virgil (70-19BC) had linked the legendary founding of Rome to the Trojan War in *The Aeneid*. Similarly then, Geoffrey of Monmouth coterminously claimed in his works that the Trinovantes, reported by Tacitus as dwelling in the area of London, had a name he himself deciphered as Troi-novant, or in other words, "New Troy." An eccentric testimony, on a par with audacious Mount Athos, allowing us Britons to proudly say, our Albion is a place where myth is entwined with history and magic: each enchantment mingling with the mundane. This is why, in appropriate measure, we appreciate its legacy much more than is usually expected.

Isolation, once this is noted, often makes the potential beneficiaries of an inheritance niggardly: an ethical outcome apparently unable to take root on Holy Mount Athos, though barely avoided in fashionable England. All meaning that we children of these Britannic Isles need to inquire why this is so? In itself, certainly, this Greek peninsula has remained one of the most unspoilt areas in the Mediterranean: a contention hardly needing justification. Its untamed and startling territories, comprising of pebbled and impassable gorges, buildings perched in breathtakingly lovely, yet unexpected positions, small scorched valleys interspersed with shadowy ravines, as well as a largely inaccessible coastline – each being a paradisiacal feature forcing British folk to inquire into the means by which Maniots have kept such big and munificent hearts. Is their secret to be unearthed in environmental extremes? Or, the Maniots' close affinity with the tiny streams of crystalline water running benevolently across the baking earth; like pulsing arteries bringing life back to the respiring soil, while their subsequent vegetable plots provide a comforting self-sufficiency to these tough, naturally dissident, denizens of Greece? Or again, is it the blistering, judicial, sunshine that beats a meanness of spirit into submission? Like Sam Fisher, the virtual Spy, unstoppably pounding his detractors into the ground.[7] Possibly, this recalled, it is the remnants of a purely Spartan outlook on life. A tragically lost kingdom envisioned as a doomed utopia of chivalric virtue, undone by the fatal flaws of internal treacheries. Indisputably, the knights recalled in this tradition exhibit an almost uncanny resemblance to the monks in their muscular and determined attitudes. Additionally, as an ethical reality, Faith is deeply rooted in their mutual narratives. Arguably, the crux of chivalry, Faith is a necessity in times of strife. It is also a modifying moral resource alchemically bettering the course of our daily lives. Furthermore, as a mysterious virtue occasionally defying interpretation it is, ultimately, one of the ways in which a man, woman, or child, can evaluate the very structure of their own Being. Few concepts revealing the superstructural parameters of our mortal condition with such effect! This attribute, thenceforth, must be understood to have both a cultural and individual tenor. The ethic that a specific society admires most, in the final analysis, depending on its material aptitudes and inevitably derived spiritual thirsts!

The position of knights in European feudal societies, literature tells us, brought it about that the three core chivalric virtues should be loyalty, prowess and generosity. Every one of which was to be developed in "good faith." Exactly as the monks of Athos, it may be commented, these warriors felt that through the pursuit of fealty, civic obligations were upheld and the social hierarchy maintained. Duty to one's Lord, either Celestial or Temporal, coupled with the cultivation of private honour, being praised as an unwavering indication of a man's moral worth: his own personal metal. Such loyalty, they collectively upheld, always outweighing the gratification of temporary whims and immature caprice. On a practical level, it was equally due to the knowledge that there were so few means of compulsion in the hands of brother Nobles regarding their confreres. Finally, prowess, contextually understood as the ability to win battles, on the field of honour, or within a knight's conscience, was proffered as vital to a gentleman's self-expression; since a knight's mission was to win at warfare – precisely as the hermits of Holy Athos engage with their unclean spiritual enemies. Maybe this is the rationale underpinning generosity as intrinsic to public magnanimity in our aristocratic, as well as saintly, forebears. Because gifts, betokening love, or at least those presents marking respect for the theoretical force wielded by another, often evinced excellence: a knight never wishing to be seen as merely the biggest and strongest animal in a given territory.

Truly, the monks of Mount Athos are knights of an effulgent Faith. Inheritors of an ennobling, multifaceted cultural current: circulations of which again bring to mind the turbulent, but ingenious, Swedenborg. An author who insisted that the adoption of such attitudes encapsulated an honest enough metaphysical stance in our millennium! A connection surprising to some, albeit an obvious link to armour forged in the moral foundries of Sparta, the Egyptian Desert and the aristocratic, or monkish, elite of Medieval Europe! Their Athonite vows of Chastity, Poverty, Stability and Obedience imitating long lost trials of endurance. Plainly, in Orthodoxy, although the oaths now taken were not part of the earliest monastic foundations, they did come to be accepted as a routine element in the Tonsure service. Previously, one would only need to find a spiritual guide and work under his religious direction; learning the ecstatic joys of religious repetition. Little more than this was actually asked for! However, with the passing of centuries contemplative conventions took ritual form. The vows themselves finally becoming administered by an officially recognised Hieromonk, or sanctioned Abbot! These days, following a period of intense training, the Rassophore (one who wears the Rassa), the Stavrophore (one who wears the Cross), and the Schema-monk (one who wears the Great Schema, or full monastic habit) take their rightful place as recognised adepts guiding their pupils up the steps on a ladder of prayer leading to a resolute life of blessed ministry.[8] Innumerable, therefore, appear to be the ways that the Holy Mount, itself, encourages this unendingly bellicose stance. The Mediterranean heat teaches it. Maddened geologies enjoining to manufacture a combatant's ring. Even though, unlike previous aristocratic knights who gambled their physical lives without the slightest hesitation, for, oftentimes, ignoble reasons, the monks of Holy Athos are quietly confident of their virtuous victory. Assured, some would say, by the fact their carefully honed spiritual protections will serve them as a reinforced sequence of defensive measures. Quoting St Paul (5-67 AD), as they often do, in his letter to the Ephesians, the monks recite:

Put on the whole armour of God, that you may be able to stand against the wiles of the devil. For we are not contending against flesh and blood, but against the principalities, against the powers, against the world rulers of this present darkness, against the spiritual hosts of wickedness in the Heavenly places. Therefore, take the full armour of God, that you may be able to withstand in the evil day, and having done all, to stand. Stand, therefore, having girded your loins with truth, and having put on the breastplate of righteousness, and having shod your feet with the equipment of the gospel of peace; besides all of these, taking the shield of faith, with which you can quench all the flaming darts of the evil one.

Bitter, yet rallying words from the mouth of an old Warhorse! Corroborating the evidence, that it continues to be unwise to think of these monastic pugilists as either soft, or lazy, or weak, as those visitors befogged by materialistic eyes have recently done! But instead, like the chivalrous knights of antiquity, and the virile Maniots of today, the Athonites breathe each moment from the depth of their hearts. Reinforcing, as this martial stance does, the antediluvian proclivity, preserved in Latin lexical items such as *cor,* which denote a fearless and courageous heart: the real seat of our governing passions. The divine Plato (428-348 BC), himself, defending congruent concepts of courage in his *Republic*, where it is understood to be the specific virtue of a Guardian Class. Prefiguring, as this grandfather of Orthodox theology did, the conclusions of later Christian Fathers! Although, even he may have missed the mark in this individual case, because these monks, exactly like the Grail Knights, Sir Percival and Sir Galahad, are on a sacred quest! Their intention being to stride into utopia and rebuild our decimated union with the Supernal!

Sitting in a country pub and dreaming of remote, magical, destinations, is a national preoccupation for us Britons. As birds sing in springtime on Oak tree branches, a pint of foaming ale merely adds lustre to the process. In addition, as everybody knows, within distant countries there are wonders beyond measure, accompanied as they are by signs of grandeur. Such emotions hiding, of course, the semi-conscious sensation that in our indigenous and time-honoured land the remaining marks of sanctity have come to seem scarce! There are some shrines to the Miraculous, it is generally agreed, and even native hills where the Holy has been experienced by a fortunate few. Yet, debate neither favours this side, nor t' other, when considering the notion of a nationwide hallowed topography. Specific places, without doubt, as most would admit, but an entire terrain? Such an idea would probably meet with an incredulous stare in these decadent days. A garden where the Mother of God has trodden? Well, "maybe," a sizable minority would whisper. But, an entire peninsula where whole monastic communities live with experimental attitudes similar to those of NASA? "Oh, come, come, now, hardly," would be the confutation! The now infamous channel tunnel, ecologically brutish even though cheap airfares, as well as a superficial and bewildering familiarity with foreigners, all giving a false sense of internationalist perspective. In which case, concluding deliberations on the nature of Mount Athos, like the enigma itself prove frustrating. Once described, they appear unending and open continua without any form of critical closure! In a way parallel, it should be adjoined, to standing back from the intricate frame of an Old Master, and trying to voice a summarising statement, or tract, about something abiding in its own inscrutability. Meanwhile, Mount Athos is a place where mystical puzzles implore religious truths to speak their mind across acres of space-time. It is a blank page exacting literary responses from the unwary; the genius loci of the place insisting that due respect is still paid to them in verse and story.

At that point we have come full circle. Any writer of worth being left with subject matter that is not as fleeting as the short lives of human beings, and ostensibly ego-free, is cursed and blessed by the same yardstick. Or maybe it is the positioning of these brief and all too human motives in raw environments that creates heroic literature. Perhaps it is all of them. There is a wealth of authorship, when all compositions are collected, about mountains, and it is easy to see why. Truly, one only has to think of Mount Athos for powerful adjectives to tumble from the tongue. It is a solitary phenomenon, vast and godlike in its own right. Just as legendary rivers were used to represent the flow of life, so Athos is a handy image to show human vulnerability. Its minerals themselves reminding us that ours is a planet constituted around Nature's awesome violence! Struggling to survive then, is integral to our existence. Literature on these issues, transforming rock and boulder into a subjective mountain, where fleshly mountaineers set forth, in the blinding brilliance of an alpine dawn, to ascend their own transgressions, remains telling. Breathing in, when nearing the top, to smell the pure air of spiritual comprehension: of heady intrinsic freedom, only to descend, once more, into the obscure and the pedestrian – notwithstanding personal transformation! In this way, indeed, Mount Athos transfigures many a man.

Undeniably, keeping the Byzantine calendar as a means to count such strivings on Athos is far from trivial in its intent. Or romantically antique. It is an attempt by the Fathers to cultivate time itself: to fix the passage of their proceedings to an agreed, elevated, standard. As such, they are aware that one of the practical tasks of the first oecumenical Councils in 325 AD was to affirm a workable calendar for all Christians, without ever relinquishing the knowledge that it was equally convened to tap into the enduring continuum of archetypal time; where problems posed by divergent dates for either Easter or Christmas were finally resolved. If conversation on these matters were to start on Mount Athos, the Fathers would, respectfully, tell guests that in order to achieve this, the Councils established Paschalia-tables for the dating of the Passion as a way to strengthen the unity of the Orthodox Church and put an end, once and for all, to schisms, as well as disputes, regarding the calendar overall. In this manner, the Athonites would explain to us, it was decided there was but a single way to accomplish such a purifying task; they must base their calendar of the person of Christ and his Saving Works. Predominantly on the central event in his personhood; the Resurrection! So, the monks merrily paraphrase these ambitious holy men. Scholars who went to unbelievable lengths to explore those events, which, in chronological succession, preceded the Resurrection; determining dates through Byzantine calculation! A technique, these sages felt, that would re-establish harmony to the universe through cosmic notions on a restored humankind. Thusly, as scientists invest their hours in a laboratory to test the conditions of truth and businessmen labour in their offices to accumulate as much profit as conceivable, the monks of Mount Athos battle in Byzantine time to consecrate each moment. They scrimmage towards the palpable marvels of Faith, both within and without, as they stride towards palaces of perfection above the contaminations of our claustrophobic society; English literature paying homage to their investment at every footfall.

SELECTED ENDNOTES

1. From *Later Letters of Edward Lear: to Chichester Fortescue (Lord Carlingford), Lady Waldegrave and Others.*

2. Chatwin was a self-proclaimed bisexual in a life affirming and rather British way.

3. *Granta* is a literary magazine and publisher in the United Kingdom whose mission centres on its "belief in the power and urgency of the story, both in fiction and non-fiction, and the story's supreme ability to describe, illuminate and make real."

4. On a personal level, I need to confess to my Quagan, egalitarian, discomfort with this ban on women entering Mount Athos. After all, as the Holy Bible itself tell us "Male and Female made He them."

5. In slightly less poetic terms, Byzantine time is simply the Julian calendar. Pope Gregory VIII established a reformed calendar in 1582 and brought seasonal calculation forward by two weeks. The Orthodox merely kept the old calendar. On top of this the Turks had defeated Byzantium as a rival political entity by this period, so to say "Byzantine" in a political sense would merely be inaccurate.

6. The Gigantomachia in Greek mythology was the symbolic struggle between the cosmic order of the Olympians led by Zeus and the nether forces of Chaos headed by the giant Alcyoneus. Heroic Heracles fought on the side of Olympians, who defeated the Giants in accordance with Hera's prophecy that the gods' victory would not be accomplished without the participation of the son of a mortal mother.

7. Sam Fisher is a fictional character from Tom Clancy's Splinter Cell.

8. Generally, it can be said that there are four levels with regard to Orthodox monks; although even these divisions can vary from place to place: a) Novice, b) Rassophore Monk (lit. "Cassock-bearing Monk"), c) Stavrophore Monk (lit. "Cross-bearing Monk"), d) Schemamonk.

"My father considered a walk among the mountains as the equivalent of churchgoing."

– Aldous Huxley

Problem III.
Never Judge by a Cover

HOMEGROWN BRITISH STORYTELLING IS FUNDAMENTALLY religious in theme. An immemorial obsession revealed by rhymed Scripture and prose epistle across the nation. Like the very first "canonical" poems written in English, they continually tell us of metaphysics and men. Of every woman's broken heart and of each child's special adventuring! As a Quagan fact, this was brought home to me many innocent years ago when travelling up Brixton Hill. Noticing, as I did, someone had painted on shutters outside the George IV pub—in extremely large black letters—that this Country's future "belonged to the Philistines." Moreover, above this slightly disturbing slogan was the image of a young girl with unsettlingly glazed eyes. She appeared to be the very depiction of a brainless debauchery dominating club culture in those dismal days. A shockingly self-contemptuous serf! However, the full implications of this sigillum did not really strike me until a few days later. The artist in question had consciously sought to eulogise a contemporary abandonment of every superior quality in human nature. From his, or her, truly blasphemous perspective all that mattered in life was the simple gratification of gross desires on a regular basis. Any attempt to achieve the Nirvanic condition clearly regarded as a consummate waste of time.[1]

Browbeaten beneath these hellish ploys, some (softly) said such mental shadows were first cast in the far past. That the heaviness of feudal oppression, wherein the organic unities of our heartfelt Culture were lost and the nation divided into master or varlet, never really dispersed. A time when so-called Christian equity broke into a radically disempowered laity and overly supercilious clergy! Back then, castles, as highly-secured military compounds, were built far and wide in a country where any similitude of right conduct in the affairs of government, had retreated into the oral confines of rural village folklore: the codified memory; that is, of our broken, but astute, peoples. Each one of the Shires constantly groaning under an oppressive mantle, shamelessly carried by our cruel Norman cousins, as they crossed the protective and tempestuous waters moating this once holy domain!

From that turning point, an authentic spirituality had itself become more difficult to attain; it was argued. Untold droves clearly abandoning the worldliness of "The Church" to seek their paradise in thoughtless, fleshy, pleasures! Looking retrospectively, hermits, nuns and monks sadly came to represent little other than political victims escaping into pointless abstraction. Although the betterments of a palpable mystical endeavour were never disparaged; unlike nowadays! Tangentially, of course, because the lower orders of priesthood were once recognised as pioneers of an empowered sentience. Also, they tended to hail from our own downtrodden aboriginal ranks. Merry Old England, on this trajectory of disintegrating social affairs, having become profoundly enslaved, in actuality and in essence – thanks to the conspiracy of conniving aristocrats and their servile lackeys. Dictatorial men, it requires stating, so absorbed in their lust for self-aggrandisement and earthly riches, that when they looked at enchanted Oak Groves and Saxon Churches they only saw places of potential ideological rebellion. Thenceforth, the bohemian traditions of England were quickly buried beneath an unofficially sanctioned debauchery: our folk painfully yielding to ever more ugly disfiguring oppressions.

Not until the imperial hegemony of Catholic Rome fell piecemeal into mutually hostile factions, during the fourteenth century, would our Nation experience a comparable need to strive for its own recovery. Gazing back, therefore, our Master Builders took the initiative by attempting to rehabilitate ethnic sentiments through a delicately prescribed lightness in their architectural stonework! Whimsy, along with irregularity, becoming the delightful order of their constructive day! A characteristic of our havened people, eventually finding free expression in sculpted carvings, dramatised religious tableau, heraldic tapestries and poetic oratory! As such, we came to celebrate our joyfully disobedient history in tall tales about Robin Hood, or in less disguised words, those who refused to bow to enforced conformity by choosing to live on the margins. One of our Bards, Geoffrey Chaucer (1343-1400), even writing of the mixed motives behind pilgrimage in his astonishing *The Canterbury Tales*, wherein, he cryptically remarks of those journeying to the shrine:

> And smale foules maken melodie,
> That slepen alle night with open eye,
> So priketh hem nature in hir corsage;
> Than longen folk to goon on pilgrimages[2]

Amused, although in widespread agreement, Chaucer's half-Orthodox audience nonetheless intuited that one day we would be completely restored as a people! Their thrilling coequally preserved through the penmanship of William Langland (1332-1386) in his exceedingly devout vision of *Piers Ploughman,* the oracular labourer of wide and fertile acres, who, "On a morning in May, amongst the Malvern hills, tired by his wanderings and laying down to rest under a broad bank by the side of a stream, dreamt a marvellous dream ...." The scene thus set, images of an Anglo-Saxon Shangri-La were put into circulation; configuring a true, intact community of blessed kith dwelling within the People's gracious bosom – and revived in occult longings for a shared wholeness interior to even the poorest cottager.

Assuredly, this reconstruction of phyletic affiliation is always at the core of our British revolutionary zeal. Tyrannical yokes come and go: century in, century out. We know this as a factor of besieged Island history. Occasionally they are even removed, in part, by a variety of competing Reformers. Our harness is, nevertheless, quickly replaced by innumerable Commissions, Protectors and Sovereigns. Necessitating, in its turn, subsequent retreats into the inner sanctums of our collective identity; retirements being measurably cyclical, but always alongside apparitions of a promised Elysium, which all men of goodwill have strived to attain through the ages. So, in a manner reminiscent to taking national breath, repeated exertions by the pious to personify righteous conduct in their daily lives presented a developing hope that superior forms of existence could, and would, be uncovered. An inspiration driving that great soul toiling among us, William Shakespeare, in his unprecedented theatrical productions! Resolutely, as a playwright, actor and dramaturge, he expressed through the medium of lyrical words, subjective strivings within us all, his own people, and the beauties, which we appraise. Without argument, such ethnic divinations additionally elevated the mind of Thomas Traherne (1636-1637) into finding *The Way to Blessedness*, whilst nourishing in earnest and altruistic men like Henry Vaughan (1621-1695) and George Herbert (1593-1633) their innate sense of British sodality.

Yet, straps to our bridle kept changing malicious grip beneath the noses of these wise men. For such is life! Some despots, in spite of this, accidentally leaving a political vacuum that allowed power to pass into the callous hands of the burgeoning business classes. At least for a while! One mechanism of social oppression, in other crushing words, had lost its efficacy to another type of autocracy. Coincidentally, or perhaps not, a few of our Sacred Scriptures had been translated into Common English by this time and were instrumental in keeping morale from weakening any further. Those living closest to the soil, surprisingly, finding real comfort in these literary unfoldings! Centuries later, analogous dissenters found euphonious descriptions of superior dimensions to our Earth, as well as "England's pleasant pastures" here below, from that savant of poetic seers, William Blake (1757-1827). A man who bitterly decried the "Dark Satanic Mills," constructed under the direction of industrialists, who intended to betray all notions of a terrestrial garden by assembling an Empire without Faith. Incapable, as the factory owners were, of seeing the "New Jerusalem," they sought instead to employ all that was finest in the realm as a mere resource: leaving it to peasant poets like John

Clare (1793-1864) and, slightly later, the priest William Barnes (1801-1886) to record how noble Britons had been systematically humiliated and brought low before ruthless, international, plutocrats.

So, in our age of sobering sorrows, we ethnics have turned, once again, to the promise of sublime protection; eulogised with unfailing melodious skills by the Poet Laureate, John Masefield (1878-1967), when he wrote about the great martyr-saint of England, St George:

> For they felt that such a man lived on after death, and would surely help all holy and beautiful and manly men for ever and ever ... The spirit of England is the something of the spirit of St. George, a manly and beautiful spirit, ready to help someone weaker, and something of the spirit of Shakespeare, a just and tender spirit, fond of fun and kindness and of the rough and busy life of men.

Fascinatingly, Mansfield goes on to say of English quintessence that:

> It is in the little churches of the land, the old homes, in the churches, in countless old carvings, in old bridges, in old tunes, and in the old acts of the English, a shy, gentle, humorous and most manly soul, that stood up for the poor and cared for beauty. No finer thing can be said of men than that they stood up for the poor and cared for beauty; that they cared to be just and wise.

Rich, as these sentiments are in an unabashed spiritual patriotism, ever beloved of honest Bards in every generation, these sweet-pea memories of rambling gardens, honeyed-beehives, apple orchards, and lush English water-meadows full of dappled daisies and buttercups, either ignored, or somehow diluted, the repressive, irreligious, darkness imprisoning our Island home. A place whereon usual Biblical purgatives seemed to offer but cold succour for our communal maladies.

Take the Israelites, referring to a previous point, as the (so-called) ethical polar-opposite to Philistines. Through untold centuries, Hebraic commentators have laid loud claim to a sophisticated, prosperous and grounded spirituality, through both written text and memorised fable. Adjoining, beneath their decidedly foreign breath that, according to Semitic writ, such benefits are for the descendants of Abraham alone! The Old Testament, itself, warning British gentiles that Judah "Shalt consume all the people which the LORD thy God shall deliver thee; thine eye shall have no pity upon them." Obliged then, to obscure belligerent themes in their own ethnocentric tracts, these sons of the Holy Land tended to operate outside the governance of officially endorsed trades. Consecutively, even if understandably, deceiving Christian hosts, whilst concurrently breaking Mosaic Law, in order to become bankers, druggists, or jewellers. To be fair, European Jewry did not appear to foresee finance becoming the sole measure of a man's moral worth across the West. Nor that collateral could be used as a tactical weapon by the greedy middle classes against aristocrats who refused, point-blank, to reach any political accommodation with their own people whatsoever. Nonetheless, an untrammelled Capitalism was the only possible outcome to this inevitable, even though socially explosive, enterprise. The inordinate economic influence achieved by certain contemporary tycoons, indisputably, a by-product of blameless revolt. Speculatively, this explains why perennially corrupt characters in our Literature, like Shylock in Shakespeare's *The Merchant of Venice*, epitomise dissonant ethno-cultural realities. He is, after all, either the victim of a rampant prejudice consistently defining him as an "impenetrable cur" and a "cut-throat dog," or a bloodsucking parasite living as an unwelcome guest in European lands. Relishing, thereby, his demand for Antonio's "pound of flesh" in sanguine disproportion to his suffering!

The figure of Fagin additionally offers another instructive representation of dubiety towards Jewry. As one of the most memorable characters in Charles Dickens' (1812-1870) vibrant morality tale *Oliver Twist*, this misshapen, avaricious and simpering thief remains a depiction of unabated villainy. Elaborately drawn as a "loathsome reptile" and as having "fangs" such as should have been a "rat's," Fagin is the veritable avatar of distorted infantile fears. A child-catcher, leading his youthful victims astray as a means to his own repellent ends: other characters ominously referring to him as "the old one," a popular nickname for the devil in Victorian

London. Interestingly, twice, in Chapter 9 and again in Chapter 34, Oliver wakes up uneasily to find Fagin hovering nearby; the boy encountering him in those foggy spheres between wakefulness and sleep. At the precise moment, one might say, when nightmares are born from the "mere silent presence of some external object." With this in mind, Fagin is meant to instil primal anxieties in adult and infant readers alike; his very person, warning us of the depths to which the desperate will descend in their struggle for survival. In this sense, Chapter 52 is especially disturbing because we enter Fagin's head for his "last night alive." The gallows forcing this wicked oriental magician to finally confess the fathomage of his own depravity!

Neither is mention of Muslims unknown in our English Oeuvre, as adherents of that other desert faith claiming to proffer a solution for our murky spiritual woes. Shakespeare's noble Othello easily standing proud in this respect, along with George Peele's (1556-1596) unjustly vilified Muly Molucco and E. M. Forster's (1879-1970) deeply misunderstood, but thoroughly decent, Dr Aziz. The latter, nonetheless, typifying turbulent cross-cultural confusions! Unquestionably, this young Musulman's chief drawback being discovered in his inability to view a situation without overwhelming emotion, which, Forster suggests, is a temperamental flaw of the Umma (community) itself. Sincerely, the author chides Aziz with humorous ironies, by commenting, "He did not realize that 'white' has no more to do with a colour than 'God save the King' with a god, and that it is the height of impropriety to consider what it does connote." Jibes aside, Forster treats Dr Aziz H. Ahmed with kid gloves. Inadvertently validating accepted scholarly opinion that Islamic figures tended to be held in a testy, albeit courteous, light. Until, that is, quite recently. Nowadays, self-righteous caricatures must be seen to lord it over their former British rulers, or death threats are apt to follow publication. Conversely, clown-like stereotypes are allowed to relentlessly deliver page after page of basic philosophical admonition to stupefied audiences, whilst cowardly commentators turn a blind eye to Koranic injunctions claiming:

Arabs are the most noble people in lineage, the most prominent, and the best in deeds. We were the first to respond to the call of the Prophet. We are Allah's helpers and the viziers of His Messenger. We fight people until they believe in Allah. He who believes in Allah and His Messenger has protected his life and possessions from us. As for one who disbelieves, we will fight him forever in Allah's Cause. Killing him is a small matter to us.

Thence, for a sizable number of literary reviewers, these aforementioned repulsive textual gargoyles signify accumulating intensities in a previously hidden culture-war. Operating, one may suggest, as an indirect yardstick for the devastating effects of civic sterility in the British Isles.

Injury is unfortunately combined to insult at this analytical crossroads, since centuries of institutionalised Western Christianity, almost unarguably, have estranged us from the delectations of sexuality, unrestrained intellectual excellence, and the secrets of our inward individuality. An excessive number of its adherents finding themselves reduced to what can only be described as a mechanically driven "Churchianity." Wherein Dogma gradually replaces an expansion of personal Being. Markedly then, like the Russian philosopher Peter D. Ouspensky (1878-1947), I have come to grudgingly admit that mumbled creeds and cultic quibbles can divorce the soul from its celestial journeying. Blessed be the days, that acquiesced, when a giddy disorientation could be delightfully experienced in reading about an author's private hell-raising and enjoying his ethically enlightening books; understood as an enunciation of personalised religious striving. Staggering poetic achievements, Ouspensky would have agreed with me in bemoaning, by Maestros like Christopher Marlowe (1564-1593) – now seen as decorous idiosyncratic statements belonging to a rapidly disappearing, non-politically correct, era. No longer, we could equally murmur, will students of Literature luxuriate in cosmopolitan eroticisms such as:

Come live with me and be my love,
And we will all the pleasures prove,
That valleys, groves, hills, and fields,
Woods, or steepy mountain yields.[3]

Nevermore, we would synchronously decry, will non-specialists fully comprehend, either the psychological acumen, or versified precision, behind John Milton's (1608-1674) portrayal of the Devil, when the Poet makes him mouth:

Me miserable! Which way shall I fly
Infinite wrath and infinite despair?
Which way I fly is hell; myself am hell;
And in the lowest deep a lower deep,
Still threat'ning to devour me, opens wide,
To which the hell I suffer seems a heaven.[4]

For Churchianity, recognised as an instrument of cultural control, flights of fancy, alternative religious faiths, or a free imagination, testify that there may be multiple pathways leading to Universal Totality; an acknowledgement frightening its dogged adherents into ever-deeper incarceration. The quizzical, healthy, and examined subversions of past sages openly rejected in order to encourage a contrariwise diminution of rational faculties.

Western Christian writers, consequently, under the dead weight of misunderstood doctrine, have themselves fallen into an irretrievable fissiparousness. Their problems depressingly linked to fixed theological motifs. And as such, the initially romantic glow of dissident quills has become successively dulled betwixt puritanical factions vying to resist intercultural breadth (viewed as defilement) and liberal assemblies interpreting pragmatism as an inclusive Ideal. Posited so, the worldwide charm of John Bunyan's (1628-1688) uplifting allegory *The Pilgrim's Progress* is unlikely to be reproduced any decade soon. Elegant lines like, "And behold there was a very stately palace before him, the name of which was Beautiful" no longer finding popular approbation! Although repugnant characters like Mr Collins, a clergyman and the nephew of Mr Bennet, in Jane Austen's

(1775-1817) novel, *Pride and Prejudice,* will undoubtedly abound. Foolhardy figures, as they are, serving as comedic foils to further ridicule an imprisoning religious conglomerate itself in crisis.

On top of that, actual Radical Tradition has been put aside for the sake of structural survival. Observing this, some prominent theological commentators contend that the heady experimentation of early Protestantism has degraded into a series of pedantic credenda, on the one hand, or purely subjective testimonies, on the other. Sturdy Catholicism standing alone: by encouraging contradictory streams within its overall ecclesiological framework – even though for a number of slightly nervous reasons. Defending, as this stance can only do, an authority-based paternalism appealing to clerical paradigms of prerogative and descriptive prose, while anxiously supporting, in the meanwhile, a maternal, poetic, and supra-logical attitude among the laity! Heavily doctored, as Church History manifestly is, this mildest of genres has suddenly become a veritable battlefield for every group in turn. The concluding jape, on the part of outsiders, being that each of these denominations has claimed righteous vindication as a persecuted sect holding fast to Evangelical transmission despite opposition from the others! Instead, as genuine sympathisers may puzzle, of proudly evolving into enlightened spiritual congregations intoxicated by the mysteries of Consciousness as it passes through timeless veils of Energy.

As a result, ours is the most benighted hour before the promised dawn. Perhaps it is Oswald Spengler's (1880-1936) much feared "Winter," wherein tectonic expectations crumble into ruin, and chill dissolution rules the night. Precious few even realising that something valuable has been abandoned as associated standards of decent living rot away under the pretext of enforced subsistence. Taken apart, as it were, before the wanton ethical caprice in our midst, seeking to replace both honour and duty as the dominant social norm. For those reasons my intention is to sprinkle purifying hyssop water across recently received literary canons, before begging fellow Quagan freedom fighters to grasp the implications of vital questions such as: why should choosing between demoniacal licentiousness, theocratic servitude, or a deliberately reinterpreted past be portrayed as the complete range of our spiritual options? Secondly, in what way has the vocabulary of Near Eastern Morality come to dominate our Occidental religious imagination? To the baffling extent, moreover, that some practising Christians have adopted the startling habit of greeting confreres with the word "Shalom!" Thirdly, why have our own indigenous approaches towards the Ground-of-Being been undermined, as well as bitterly vilified, throughout the ages? And lastly, what are the alternatives? At the end of the day, Abrahamic textuality is either formed from the edicts of a celestial Tyrant (dominating European peoples), or from the sublime guidance of a loving Mother-Father to place spiritual things at the helm of affairs.

Formulating these questions is, that contended, therapeutic. Examining, as they do, the grievous wounds inflicted on our national psyche by a slow withering away of British ipseity. Rancorous and unresolved class-based afflictions admittedly further warping indigenous literary sensibilities out of all recognition. Clearly, our entire Body Politic has fallen as easy prey before insatiable financiers, those new Robber Barons, and their resuscitated henchmen in the form of Wall Street, along with its military-industrial-entertainment complex. In which case, far from enjoying a greater independence than our grandparents, contemporary citizens have become more deluded in their servitude than any previous generation. Somnambulant automata, many critics have observed, sadly allowing slavery to be packaged as liberty; the chicanery of cheap alcohol, soft drugs and casual sex making most Britons mindlessly thrall to these types of trivial indulgence. Each factor preventing, in its turn, a full flowering of the inmost Self. Such a populace, it hardly needs stating, is estranged from all notions of a historical continuum that doubtlessly emancipate a man. In fact, they are merely members of a restless political undead. Believing, quite inaccurately, that their deeply disoriented wits have found a futurist's utopia through the medium of cultural dissolution! So, cut off from antiquity and psychologically disabled through elitist machination, such narcotised natives taste little apart from death between their already dry, blackened, lips.

Still, with these dark musings in mind, it seems as if a nation sometimes needs to retrace its footsteps in order to go forward. Withdrawing from an actual cul-de-sac by carefully scrutinising precedents, palimpsests, as well as faded prototypes, to clarify the view ahead! In this way, history reminds us that the veneration of our ancestors, along with "Swedenborgian" subjective mountains, were once facets of a single complex system of worship. Undoubtedly, having preserved fallen brethren in a symbolic edifice of this kind, people, Britons and otherwise, shared a common, continual and communal allegiance with their forebears. The importance of which was etched into mound, or mountaintop, connecting regional inhabitants with their deceased. We are, after all, participants in a single landscape intimately binding us together. Honestly speaking, nearly the entire genealogy of our British ancestry can be told by simply pointing at specific hills and recalling local events as stories passed down through engendered kinsfolk. The exultation of our ancestors, and places of prayer, being largely inseparable in these shores as an interconnected, uncanny, and wonderful web; woven by the spectral pins of narrative, landscape, and ethnicity. Equally vindicated, as these British practices are, by analogous Hindu beliefs that areas, like Mount Kailas, are the final resting places for the souls of their dead. Along with sites like the large communal cemetery on Mount Koya-san in Japan – implying in its turn an identical mindset to our own! Congruently, the monks of the Romanian Sketae Prodromos on Holy Athos have only one gravesite. It is a basic one, and is prepared for all the monks who have passed away. This is, primarily, for two reasons. Firstly, the lack of space for a sizable cemetery on the mountainous terrain and, secondly, the fact that these human remains may be holy relics! Exhuming them, therefore, is a method of publically acknowledging this post-mortem status and treating them appropriately. On Athos, customarily, bodies are exhumed following three years' interment and, since no coffin is used in the burial, the physical remains decompose quickly. Bones eventually being kept in a nearby ossuary!

In terms of our ageless British Ancestral Faith, Orthodox attitudes towards decay and mortality are demonstrably educative: holding firmly, as these dispositions do, to new Life coming out of death. The monks of Holy Athos, in particular, instructively loyal to this traditional worldview, by circuitously reminding us that many early Christians, when persecuted for their beliefs, took refuge in Roman catacombs! All resulting in the practice that their prayers were comfortably said by, and in, tombs; alongside the bodies of their Pagan loved ones! When possible, they even sought sanctuary among the corpses of the dead to meditate; occasionally using coffins, or a specific crypt, as an altar on which to celebrate the Eucharist. This accounts for the reason why, from Apostolic times onwards, the Church has held a respectful veneration for the Blessed Dead. Certainly, miracles like the aroma of perfumed myrrh exuding from skulls, or an unexpected healing linked to the bones of a martyr, were frequently reported in connection with these places of repose. Phenomena, of course, manifestly combined with their Christian conviction in the bodily Resurrection of Jesus Christ, along with the future revival of all believers: whilst divergently teaching us sinners about the vital value of each link in a family chain. The paranormal, notwithstanding, all seen as aiding the laity in the explanation of higher truths! Additionally reminiscent, maybe, of discourses overflowing on Mount Athos regarding deceased Christian leaders – seen as supernatural great-grandfathers in faith, or Wyrd family elders, who can be approached to intercede for the living! Psychic activities demonstrating, in their turn, Platonic concepts that this brief and transitory life is merely a preparation for one's death! And that the Saints should take a radiant pride of place among our common ancestors; honoured by days of feasting and religious fast.

Fragments of this Ancestral Faith, furthermore, are scattered everywhere in Greek, Russian and British popular Tradition. They are sagaciously recounted by numberless old men in rustic taverns, who have had unbelievably few hours of formal schooling. Likewise, they are conveyed by grey-haired countrywomen as they nurture the young in our nurseries. Without doubt, they are also mouthed as a series of subconscious mantras by Anglican clergymen to their curates in leafy, Acadian parishes. Recounted coequally, it is often espied, by courageous fishermen to their extended families on rainy days in the autumn! Over-steaming pots of Indian tea served with buttered scones, whipped cream and local strawberry jam: causing those listening to such narrations to say they have never heard tastier fables to fall from the tongue of unlettered folk. For nearly five centuries, that bequest acknowledged, Englishmen were in full communion with the Orthodox Church. Evidenced, as this is, by the extraordinarily close cultural contacts with Eastern Christendom; two half-digested examples curiously leaping to mind in this connection! First, the sainted English Archbishop, Theodore of Tarsus (602-690), was actually Greek by birth. Unmistakably, when living in England, he, along with other holy men from Greece, wove a number of vibrant fraternal bonds between these Sister Nations. Secondly, proud Gytha, daughter of King Harold Godwinson II (1022-1066), married her Orthodox spouse in Kiev. This half-millennium, then, proving to be a long and uncommonly eventful period, wherein timeless places of British worship were constantly redefined as one sect gained temporary ascendancy over its rivals! Social historians noting that such transfers of religious power became distressingly brutal throughout these saddened Isles, following, as they did, the remorseless precedent set by the Norman invasion, as sponsored by the Roman Church, in 1066! Clout and cudgel, disgracefully, reigning supreme as tools of dialogue, throughout the English Reformation; under the auspices of Tudor dictators such as King Henry VIII (1491-1547), Elizabeth I (1533-1603) and much later the "radical" Protestant iconoclast Oliver Cromwell (1599-1658)! Yet, the remodelling of received custom to suit political expediency was fully chronicled, as well as the subsequent loss of Soul-quality, or as some described it, the deformation of aesthetic texture. Fortunately, this process did not happen everywhere at the same pace, but after the fluidity patterns of a slowly freezing river.

Strangely static, our Ancestral Faith thus endured in specific vestiges. In the stock of accepted folk wisdom, proverbial anecdote, "diacritic" village practices and ethnic memory as parable! That which was understood as "traditional," managing to survive, not to mention outsmart, later liberal speculations and an enforced, aggressive, multicultural corrosion. Indisputably, our Ancestral Faith, which had become incarnate in the "Christian way of life", could only be uprooted, it was felt, if the urban cult of "tolerance" penetrated into the midst of gentle-hearted countryside culture and its bucolic ways. Although even then, if Northern Europe is taken in its entirety, these modes of "split" Quaganry proved to persevere by unexpectedly weathering such icy storms. Commentators becoming aware of suchlike survivals in small English villages wherein Saxon foundations stand, or where a Town Hall and a local Post Office surrounded by tiny, clustered, parochial shops, continues to be the measure of a genuine neighbourhood! In Hampshire, this noted, some farming families unceasingly celebrated "Old Michaelmas" until the tragedy of the Second World War finally devastated these customs. Similarly, in places where local parish fetes were kept according to the "English Style," it is evident such conventions went back to an era when England had a virtually Athonite predilection towards Orthodoxy!

Preserved, as this type of faith must be, in regional folktales amid blackened Oak beams and ecclesial piety, we are taught that on his way to execution, the fourth-century Christian martyr, St Blaise, prayerfully touched the throat of a boy choking on a fishbone with one of his healing hands. Miraculously, it was affirmed, the young man recovered. To commemorate this saving event, the Blessing of the Throats service held at St Etheldreda's Church on the Saint's day (3rd February) continues to the present. Undoubtedly, people suffering from throat ailments still kneel at the altar rail, while the priest imitates the holy man by touching their throats, albeit with two candles, tied together in the form of a cross. Incidentally, Ely Place, where this beautiful old redbrick building is situated, was once the residence of the Bishops of Ely, and remains one of only two areas in the City (the other being the Temple), over which the Lord Mayor has no jurisdiction. Even nowadays, it proclaims its continuing independence by having a liveried Beadle ritually lock its gates at 10 pm each night of the week.

A colourfully Orthodox aura, aligned with the Nativity of Christ, was, debatably, best conserved in our market towns and hamlets. Almost certainly, declared those marketing, there is a moment on this specific anniversary, when Creation itself stood completely still. When birds stopped in their flight and rivers ceased to flow. Immediately following this Cosmic Hiatus, however, church bells were said to ring spontaneously, whether or not their belfries had vanished beneath the waves; as had been the case at St Wilfred's Cathedral off Selsey in Sussex. Furthermore, Bumble Bees buzzed for joy, Cocks crowed in exaltation, and Dogs would loudly bark in full praise of their Divine Architect. Poignantly, on the evening of Christmas Eve, candles were placed in British windows to guide St Joseph and the Mother of God on their journey, because there was no place for them at the Inn. Similarly, Holly and Ivy decorated native homes with their evergreen leaves to remind us of Life Everlasting, whilst Mistletoe was hung in our parlours – although never in church, as it was rumoured to be the wood from which the Cross was constructed.

Domestic necessities, all these things being known, needed to be prepared before Christmas Day. In the sure knowledge that any work done on the day itself, would turn out badly. So prepared, the foods eaten at Christmas, such as plum pudding, customarily had thirteen ingredients: one for Christ and one for each Apostle. Plates of mince pies, made from meat and oriental spices, typically covering the table. Learned relatives, everyone agreed, as they built up to making a wish for good fortune in the year ahead, reflected that their oval shape recalled the manger where the Saviour was laid in swaddling-clothes.

Like Serbian folk songs, or the Little Russian *koliady* of Orthodox tradition, British Christmas carols were taken from home to house by children eager for seasonal treats. Slices of Christmas cake, fruits, nuts and small coins sufficing as a justifiable reward for their toothsome melodies on clear, but chilly nights, sparkling with heavy frosts! Sometimes accompanied by an adult, although by no means always, the carollers tended to have a ponderous Victorian guise; a torch, or makeshift lantern, being meticulously balanced above song sheets beclouded by their visible, steaming, breath! The more vigorous choirs, looking disturbingly like turbine engines from the Industrial Revolution as they exhaled in unison. Inexplicably adding, as this did, to the thought that a few of these harmonies were very old indeed and originally used to celebrate each feast, in its turn, in greater theological depth.

All the same, those traditions connected with the Lenten cycle and their joyful culmination at Easter, formed the majority of Orthodox cultural residues. Just as the Russians have coloured eggs blessed at Easter, so Britons had "pace-eggs" which were presented to parishioners in church before they were quickly consumed. Younger members of the congregation, that remembered, felt these paschal eggs should be rolled down a hill instead of eaten; a playful custom encouraged by their local priest under the pretext of representing the stone rolled away from Christ's tomb. On Easter Sunday, referred to in some parts of the country as "Holy Sunday," or "God's Sunday," new clothing would be sported as a token of fresh beginnings! Easter bonnets adorned with Spring Flowers and trimmed with bright ribbons, being the preferred item of sartorial splendour for young Ladies! Also, comparably to the Greeks, our native Easter breakfasts, which people ate around midday after the morning service, consisted of dyed eggs and lamb. Garnished, as this was, by mint sauce, alluding to the previous sufferings undertaken by the Lamb of God! It was commented by rural scribes that before Industrialisation, boys and girls would wake up at the crack of dawn to watch the Sun dance with bliss at the Resurrection: a consuetude existing until recent times in Russia, as well as here.

Graveyards, moreover, were decked with flowers at this time of year. Our dead, unlike nowadays, included in the festivities! Those knowledgeable in tree-lore, along with its half-remembered alphabets, pointing out that the Yew, a mark of the Eternal One, since it lived for a thousand years or more, was used to dress churches at Easter. Blossoms, as personal love offerings, were placed on tombs, while the practice of "heaving" at Hocktide (the Monday or Tuesday of the following week) was playfully observed. Muscular young men, in a fashion similar to the Russian "Radonitsa,"[5] being expected to lift one another from the ground to enact the coming general resurrection of the departed! Manifestly, we too had our indigenous athletes of the Spirit.

Curiously, the light of the risen saints occasionally casts unexpected shadows. All explaining why timeworn rituals surrounding death were understood as methods by which the living could be protected from the Unknown. Beyond question, relatives and friends always tried to ease the passage of a dying family member and, upon death, strove to assist his, or her, soul along the difficult road to the next world. What is more, it was civically assumed that every human body should be laid to rest with both respect and honour. This was done as a duty, of course, not to mention out of private self-esteem. Social position, when all mouthed and finalised, as well as affection felt towards the deceased, demanding good manners. So, it was insisted, obviously, that the dying urgently needed the help of their nearest and dearest at this ultimate moment of personal crisis. Proportionally explaining the unsettling emotional adjunct to these customs, in that an angry ghost might return to haunt village folk if the necessary assistance had been denied! Similarly, many theologically confusing funeral rites seem to have their basis in the ancient assurance that justified, even though departed, spirits have no need to return to the lands of the living. Unfortunately, that agreed, a large number of the family observances common half a century ago, have already vanished from contemporary England, portending disastrously for our sense of ethnic longevity.

Burial customs, truly, were always acknowledged as hard, Quagan, and difficult processes, which ought to be shortened once the end was fully guaranteed. Assented so, death was nevertheless seen as a part of life's organic patterning. Consequently, in North East England, as in Romania, the funeral clothes of a bridegroom and bride formed an integral part of any wedding trousseau. The common burial garment usually understood as being a shroud; normally made of linen – except between 1666 and 1814, when the use of anything other than wool was forbidden (by British law) in order to benefit the burgeoning textile trade. There were equally precedents for a dead person to be dressed in his, or her, own clothes. Monks, priests, and nuns, for instance, were buried in their Habits, while members of the armed forces are still laid to rest in their uniforms. Gypsies are dressed in their best clothes as a rule, and sometimes a bride who has died soon after her wedding is buried in her bridal dress. Tears in the death chamber (even in this case) needed to be restrained, however, for they hindered the soul's departing by reasserting its earthly ties. On a par with this, an excessive display of sorrow on such occasions was known as "crying back the dying" and seen as a selfish, unkindly, act. Synchronously, an allied belief in coastal areas seems to have encouraged the contention that no one could die unless the tide was actively running out. If a sick man lived through one single ebb tide, he would linger on until the next, they said – whilst those landlubbers faithful to our ancestors in the West of England were understood to place Rue and Wormwood in coffins as signs of repentance for unresolved misdemeanours.

Other rural authorities claimed that if a sick man's bed lay across the lines of the floor-boards, it had to be turned to line up with them, for the Angel of Death (Azrael) would not come quietly if the living were unprepared and the bed stood "athwart the planshuns." Further, dove, pigeon or game-bird feathers accidentally included in the pillow, or mattress stuffing, could additionally keep Death away. Thus, as a cherished folk precaution, pillows and mattresses were often removed from the room: even though if a good friend, or close relative, was known to be coming and might arrive too late, a small amulet of feathers was conversely placed between the sheets to preserve life for a few hours longer. Outrageously, by contemporary standards anyway, affectionate relatives would sometimes lift a dying elder out of her, or his, bed and lay him, or her, on the cold floor to hasten the inevitable journey. Contact with the earth, it was contested—from which all humankind springs—proving effective as a means of easing this passing. By origin, such customs seem to have started in those far-off days when cottages still had floors of beaten earth.

Fascinatingly, our ancestral teachers maintained that as soon as death occurred, a number of things had to be done to allow the departing soul free passage into the mysterious Beyond. Doors and windows, anecdotes recount, were opened. Knots were loosened and animals put outside until after the funeral; in order to prevent the passing spirit from accidentally entering into them. During the warmer months, even the hearth fire was put out, because it represented the life of the house. Atop this, clocks were stopped, since the dead have nothing to do with time: perishable foods in the room being immediately thrown away to prevent the spirit from corrupting them. Likewise, mirrors were veiled, or turned to the wall, for fear that the soul might become entangled in their crystal reflection and a green tuft of paper, or salt heaped upon a white porcelain plate, was then placed on the dead person's breast. Widespread explanations for this otherwise baffling custom were elaborated by claiming that it prevented the body from swelling, even though, prototypically, there was a deeper meaning. Fire, Salt and Earth having always been regarded as antidotes to evil, as well as a protection for the soul from any unclean powers, which might try to dominate proceedings.

Another deeply anchored notion, which still survives, is that a corpse should never be left alone between death and the funeral. Resonances with Orthodoxy in this matter becoming profoundly clear. Even now, to have a corpse in an empty house, especially at night, is commonly regarded as a shocking neglect of essential obligations. Coupled to this, it was felt that if only one mourner was at home and unexpectedly compelled to go out, then this absence must be as brief as possible, and the house door, along with the door to the death-chamber, must be left unlocked. Formerly, this noted, an unbroken vigil was kept by the coffin: neighbours and friends joining in, partly to allow relatives to rest and additionally to show their regard for the dead person. This traditional "Wake" or "Lykewake" continuing to abide in remote parts of Scotland, Wales and Western England! Yet, people being people, once a large assembly slowly gathered about the corpse, it became an occasion to eat, drink, sing and dance, tell stories, play cards and indulge in practical jokes; all considered vital gestures of love and respect for the deceased person, as well as providing comfort to the bereaved. Unarguably, until about a hundred years ago, a small coin was still placed in a dead man's mouth, or in his hand, so that he might pay his way on the passage between the worlds; exactly as in Greece. Coequally, as across Eastern Europe, objects were sometimes placed in the coffin – a candle to give light, food to sustain the deceased, and sporadically, a hammer with which he could knock at the Heavenly Gates when he reached his destination: A Bible or Sunday-school certificate showing that the dead man had kept to his Ancestral Faith while embodied. Tufts of wool were even placed into a shepherd's hand in order to prove, at the Last Judgement, that his irregular churchgoing was due to the demands of work. Tragically, it was not unusual for toys to be buried with children, or some cherished possession with lonely adults, although this highly symbolic custom is currently straining under the pressure of enforced commercial sentiment.

Upon close scrutiny and careful inspection, the correspondences uniting our British Ancestral Faith with virile Russian Orthodoxy and Greek Tradition are unending. Be they recovered in our playful rhyming slang, cultivated clan memory, or revered national narrative. Attested so, when saying our last tearful farewells at a graveside, it should not be forgotten that the superficially bleak expression "Goodbye" actually means "God be with you," whether whispered by a bored aristocrat, an alienated drunkard, or wellborn yeoman. Moreover, disappearing communal customs such as leaving the doors open when a funeral party is absent continue to act as a sign of neighbourly trust in adverse times. In rural districts, the practice of presenting sprigs of Rosemary, or Evergreen, to the mourners before this sad procession sets out endured as a tactile promise that the deceased will not be forgotten in the streets where she, or he, lived. Each of which remain fragments of a single, perennial, witness.

Easily recognised when considering conventions like "Touching the Dead," whereby chance visitors calling at a house where a dead body reposes are asked to enter, view the corpse, and then to temperately touch it. Suchlike customs continuing from those times when England was called "Merry" in the fragrant archaic sense of "blessed!" For those visitors who did not know the dead person, this request was sometimes startling, or, more probably, embarrassing. That acknowledged, it could not be refused, because this could give lasting offence. One explanation offered for these eldritch practices found in the perception that to dutifully touch the brow or the hand of a corpse, gently and reverently, was a final act of communal courtesy, which no one ought to withhold; a type of social absolution rooted in the sweetly vociferous language of lost ancestors and steadily fastened in our lasting communication with their worldly Being.

Traditions like these, without causing too great a controversy, consummately anointed this land as translucid cultural remnants of our forebears. Demonstrating, in their turn, an Old English, but unarguably non-Byzantine, Orthodoxy, that avowedly declared spiritual unities amid All with All! An awareness equally existing beneath the habit of gifting our young with their own colourfully illustrated copy of the Bible: either upon Confirmation, or at the successful end of the school year on Prize Day; a practice always boding well for our unbroken British custom of storytelling. Games would then be played to mark the successes of smart pupils, whilst proud parents would loudly brag among themselves about their child's peculiar talents, over a table groaning with freshly squeezed lemonade and cut cucumber sandwiches. In this way, our Ancestral Faith was taught through the beat of blank verse, dramatised philosophical discourse and bold, brashly pigmented, pictograph. Obstacles in life, metaphorical and otherwise, theatrically described as mountains, earthquakes and oceans. And as Aristotle (84-322 BC) wryly attested, to metaphorise skilfully is the work of genius in the literature of any language.

SELECTED ENDNOTES

1. Cultural themes analogously touched by the Albanian author Ismail Kadare when he spoke at the French Institute in London 2006. See Appendix 1 for my impressions concerning this occasion.

2. In modern English this will read:
   And little birds are making melody
   And sleep all night, eyes as open as can be
   (So nature pricks them, in each little heart),
   Our pilgrimage then folks desire to start.
   (*The Canterbury Tales. Prologue. Line 6*)

3. Christopher Marlowe's *The Passionate Shepherd to His Love* (probably composed mid-1580s).

4. John Milton's *Paradise Lost* 4:73-77.

5. Radonitsa is a commemoration of the departed observed on the second Tuesday of Pascha or, in some places, on the second Monday of Pascha.

"Faeries, come take me out of this dull world. For I would ride with you upon the wind, Run on the top of the dishevelled tide. And dance upon the mountains like a flame."

– W. B. Yeats

Problem IV.
Inheriting Our Orthodox Tongue

OWADAYS, EVEN SERIOUS CRITICS ARE ON THEIR KNEES
before the blogosphere. A situation reducing the reading
public's appreciation of literature to that of a mankurt.[1]
Quite apart, of course, from obscuring otherwise tantalising parallels
existing between Quagan writers like Emanuel Swedenborg and
(arguably) Soren Kierkegaard.[2] Each an author, at the day's end,
pioneering related, but untried, spiritual trajectories into our
understanding of sentient conditionality. A datum, furthermore,
made significant by the fact Scandinavians are etherically, as well
as ethnically, kith to us Britons; by word, blood, gesture, deed and
marrow. In themselves, telling characteristics when we recall that,
as a dashing young neoteric author, Kierkegaard once wrote, "What
is a poet? An unhappy person who conceals profound anguish in
the heart but whose lips are so formed that as sighs and cries pass
over them they sound like beautiful music." Regardless of this
wistful conceit, however, few pursuits in our deconstructive period
are perceived to be as pointless as composing Poetry. An activity
upheld as conducive to little more than pleasantly passing time away
in a café; or read as a series of brief, uplifting, versicles in birthday,
Christmas, or "deepest sympathy," cards! Indeed, it is seen by the
majority as neither truly entertaining, nor, for that matter, relevant!
Merely textual composition on the aimless scale of pretentious
verbosity: or the literary concern of someone who cannot really write
good prose. To the present Anglo-Saxon mind, versification tends to
be understood as a linguistic skill anyone can acquire and at which

everyone, given a little time, can excel. A trivial art for frivolous amateurs! Likewise, the very idea of raising consciousness to new and unexpected heights, thereby beautifying our world through symbol, evocation, mystery, rhythm and rhyme, is either rejected, or ridiculed. Hence, misunderstanding Hamlet's intentions, bemused audiences now publicly retort, "Words, words, words" back at urban chanters.[3]

In itself, certainly, a poem is simply a word-composition in verse. And, admittedly, even in the hands of amateurs, poems can make an impressive use of the latent aesthetic qualities within language to suggest differential meaning; not to mention evoking emotive responses in their readers. Equally, poems rely heavily on imagery and metaphor; usually having a rhythmic structure based on patterns of stresses, or on patterns of different-length, syllables (as in classical prosody). Moreover, they may, or may not, utilise rhyme. In which case, due to the huge diversity of British poetic forms and structures, poetry can be problematic to characterise. Typically though, poetry as a form of literature makes use of the formal properties of the words it uses—the attributes of the spoken, or written, form of the words—independently, sometimes of their "elemental" meaning. For example, rhythm can be established by the number of syllables in the words, or how these syllables are stressed; alliteration and rhyme, it needs to be observed, depend on the sounds of the words. So explained, poetry of a sort recognisable to us moderns appears to pre-date other forms of literature: early instances including the Sumerian Epics of *Gilgamesh* (dated from around 2700 BC), parts of The Holy Bible, *Manas*, and the grand Indian epics *Ramayana* and *Mahabharata*. Demonstrably, in cultures based primarily on oral traditions, the formal characteristics of poetry often have a mnemonic function for socially important texts, be they moral, legal, or genealogical. Meaning, of course, they may initially materialise in verse form. As such, some poetry uses exactly specified forms: examples being, the sonnet, the haiku, and the limerick. Developing this line of reasoning, traditional Japanese *haiku* contains seventeen *onji* (syllables), distributed over three lines in groups of five, seven, and five, and should also have a *kigo* – a technical word indicating a season, whereas a limerick has five lines, with a rhythmic scheme of AABBA, and line lengths of 3,3,2,2,3 stressed syllables. By convention, this stated, limericks have a less reverent attitude towards society and the world around us. Lastly, it needs to be added that poetry not adhering to a formal poetic structure is called "free verse," since it is said to reflect subconscious motivations.

Obviously, language and inheritance dictate most poetic norms. Persian poetry, this contended, always rhymes, whilst Greek poetry rarely does. Additionally, some languages contain more rhyming words than others. Italian, as a case in point, has a rich rhyming structure permitting the use of a limited set of rhymes throughout a lengthy poem. The innate linguistic opulence of these compositions often resulting from word endings that follow regular forms! Contrastingly, English, with its irregular word endings (adopted from other languages), is less sophisticated in rhyme. Perhaps, explaining why present-day English poets writing about Mount Athos, such as Clare Cameron, appear almost in thrall to endless variations of blank verse. Of extra note, some languages prefer longer lines, whereas others favour shorter ones. Each convention resulting from the ease of fitting a specific language's vocabulary and grammar into an inherited and specified configuration; rather than into others. Interestingly, this may occur when a language typically has longer words than other languages – like Greek and German when compared to English, even though linguistic "accidents" frequently occur; wherein speakers of a language associate good poetry with a verse form preferred by a popular poet, or skilled lyricist. Relationally, works for theatre, historically, took verse form: an increasingly rare custom nowadays although many reviewers would argue that staged language remains intrinsically poetic. In more recent years, this argued, digital poetry has arisen, which takes advantage of the synthetic qualities inherent within digital media.

Wordsmiths notwithstanding, if Poetry is as the populace deem, then it is inside the realm of projected possibilities that Mount Athos doesn't really exist in literature. Not, in any case, as an evocative image of the Sacred in English language publications. Instead, kitsch depictions of this under-utilised mountain location would be seen to spread across the virtual pages of potential holiday-makers; a position more or less asserted in *The Pilgrim Tourist* by Eric Garcia McKinley. In effect, therefore, even on those overly sparse occasions when this pinnacle of perfection was tentatively scribed, its peaks could be little other than invisible: dedicated as they are to the worship of a Christian Saviour (who is nearly forgotten) and set apart for the unending service of a remote Deity. Any thought among readers that these territories are duly entitled to our literary respect by inviting a textual Presence to manifest itself before us would simply be stupefying. All commentary commanding a contemporary bookworm's imagination with religious inferences, hallowed associations, and mystical nuances, along with a sense of rightful awe – let alone a fully justified veneration, could only be registered as narratorial fluff.

From this plebeian perspective, Mount Athos would be far too perfect to be real; like a Unicorns' magical alicorn, or the sparkling magnificence of a pixie's beard. Aligning Athos, as this idea does, to other enchanted artefacts and domains. To magical lamps in Sir Richard Burton's (1821-1890) unexpurgated translation of *One Thousand and One Nights*. In addition to *Chitty-Chitty-Bang-Bang: The Magical Car*, which Ian Fleming (1908-1964) tells his admirers can develop flotation devices at the drop of an anchor, and fly through the air when required. One could even comment that Blessed Athos suddenly becomes akin to Rivendell, the Elfish Kingdom of Elrond: described by Professor J. R. R. Tolkien (1892-1973) in his magnum opus *The Lord of the Rings*. A geoscape where chastened fairy warriors prepare to battle for a better day in future times!

Yet fantasy proves to be the doggerel of human creativity, as well as a poison in the Poetic Arts. Pointedly so, if it makes ancestral Athos equivalent in eccentricity to the wayward, albeit confessedly hypnotic delusion, of unabated happiness without labour, or success without germinal sacrifice! Or for that matter, private triumph regardless of specific, individual, consequence! Obliquely purporting, as these chimeras do, that the Holy Mountain cannot be related to the sort of psycho-geography woven into shape by needle-thin anomalies and bold, strapping, paradox! Stated honestly, any such dreamlike depictions of transcendent Athos are actually veiled attacks upon the religious realities of those adorable Hellenic peaks. By debunking its solid existential basis, after all, the marvels worked upon its slopes eventually become the stuff of random improbability and superstitious conjecture.

But Poetry, when it is worthy of the name, is an articulation of purest Being and not merely emblematic flotsam and jetsam unworthy of our European artistry. As literature, it personifies the ever-living Elements around us. By giving name and form to hylozoic materials, it weaves narrative around complex ideas in the form of Myth and Symbol. Comparable then, to the *Veda* of Ancient India, true English poetic text explores our sophisticated and abstract relationship with living biospheres: as it coequally does our core-identity as human beings. The very reading of elaborative paeans, when sculpted well, resulting in an enlarged stratification of the mind and a subsequent emboldening of the heart! Without any overstatement, the minute someone with a Quagan attitude starts to ask ontological questions, real poetry is born. Almost certainly, this is why established literary savants continue to contend that following an aesthetic path of this type leads to Divinising experiences. An unveiling of new vistas, so to speak, beckoning every and each one of our devout progenitors with alchemising assurances of their own transmutation! Mount Athos, grasped thusly, is affirmed as a "geologian" and teaching Guru in its own right. The surly type of savage, even though cultivating, territory about which Thomas Berry (1914-2009) could happily wax lyrical: if he were to momentarily pause, that is, regarding the integral part played by meter, lyrical reverie, and scientific rapture, behind his well-reasoned Ecotheology.

Seen in this brilliance, Poetry—from the Greek *poiesis*, ποίησις, meaning a "making" of word play—is innately religious in character and evolves from the perceived need to worship, recount significant oral epics, and offer sacred context. As in the case of the Holy Gathas (first recited, probably, in the first half of the 2nd millennium BC) originally composed by the Zoroastrian Prophet, Zarathustra. Beyond question, therefore, it has been recognised from the dawn of humankind that poetry, leaving aside its practical application as a memory aid, should be regarded as a creative act of potentially sacred language production: thenceforth elucidating the historical concentration by poets on metaphysical linguistic conventions – which engage powerful emotive responses. Particularly useful in this respect, devices such as onomatopoeia, assonance, and even dissonance were, and are, used to achieve prayerful and, dare one say, incantatory, effects. Grasped so, the use of irony and ambiguity, along with other stylistic elements of poetic diction often consciously leave a poem open to multiple interpretations; especially on this highly abstract level. A magical use of metaphor, metonymy, and simile, all assisting in the adaptation of resonance between otherwise disparate images – a layering of meanings, as well as connections previously unapprehended, becoming apparent. Because of this, it has been argued that some poetic evocations cannot be understood at any depth outside of their indigenous cultures. In real terms incapacitating readers through an unavoidable inability to intelligently respond to these alien language-dispositions within which a foreign poet writes. A possible instance being that even educated Western audiences accustomed to identifying Sufi poetry with Rumi (1207-1273) may have encountered incomprehensible imagery composed in lines based on unknown rhyme and irregular metre, even though they were still overwhelmed by its lullaby-like euphony.

Contrariwise, much modern Western poetry reflects a critique of poetic tradition itself: playing with and testing, among other things, the overall principle of euphony – sometimes altogether forgoing set rhythm, along with rhyme. Above this, in today's increasingly globalised world, poets frequently tailor techniques, styles, and forms from diverse cultures and languages. Some twenty-first century literary theorists, that agreed, have come to rely less on the theoretical opposition of prose to poetry, and have gone on to claim that a poet is simply one who creates linguistic cadences and wordscapes by using associative language tools. Ironically, the underlying concept of a poet as "primal" creator is still not uncommon, and some postmodernist poets, de facto, refuse to distinguish between the creation of a poem in words and other creative acts in unrelated media. Genuine radicals, however, like the exponents of DaDa, challenge the very attempt to define poetry as something ultimately misguided! By and of itself, this rejection of European tradition, allied to DaDa metaphysical claims, has had a domino effect on those writers already given to semantic experimentation, thereby producing further intellectual upheavals permitting linguistic dislocation (in the deepest sense), whereby authors abandoned every distinction between poetry, drama, and prose. So, numerous modernist poets have written in non-traditional forms, or in what traditionally would have been considered prose; even though their authorship was usually infused with theatrical diction. Frequently, with a tone and rhythm established by non-metrical means. Admittedly, there was a substantial formalist reaction within the modernist schools regarding the "breakdown" of linguistic structures, even though this reaction focussed as much on the development of new informal structures and syntheses – as in the revival of older forms and conventions. This does not imply, that attested, contemporary poetics lack narration, or is fundamentally illogical, but instead that these types of poetry attempt to render semantically sublime, or lexically beautiful, sensibilities without the theoretical burden of necessarily engaging reductive, or pedestrian, thought processes. Helping to explain why, a little earlier in time, the English Romantic poet John Keats (1795-1821) designated this intriguing escape from logic, "Negative Capability," whilst his personal approach blended lyrical form with Pagan themes. His subtle experimentation possibly due to his feeling that form was both distinct, as well as abstract, when compared to any underlying notional logic. And it is this approach which has remained influential into the twenty-first century.

Stepping back, an adoration of Great Nature has always helped to formulate the anatomy of Romantic, or Pastoral, verse through its long and unexpected affiliation with English Perennialism!

Confessedly, anyone visiting our English Shires, who walks along a narrow, curvaceous, lane, with green grassy banks speckled with bluebells and ramsons, only to suddenly look out over the wide rolling verdant countryside, will readily understand this vital connection. It is as though these types of genre naturally complement each other. They are closely allied. Not merely related through the engine of folk expectation and made into the type of traditional "fairy telling" that expressed small-scale mysteries: especially throughout the media of generic public spectacle. Appreciably so, way back when, in Victorian pantomime, or seventeenth-century masques, wherein allegorical figures were associated with unbaptised passions; to say nothing of Libertarian celebrations of flagrant sexual ambiguity. What's more, dating back to the time of Classical Theatre, such "fairy" motifs were woven around popular village stories, which had gained a coherent design thanks largely to sixteenth-century *Commedia dell'arte* in Italy, as well as other European and British stage traditions. With this securely in mind, it is unsurprising to find the silvery-tongued British demos attaching names from cleverly constructed legend and openly symbolic lore to some of their occasionally uncouth national attributes. Following the French, for once, by embracing these licentious images of psychic transformation as representations of escape from conventional habitations into the outer sanctum of a Sur-Reality![4]

Puns are repeatedly discovered as the key to unravelling this elaborate entifying cant. Coupled, as they are, with witticisms and dateable wordplay! Every lexical-item of which offers an expressive, cerebral, release, wherein British poets have composed some of the most memorable, as well as quixotic, stanzas in the entirety of our Western lands. Aided, as this has been, by the lick of our noble tongue across both linguistic hemispheres! Consequently, the phrase "English poetry" has become unavoidably equivocal. It can mean rhyme written in the English language, whatever this implies, along with any one of the colourful, colonial pidgins: or contrariwise, that type of poetic discourse written in the domiciled regions of physical England. No matter how it is interpreted, everything said, the earliest poetry (being orally transmitted through performance), as I have discussed elsewhere, as well as latterly written down in manuscripts, yields to an approximate chronology. Showing, as this must, that a large number of lost treasures left little apart from slender linguistic traces, as quotation, or reference, through the inevitable decay of passing Millennia! Like inkling tracks across scant vellum.

Speaking practically, hereafter, any examination of the dates on those manuscripts luckily preserved, against ideological adversities and careless odds, appear to show very little surviving material predating the tenth century: one or two collections of poetry written in Brythonic (a predecessor of modern Welsh) along with Latin, dating from the sixth century, representing nearly the whole field. A few fragments of Anglo-Saxon verse, interpreted as the most direct ancestor of modern English, seem to resound from the seventh century: although opinion is becoming more and more divided on this issue. The dulcet voice of our earliest ancestors being drowned behind the less operatic tones from prehistoric British choirs! Evolving this discordant theme, it is fair to argue that the first ascribable English poem is a hymn on the creation. The Venerable Bede himself attributing this song to Caedmon the Singer (658-680 AD) who, according to Church Tradition, started out as an illiterate herdsman caught up in the Spirit to the extent of exhaling sublime poetry at a monastery in Whitby. A character-type any adherent of Orthodoxy will instantly find recognisable, not to forget the start of Anglo-Saxon poetry as an identifiable text-type. Stunned so, admirers of this melodist would have heard:

> Now let me praise the keeper of Heaven's kingdom,
> The might of the Creator, and his thought,
> The work of the Father of glory, how each of wonders
> The Eternal Lord established in the beginning.
> He first created for the sons of men
> Heaven as a roof, the holy Creator,
> Then Middle-earth the keeper of mankind,
> The Eternal Lord, afterwards made,

The earth for men, the Almighty Lord.
In the beginning Caedmon sang this poem.[5]

Further evidenced, as a remnant of an indigenous poetic flow, by the dates accredited to the great epic *Beowulf*, since they range from the eighth through to the early eleventh century!

Regarding *Beowulf*, of course, we need to take a momentary pause. Consisting of 3182 alliterative long lines, this anonymous verse masterwork, named after its protagonist, the heroic Beowulf, is conserved as a single manuscript known as the *Nowell Codex*. By story, its pages chronicle the adventures of this champion of the Geats, who pledges his help to Hrothgar, King of the Danes. A monster by the name of Grendel, the author tells us, has been attacking this nobleman's mead hall and Beowulf must grapple with him. So, following his defeat of this gruesome beast, and then his coequally grotesque mother, Beowulf returns to Scandinavia where, after fifty years have passed, he even overcomes a dragon. Yet, the poet finds himself driven to pensively ponder on the transience of both heroism and life:

O flower of warriors, beware of that trap.
Choose, dear Beowulf, the better part,
eternal rewards. Do not give way to pride.
For a brief while your strength is in bloom
but it fades quickly; and soon there will follow
illness or the sword to lay you low,
or a sudden fire or surge of water
or jabbing blade or javelin from the air
or repellent age. Your piercing eye
will dim and darken; and death will arrive,
dear warrior, to sweep you away.
(Lines 1758-1768)

The previously scripted folktales having added extra emotional impetus to the interweaving allegories in a composition that created a seminal oeuvre! Other celebrated Anglo-Saxon textual jottings, deepened by the presence of heraldic animals (or not), being *The Dream of the Rood*, written, as it was, before AD 700: a demonstrable fact, due to excerpts of this piece having been carved on the Ruthwell Cross. Along with poems on historical events, like the Battle of Brunanburh and the Battle of Maldon, which were apparently composed shortly following the events they commented on. Meaning, when all is collated and combined, they can reasonably be dated in sequence. All the same, in practical terms Anglo-Saxon poetry is usually categorised by the manuscript within which it appears, rather than its possible presentation before an audience as either performance, or read, verse.

Apart from the Caedmon manuscript and the *Beowulf* manuscript, as two of the four great poetical codices of the late tenth and early eleventh centuries, the other most historically illuminating manuscripts of this period are the *Vercelli Book* and the *Exeter Book*. Catalogued so, these vestigial poetic papers are limited in number, even though captivatingly wide in breadth of subject! Incontestably, *Beowulf* remains the only heroic epic extant in its "entirety." Despite the occasional reminder, from other works like the famed *Finnesburg Fragment* and *Waldere*, that it must have been one of many comparable scripts! Appended collections, continuing this allegorical theme, incorporating a great deal of religious verse and Biblical paraphrase from devotional works! Elegies, such as *The Seafarer*, *The Wanderer*, and *The Ruin* (frequently taken as descriptive of the Roman ruins in Bath), along with innumerable riddles, charms and proverbs, equivalently abound in these documents! With one notable stylistic exception, known to us moderns as *The Rhyming Poem!* As a work of 87 lines found inside the *Exeter Book*, it is distinctive for being written in rhyming couplets. Unarguably, that noticed, rhyme is otherwise virtually unknown in Anglo-Saxon literature, which used alliterative verse as its preferred medium.

In leitmotif, this poem concerns the life of a ruler: from the occasion of his birth, through his prosperous affairs at Court, to his inevitable fall from social grace and eventual demise. Ending, as readers can see, with cerebrations on the Eternal rewards awaiting those who seek the solace of penance. Probably inspired by the

Biblical *Book of Job*, this poem remains a tour de force with regard to its versification in a nearly modern sense of the word. But there's the rub! These materials themselves have managed to mask their own hidden significance, in that they all stand as testament to an Anglo-Saxon Church with a visibly Orthodox flavour. Roman Catholic apologists may like to gloss over such socio-historic details as insignificant, and present all Western Europeans as tantamount to card-carrying "Romans" before the Great Schism, yet careful textual analysis reveals the "signature" of Orthodoxy throughout Anglo-Saxon poetry. Particularly in the plethora of textual minutia, like rhyme being considered as a technique of unnecessary ornamentation.

Inspected from this different angle, Geoffrey Chaucer is seen to wield a cunningly "Orthodox" plume in English poetry. Assuredly, when sitting down to begin writing *The Canterbury Tales* it is unlikely that the Poet was merely trying to compose an innovative set of sweet-sounding mini-sagas designed to amuse those educated enough to read between the lines. A number of scholars, this safely intuited, who have studied his myriad inferences, on top of meticulously planned secondary and tertiary discourses, never really seeing the fulsome implications of his dogmatic couplets and doctrinally slanted polysyllables in a *chef d'oeuvre* comparable in complexity to Occult codifications.

It is unsurprising, so said, that Chaucer undertakes colossal efforts to elucidate deduced personal arguments to his readers, whilst unveiling private religious qualms and idiosyncratic theologies in a variety of ways. One of his principle descants, delivered in the form of fictive characters, mirroring a debauched secession of irresponsible leaders within the overall Communion of the Church. In Chaucer's day, it must be remembered, scarred as this was by geolinguistic polarisation, as well as mass psychological enslavement through (highly-controversial) practices such as Indulgences, a method by which sins were expiated like a financial debt to theocratic creditors, even notions of fellowship could be used against the People: a social fracture eventually sparking Martin Luther's (1483-1546)

Reformation. Nearly equal in protest, Chaucer uses his literary pawns to expose the spineless ineptitude of Christian clergy. As a brilliant tactic, the Poet positions himself (as a character) in the General Prologue. A masterstroke, allowing Chaucer to share his first impressions of the other pilgrims he encounters at the beginning of his journey with his audience. In doing so, of course, he gives away far more information than initially meets the eye. Outwardly respectful to all, "pilgrim Chaucer" nevertheless cannot contain his distaste for certain members of his party. As we may read concerning the Pardoner, "For wel he wiste, whan that song was songe He moste preche, and wel affyle his tonge, To winnw silver, as he ful wel coude – Therefore he song the murierly and loude." (General Prologue, 711-714) In other words, this loathsome wretch would put on a pious act in order to gain admiration and respect from those placed around him. Certainly, he was aware that through his passionate, even though insincere, singing he could earn extra money from the gullible. In this unveiling, Chaucer worked hard to present the Pardoner's wicked intentions to both the other pilgrims in-text, along with his actual audience.

Healthy and irreverent British tradition, firmly to Chaucer's mind, should always act as the barometer of our affairs! This may additionally be one of his motivations in helping to restore the English language of his era as a veritable laboratory of literature. Indisputably, Anglo-Norman, or Latin, were still preferred in the public activities of Church and State, meaning that "English" was weakening as a common linguistic medium: even though a number of important demotic texts were written during this reformative period. Patently, around the turn of the thirteenth century, the priest Layamon wrote his *Brut*, also known as *The Chronicle of Britain*, largely based on Wace's twelfth-century Anglo-Norman epic of the very same title. Yet, admittedly, whilst Layamon's language is clearly recognisable as Middle English, his prosody shows strong residues of Anglo-Saxon parlance and, as such, secures his linguistic importance. On a related note, quite a few transitional works found themselves preserved as popular entertainment; including a variety of lyrics and romances.

Regaining prestige, therefore, in 1362 the English language replaced Latin and French in Parliament and the Courts of Justice. Not merely politics, this cultural move marked a recovery of essential Soul in these lands.

Unarguably, it was with the unfolding of the fourteenth century that major works of literature in English began, once again, to appear in extensive circulation. Among them, the writings of the "Pearl Poet" – a name given to the author of *Pearl*, a palatial alliterative poem in Middle English. Its author, easily recognised as the "Gawain Poet," since he seems to have composed *Sir Gawain and the Green Knight*, as well as *Patience*, and *Cleanliness*: visibly giving so-called "fairy verse" totally new dimensions. Some scholars interjecting that this master of symbolist composition likewise quilled the edifying *St. Erkenwald*. Maybe so! In any case, it is the better publicised Chaucer who contemporaries envisaged as the obvious successor to Virgil and Dante (1265-1321). At the risk of meandering, the reputation of those who followed Chaucer has, unfairly, suffered by unnecessarily direct comparison, although it must quickly be admitted that John Lydgate (1370-1451) and John Skelton (1460-1529) are treasured and studied in their own right. Still and all, with minor exceptions, as we progress to the early years of the sixteenth century only John Skelton's poems stand out as transitional texts between the late Medieval and Renaissance styles! Over and above this, problematically, the new King, Henry VIII, boasted of being something of a poet himself, causing satirists to muzzle their fire to a greater or lesser extent.

External resemblances to authority figures, caricaturing or glorifying, have been the tag of fairy literature from the Medieval Romances onwards. In themselves, these ethereal, preternatural creatures offered the perfect whiteboard upon which critical statements could be inscribed. Evens-Wentz (1878-1965) himself, in his astonishing book, *Fairy Faith in Celtic Countries*, euphemistically reminding his readers that it was neither the elemental forces of Nature, nor the dead, supernatural entities, or tribes lost in our historical landscapes that (always) feature in these tales. Side by side with these depictions of those who had been blessed, or cursed, through a mystical encounter with sentient Nature are portraits of cultural malice, political pranks and social mischief. Young knight errants being especially vulnerable, according to received reflection. Heretofore, a fairy appeared to Sir Launfal, in one such story, to demand his love. Rather like the fairy bride of "ordinary" folklore, she imposed a prohibition on him that he eventually violated. There was equally talk that Sir Orfeo's wife was carried away by the King of Faerie, while Huon of Bordeaux was assisted in his affairs by King Oberon himself. Nonetheless, these fairy characters, as personifications of magical, or political, forces, dwindled in number as the medieval period progressed, leaving the field open to double-edged illustrations of enchantresses and wizards. Poets, at this point, delighting their listeners with stories of Morgan le Fay, whose connection with the realm of Faerie is heavily implied in Sir Thomas Malory's (died 1471) ingenious *Le Morte d'Arthur*.

All of which brings us to the enchanted lifestyles within Elizabethan poetry. A literary period moulded by witty young blades, pomandered ladies and gallant adventurers: along with rich textual compositions regularly overlapping Courtly assignations with the activities of nymphs and satyrs from antiquity. The re-initiation of ancient lyrical models, coupled with the slow emergence of a native Courtly poetry (often centred round the figure of the Monarch), never abandoning the evolution of verse-based drama, being among the most important advances achieved at this time. Thereafter, a broad range of Elizabethan poets wrote songs, including Thomas Nashe (1567-1601), Nicholas Grimald (1519-1562) and Robert Southwell (1561-1595). Although, the greatest of those songwriters remembered to history was Thomas Campion (1567-1620). After all, he is especially praiseworthy due to his experiments with metres built on counting syllables instead of stresses. Ahead of this, his quantitative methods were founded on Classic models and need to be understood as part of the extended Renaissance revival in Greek and Roman techniques. Generally speaking, songs of this sort were printed either in anthologies, or miscellanies, such as Richard Tottel's (died 1594) *Songs and Sonnets*, (1557), or in songbooks that incorporated printed music designed to facilitate performance: events forming both private and public entertainments.[6] Production values notwithstanding, by the close of the sixteenth century, an entirely new generation of composers, including William Byrd (1543-1623), Thomas Weelkes (1576-1623), John Dowland (1563-1626), Orlando Gibbons (1583-1625), and Thomas Morley (1558-1602), were helping to bring the art of Elizabethan song to an exceedingly high level of musical attainment.

Linked, possibly, to the consolidation of Queen Elizabeth's power, an honest sympathy for the Liberal Arts strode abroad. This encouraged in its wake the emergence of verse aimed at, and oftentimes set in, an idealised version of the Courtly world. As such, innovators felt the need to explore poesy through uplifting iambic patterns: a metrical foot, in other words, of two syllables, one unstressed (or short) and one stressed (or long). Unquestionably, our beloved Shakespeare experimented with any number of iambic combinations throughout his plays and appears to have viewed iambs, which may be seen as the reverse of the trochee, as marking a new energy and fluidity in verse forms. Amid other experimenters with this trend are to be counted Edmund Spencer (1552-1599), who wrote *The Faerie Queene* and Sir Philip Sidney (1554-1586), the author of *Arcadia*. As a point of information, annotators tend to concur that the first Pastorals in English were the *Eclogues* of Alexander Barclay (1476-1552), a poet heavily influenced by Mantuan versifiers. So, it could be said that when adopting a poetic stance, we Britannic Islanders perpetually look to previous cultural precedents as artistic justifications for our exceedingly inventive, even though heritage-based, diction. Explaining, partially of course, Sidney's deviceful representation of Mount Athos as an immortal witness to the fleeting affairs of men! As he sternly penned in his *The Apologie for Poetrie*, "Under Mount Athos in 492 BC, so Xerxes cut a canal through its isthmus." A superficially simple line which yields, with very little deconstruction, to this young swordsman's sense of an endlessly inhuman antiquity! He even manages to allude to the uncomfortable presence of realpolitik within dynastic dynamics. It was, after all, the implacable will of this King-of-Kings to chisel a canal through hardened stone, not the engineers, or slave-workers, on the ground. Theirs was an age, put differently, of brute force and unredeemed violence where, under the nose of a place devoted to Pagan gods, the Heavens nevertheless waited for the time when Christ would set his celestial foot on this Earth from on High.

During the same period, Edmund Spenser wrote an eclogue drawn almost entirely from Virgil, describing Mount Athos in terms of disturbing conundrum. Overtly, this other Elizabethan swashbuckler nearly chants these strangely complimentary lines: "Nor how Mount Athos through exceeding might/was digged down." An attempt, on his part, to draw attention to the enigmatic nature of the Mount as a natural colossus and an immovable, primeval, object! A theme Dr Johnson (1709-84) elaborated in the renowned *Samuel Johnson Collection* when reminding his own readership that, although sometimes deliberately obscure, Spenser's translation of the *Virgilian Culex* remains an evocation of neglected lore. At the risk, therefore, of adapting the Roman Catholic theologian Karl Rahner's (1904-1984) assertion that there are "anonymous Christians," I propose there is clearly a category of poets in English literature who could be addressed as a "subconscious Orthodox remnant," because the sound of their obsessions reverberates towards those intellectual streams venerated by our ancestors. So cautiously regarded, possibly even by his fellows, Sidney was not knighted until four years before his death, although he was from a family whose connections at Court were among the most exalted in the reign of Elizabeth.

Other submerged signs of an unconscious Orthodox nostalgia are discovered in small details of personal history. Family tradition has it that Sidney was tutored at home by his mother, until he was of an age to attend Shrewsbury School. Unlike many, he advanced to Christ Church, Oxford, even though he left without taking a degree. In the year after, he left for Europe as part of the entourage of his uncle, the Lord Leicester (1563-1626). As a matter of record, Sidney visited France, where he became Gentleman of the Bedchamber to King Charles IV of Austria, also eventually meeting scholars like

Hubert Languet (1518-1581) and Petrus Ramus (1515-1572). On his return from this grand tour, he served in Ireland with his father, who was three times Lord Deputy. Once back in England, he met with the First Earl of Essex and his daughter, Penelope, who inspired the sonnet-sequence *Astrophel* and *Stella*. Most certainly, young Penelope's brother, Robert, who was to become the Earl of Essex, should concurrently be remembered as the close friend of Edmund Spenser, who later became Sidney's friend when working in Leicester's household. That being said, Penelope Devereux married Lord Rich, while Sidney married Frances Walsingham. Sidney had, meanwhile, become one of the brighter adornments of Elizabeth's Court, being entrusted with diplomatic missions: some saying this was why he decided to write a masque, *The Lady of May*, in order to celebrate the Queen's visit to Leicester's House. After a quarrel with the Earl of Oxford, however, Sidney left Court in temporary disfavour, and went to stay with his sister Mary. For her entertainment, he composed his *Arcadia*, a prose romance of which he himself had no great opinion. Around the same time, he probably wrote *An Apologie of Poetrie*, wherein Mount Athos made its ominous entrance into his verses.

Sidney, at the end of the day, was a courteous, polished and courageous young man; everything someone should be if bearing the epithet "aristocrat." This may be one of the reasons why his work was not published in his lifetime, though the manuscripts were clearly circulated, as was the fashion of his day. Correspondingly, judging from tertiary evidence, they seem to have been widely read. Fascinatingly, Sidney's arrival on the English poetry scene is remarkably sudden, and brilliant (beyond doubt), even though sadly brief. Some critics bracket him with Spencer, but only due to the fact that they were contemporaries. Occasionally, commentators have argued that if Spencer had died at 32, we would only have *The Shepheardes Calender*, along with a few short poems. Still, taken together, Sidney's poetic legacy is small in terms of compositions, yet his work, according to C. S. Lewis, "rises out of the contemporary Drab almost as a rocket rises: whereas Spencer climbed slowly and painfully." As Lewis additionally points out, Sidney's work was done before Spencer had published anything of comparable worth. Indeed, his *Astrophel and Stella* is acknowledged to this day as taking pride of place among Elizabethan sonnet-sequences and its influence has been demonstrably profound. Unfortunately, *Arcadia* as well as Sidney's *An Apologie for Poetry* seem little read in these decades, except by students of Literature. The former, like Spencer's *The Faerie Queene*, because it is bewilderingly intricate, and the latter since the time for an *Apologie* is long past. Nevertheless, the *Apologie* contains a plethora of fine things and unsuspected riches for the lovers of Orthodoxy.

Before examining the residual traces of Orthodoxy in other poets, a few last observations need to be made regarding these Elizabethans. Edmund Spencer, for his part, attended the Merchant Taylor's School. The Headmaster of this venerable institution being Richard Mulcaster (1531-1611), a teacher of formidable talents, as well as a man of passionate devotions towards English as a vehicle of Literature. This appears to have been why the schoolboy Spencer is known to have been practising the poets from a very young age. As time went by, Spencer attended Pembroke Hall, Cambridge, as a sizar.[7] During his second year, he even became friends with Gabriel Harvey; newly elected as a Fellow. Their friendship endured even though Harvey had little sympathy with Spencer's work and sometimes disparaged it. Spencer, furthermore, in his first year at Cambridge, contributed to S. John van der Noodt's anthology, *A theatre wherein be represented as wel the miseries and calamities that follow the voluptuous worldlings*, a number of sonnets and epigrams translated from Italian and French. Spencer, unlike Sydney, took his Bachelor of Arts Degree, and then his Master of Arts Degree, two years later becoming secretary to the Bishop of Rochester, the Right Reverend John Bell. The year following, through Harvey's influence, the young Spencer found himself as a member of Leicester's household, becoming friends with Sidney, who was Leicester's nephew. In the same year, Spencer married Machabyas Child and completed *The Shepheardes Calender*, which he dedicated to his new friend.

It may go without saying that Sidney was full of praise towards the project, despite having reservations about his companion's "rusticke" language. A criticism echoed by many leading academicians from that time to this. Unquestionably, so admitted, Spencer's gifts were plain to see. He was a man who could make music with words; a true poet by natural calling. Thusly, when a new literary club known as the Areopagus was summoned forth to celebrate the achievements of Tudor artistry, Spencer found himself invited to join the ranks of Sidney, Edward Dyer (1543-1607) and Gabriel Harvey (1545-1630). During this epoch, Spencer also found himself completing some of his shorter poems, the majority of which were not published until some years later. He additionally began work on *The Faerie Queene* and became secretary to Lord Grey de Wilton: a man destined to take office as Lord Deputy of Ireland. He lived in Ireland for 18 years; successively, they say, in Enniscorthy, Dublin, Kildare and at Kilcolman in the beauteous county of Cork. Throughout his life, moreover, Spencer remained aware that his was an era within which lovers used to stroll under the glittering canopy of autumnal stars, fully mindful that each evening these celestial lights helped to illumine their breathy promises: that his was a time of sparkling enlightenment that gifted romantic oaths with glittering Verse. It was said, way back then, that poems were the laments sung by wounded souls trying to ease their unrequited pains. Particularly, perhaps, if the beloved in question was of the same sex! Our romantic forebears, this asserted, were more sanguine about these issues than at first appears. Their attitude seemingly earthed by an understanding that worse things happen at sea, and life was actually rather a messy business. A view that dominated both sexual and poetic discourse in periods before the Mid-Victorian zealotry for categorisation gave birth to oppressive social aberrations. Decidedly, their atavistic reasoning seems to have run along the lines that in the early stages of adolescence, as well as in one's dotage, the Heavens turn a blind eye towards sexual affections, which took unusual courses – and did not involve the possibility of producing children. The Elizabethans even felt that some highly-sexed individuals were simply carried along by the force of their own nature – into excess and ecstasy: sentiments almost prophesying the birth of Lord Byron (1788-1824) as the physical apotheosis of Romanticism.

It may come as something of a shock, therefore, that a few centuries later it was Byron who unwittingly succumbed to the presence of the Holy Mountain. Anecdotal testimony still holds that, although never actually setting foot on its slopes in person—and, probably, only having seen the mountain from a measured distance— this juggernaut against the dreary limitations of Enlightenment thinking felt moved to compose his little known fragmentary poem, *The Monk of Athos.* Uncharacteristically pious, curious audiences may read in this striking work:

Beside the confines of the Aegean Main,
Where northward Macedonia bounds the flood,
And views opposed the Asiatic plain,
Where once the pride of lofty Ilium stood,
Like the great Father of the giant brood,
With lowering port majestic Athos stands,
Crowned with the verdure of eternal wood,
As yet unspoiled by sacrilegious hands,
And throws his mighty shade o'er seas and distant lands.
And deep embosomed in his shady groves
Full many a convent rears its glittering spire,
Mid scenes where Heavenly Contemplation loves
To kindle in her soul her hallowed fire,
Where air and sea with rocks and woods conspire
To breathe a sweet religious calm around,
Weaning the thoughts from every low desire,
And the wild waves that break with murmuring sound
Along the rocky shore proclaim it holy ground.
Sequestered shades where Piety has given
A quiet refuge from each earthly care,
Whence the rapt spirit may ascend to Heaven!
Oh, ye condemned the ills of life to bear!
As with advancing age your woes increase,
What bliss amidst these solitudes to share
The happy foretaste of eternal Peace,
Till Heaven in mercy bids your pain and sorrows cease.

Strangely, Byron appears to be on the verge of adopting a view *sub specie aeternitatis* in these lines. Beyond argument, it is additionally one of his many (frequently overlooked) attempts to describe Sublime feeling within his corpus. It may be wise to remind ourselves at this juncture that Edmund Burke (1729-1792), defined the Sublime in terms of delight mixed with terror or pain, and produced by an "infinite object." In other words, it is an aesthetic value closely akin, and perhaps leading to, the Beatific Vision; whereby a glimpse of the Absolute is vouchsafed to the favoured. Nonetheless, it is reasonably certain that Byron was not seriously tempted to retreat to Mount Athos and take up a life of religious contemplation.

In stating this, Byron's love of Greece is not in question. Maybe, his overall plan was to support the struggle for Hellenic independence taking place at this time, not just to see the marvels of antiquity, but as a just endeavour in itself. As such, Byron originally seems to have sailed to Zante, but he decided instead on Cephalonia during a brief stopover in Leghorn: where his party was soon joined by James Hamilton Brown; a Scot who had served in Ionia and was sympathetic to the revolutionary cause. Once they had rendezvoused, each of these adventurers arrived at Argostoli, Cephalonia. Undoubtedly, Byron settled into quarters in Metaxata and immediately sought information about the political and military situation from various Englishman and Greeks. The British resident, Colonel Charles Napier, was especially helpful in this regard, as were George Finlay and Colonel Leicester Stanhope who arrived slightly later. Byron speedily saw how vexed circumstances were due to the conflicts between different revolutionary leaders. However, as chief representative of the London Greek Committee, he had to proceed with extreme caution. Besides, Byron needed to remain in Cephalonia with Pietro Gamba multiplying his Greek contacts and assessing the information he was gathering as a prelude to action.

When Prince Alexander Mavrocordatos (1791-1865), who eventually became the first President of an independent Greece, moved to Missolonghi he invited Lord Byron to join him and his forces. Byron decided that, all in all, this was the right move and left shortly after Christmas 1832 to join the forces of western Greece. The brief journey, this stated, proved harrowing because their passage was intercepted by a Turkish vessel, and Byron was forced to seek shelter near Dragomestre. Noticeably, archaic regional hostilities were still poisonously active, withal! Yet, arriving at Missolonghi in January 1824 Lord Byron met with a great reception in his personal honour. Memorably, as he sailed into the protective harbour, every ship in the Greek squadron fired a cannoning salute of respect as his small vessel passed them by.

Byron, always and ever eager for action, as well as pleased with Mavrocordatos, undertook to support a force of 500 Suliote soldiers for a year. Plans were variously made for expeditions including an assault on Lepanto to be led by Byron himself. But the Greeks were stubbornly difficult to deal with (especially the fiercely independent Suliote), all making Byron begin to visibly chafe under the strain of unnecessary delays; never forgetting the pointless complications that seemed to increase daily. His mood, that observed, is captured in the memorable lines, "On this day I complete my thirty-sixth year," which he wrote on 22 January, thinking of the conflicting claims of war and love, and especially of Loukas Chalandritsanos, the Greek boy he had brought with him from Cephalonia. When the firemaster James Parry arrived in February with long-awaited and much-needed supplies, Byron's enthusiasm for the cause revived; not least because of Parry's own energetic and fiery character. Unexpectedly, however, in the midst of these sudden changes of mood, came an ominous incident. Conversing with Parry and others on the evening of 15th January, Byron collapsed in a violent convulsion. Though he slowly recovered, everyone saw that his constitution had become severely weakened, whilst his spirits continued to be discouraged by the ineffectual state of the Greek military situation. Eventually, the Lepanto expedition was abandoned and many of Byron's Suliote troops decided to leave. To Parry, Byron despaired of ever being able to give practical help to the justice of the Greek cause. Moreover, the weather was wet and the low-lying area of marshy land around Missolonghi did nothing to improve Byron's precarious state of health. Thus, on the rainy morning of 10th April, after returning from a ride, Byron complained of pain and fever. Naturally, his physicians attended him closely, yet he slipped into an unexpected decline. On 14th April, Byron suffered severe bouts of delirium which became increasingly draining. By 16th April it was unmistakable that he was dangerously ill, and his room became the focus of a large group of worried friends, servants, and physicians. The next day Byron, almost clairvoyantly, told one of his medical attendants,

> Your efforts to preserve my life will be vain. Die I must: I feel it. Its loss I do not lament; for to terminate my wearisome existence I came to Greece. My wealth, my abilities I devote to her cause. Well, there is my life to her. (*Marchand, Biography*, 3.1224)

As he slipped in and out of consciousness over the next two days, he spoke of his daughter, Ada, and sister, Augusta, while making provision for his beloved Loukas, among others. Some said he rambled, as if he were in ferocious battle, fighting for Greece. Nonetheless, terminally debilitated, it was his old servant, Fletcher, who heard Lord Byron's last words: "I want to sleep now." A tremendous storm, they say, broke out on the night Byron died.

The news of his death on the evening of 19th April was a heavy blow to all of the fighting factions in Greece, even though it became a turning point in their fortunes and assisted them in uniting together in honour of a man who gave his life "that Greece might still be free." News of his death, that stated, did not reach England until mid-May, although it shook the entire nation on announcement. Unsurprisingly, and contrary to his wish to be buried in Greece, Byron's body was sent home to England – where it arrived in the Thames estuary aboard the good ship *Florida* on 29th June. Some wanted Byron buried in Westminster Abbey, but the dean, Dr Ireland, refused. Augusta, for her part, had determined that Byron should be buried in the family vault at St Mary Magdalene in Hucknall, Nottinghamshire. After lying in state for two days, a funeral cortege of forty-seven carriages escorted his hearse out of London. Events testifying that no British writer, except Shakespeare, had acquired greater fame, or has exercised more global influence.

Notorious in his time, Byron became a legend after his death: thereby, guiding the arts, music, and literature of the nineteenth century: eclipsing in authority, some say, that of Sir Walter Scott (1771-1832) himself. With this in mind, Byron's influence is ever more apparent, albeit in Europe and America, than in England. This is partly because of the evangelical moralism that was steadily gaining momentum in the poet's lifetime and which continued to configure the bizarrely insincere Victorian sexual ethos. In addition, satire, itself Byron's stylistic verse-signature, went out of fashion in the age of Queen Victoria. Byron and his work, thenceforth, accidentally reflecting the manifold hypocrisies within Victorian Society: as the ambivalent responses of the critic Thomas Carlyle (1795-1801) and the oddly lacklustre praise of the poet Alfred, Lord Tennyson (1809-1892) singularly evidence.

Ironically discerned, middle-class Victorian moralism preserved for Byron a twentieth-century legacy: as one may see in the almost scandalous event of 1924; the centenary of Byron's glorious death fighting for the freedom of Greece! A petition, finally, for a Byron memorial to be ensconced in Westminster Abbey was refused (again) by Herbert Ryle (1856-1925), the Dean at the time! In spite of strong support, it should be recalled, of outstanding literary figures like Thomas Hardy (1840-1928) and Rudyard Kipling (1865-1936), as well as three former Prime Ministers. For his part, Ryle proclaimed, "The Abbey is not a mere literary Valhalla." Consequently, it was not until 1968 that Eric Abbott, as the serving Dean, at last endorsed a petition from the Poetry Society for a memorial, regarding which a ceremony of dedication was held on 8th May 1969.

Despite much scholarship, early twentieth-century interpretive and critical work left Byron at the margin of cultural and literary studies. Critics and scholars equally appearing guilty of simplifying Byron's persona into a hell-raising radical, whose only concerns were for the flesh-pots of Europe. Undoubtedly, his repeated—all be they rare attempts to grasp our world from the viewpoint of Eternity—

were seen as either inconvenient, or confusing. This happened because Byron seemed an inappropriate writer for pedagogical and academic purposes. Still, Byron's influence remains strong, especially for pivotal cultural figures like Oscar Wilde (1854-1900) and James Joyce (1882-1841), whilst those with gothic tastes in verse and prose are never disappointed in him. "Byronism," as such, made an impact too on the images assumed by some of the more outrageous rock stars of the late 1960s and early 1970s. The fast rhythm and excesses of life-expression that became synonymous with this poets' spirit, now recognised as part of the pattern of celebrity. Overall, Byron's literary survival in the high-cultural venues of postmodernism, where satire, wit, and parody have regained social approbation, nevertheless, weirdly obscures the fact that even a distant glimpse of Holy Mount Athos challenged his worldview to the core!

Perspicaciously, every true poet needs a Muse. In this Sidney, Spencer and Byron followed lyrical tradition as impassioned (sometimes bisexual) lovers. For the record, mine is the Bridesmaid of Christ's Church: Great Nature herself. This is because She is the source of all Beauty and ethical instruction. Benevolent in Her blessings, She never proceeds by sudden leaps: which may be why I believe that sexual appetites do not conveniently start, or finish, as deemed temporally appropriate. On the contrary, the desire for sexual activity develops from puberty, and in most cases, only wanes in late middle age. In other words, adolescents, as well as the elderly, need to direct the sexual impulse away from procreation. This is done, of course, by the natural rise of homosexual inclinations at these two stages of life. What appears, so argued, as perverse and unproductive is on closer inspection of benefit to the species. Factually, homosexual inclinations have surfaced in every human community at all times, regardless of whether it is viewed with horror, or punishable by death. In enlightened cultures, moreover, which seemed to have sensed its mystery, it was tolerantly accepted, and such individuals in those societies (presumably) had no reason to suppress their urges. Unquestionably, as far as the ancient Greeks and Romans were concerned, there is little need for additional evidence among informed readers on this practice. Less known, possibly, is the data surrounding "uncultivated" peoples, such as the Gauls, or the Picts, which coequally tell us of homosexuality in easily detectable ways. In Central Asia, furthermore, the countries of that exotic region have openly discussed this tendency from time immemorial until the present day. What is more, Hindus in India, the distant Chinese, dashing Azerbaijani's, no less than the Islamic poets of Persia, eulogise the love experienced by partners of the same gender. In other words, the universal, persistent, and ineradicable character of this impulse shows us that it arises out of our human nature itself. Apart from the fact what happens behind closed doors is a private affair – and meaning, in its turn, that among authentic Quagans, Poets and Athonites, these issues are neither here nor there.

It is Emanuel Swedenborg, so acknowledged, along with Mr Jesse Thompson (as my personal esoteric mentor), who raises the attention of practising poets to a more radical—though punishingly critical—challenge. Sexuality and semi-submerged character traits are no doubt important, but living verse provides a speculum, as it were, by which to recognise the inescapable abnormality of ordinary language: a recognition making us all gleemen, even though some of us bards. As we read in Swedenborg's *Secrets of Heaven,*

> A life of faith without love is like sunlight without warmth – the type of light that occurs in winter, when nothing grows and everything droops and dies. Faith rising out of love, on the contrary, is like light from the sun in spring, when everything grows and flourishes. Warmth from the sun is the fertile agent. The same is true in spiritual and heavenly affairs, which are typically represented in the Word by objects found in nature and human culture.

Soon afterwards, among those who admire him, few could fail to grasp the poetics of everyday life as anything except supermundane. A realisation largely unarticulated between our Anglo-Saxon ancestors; all be they present in their artistic cultivation of these alphabetical territories. Stated differently, our Skalds felt that language had much more than a single purpose. Like runic script itself, there was a utilitarian, along with a magical, application running through each letter. So, it is hardly surprising that those surviving fragments of Anglo-Saxon literature bringing us most closely into contact with our wider tribal origins happen to be the heroic-poetry of our pre-Christian warrior Culture: of that community of subjects, in other words, linking indigenous Britons with a greater civilisation known to the Romans as "Germania." Essentially, the great-great-grandfather of our fluid contemporary tongue at a primary stage of development: albeit without the wealth of inflections it would one day acquire and a reduced vocabulary awaiting the force of expanded mind—as well as a courageous heart—to induce bona fide Hylozoic expressiveness. In this, pastoral imagism, the celestial music of singers, and a passionate zest for living the art of versification, became the stuff of poetic discourse. Surely, they mapped the long processes of socio-imaginative adaptation. This is not to say, naturally, that anyone who writes poetry is unusually sensitive to the mutual assaults of external or internal stimuli, or somehow strangely privileged, in the manner of someone clearly observing the subtle sorrows such monumental struggles entail. Rather, the unique power of a poet is, quite possibly, found in his or her ability to allow disembodied sensibilities to pass through the body, while exploring the Quagan implications of carefully chosen words. The closest analogue may be that of a talented jeweller placing diamonds into a pre-conceived, although devotional, crown. Yet, seen hither, or thither, Poets and Quagans are kinsfolk.

SELECTED ENDNOTES

1. Mankurt is a term referring to an unthinking slave in the *Epic of Manas*. According to the author Chinghiz Aitmatov, there was a Kyrgyz legend wherein mankurts are understood as prisoners of war who were turned into slaves by having their heads wrapped in camel skin. Under a hot sun, these skins dried tight like a steel band, thus enslaving them forever.

2. Swedenborgianism generally understood as a philosophical school attempting to describe the dynamics of human subjectivity (experienced in a person's own acts and inner happenings), shares many of the concerns of Quagnry. However, it tends to reject heavy-handed Existentialist conclusions. Hence, it may initially seem surprising that I am categorising both Swedenborg and Kierkegaard as Quagans although this epithet fits their work much more meaningfully than most of the other designations available.

3. My own mother, before the launch of my first poetry collection, *Caliban's Redemption*, had said, without thinking, that I was now in a position to write a "proper" book. A perception common enough these days in the land of Shakespeare.

4. The Surrealists were, in fact, trying to find a Sur-Reality underlying this world of fleeting phenomenon. In other words, the fundamental continuum from which everything springs into Existence.

5. Originally, this would have been:
    Nu scylun hergan hefaenricaes uard
    metudæs maecti end his modgidanc
    uerc uuldurfadur sue he uundra gihuaes
    eci dryctin or astelidæ
    he aerist scop aelda barnum
    heben til hrofe haleg scepen.
    tha middungeard moncynnæs uard
    eci dryctin æfter tiadæ
    firum foldu frea allmectigprimo cantauit Cædmon istud carmen.

6. Moreover, as a point of information, it was Thomas Wyatt (1503-1542) who was among the first poets to fully master sonnets in English.

7. A sizar is a student who receives some form of assistance such as meals, or lodgings, during term time, or lower fees.

"His expression may often be called bald … but it is bald as the bare mountain tops are bald, with a baldness full of grandeur."

– Matthew Arnold

Problem V.
Inklings of Jerusalem

OUR ANCESTORS TAUGHT US THAT WE COULD LOVE THE actively Sublime best through place and space. Learning thus, about the "spiritual geography" of Briton, a geography where Anglo-Saxon earth rises up to meet an English Heaven, and where this Heaven showers its dew-soaked blessings on our British soils, these lessons remain a native Idyll. In hoary Titchfield where distant kinsfolk experimented with Christian dogma in their attempt to climb Jacob's Ladder into the Uncreated Light: or around Canterbury, as one of our spiritual Capitals (the very cradle of English remembrance), where these admonitions were taken into our blood and bones. Confusedly so, since they sounded so close to our native Quaganry! Also, in legendary regions, like London, that mighty city where Princes still debate the future of Kingdoms East and West! For us, then, any Athos of England would not be a mountain, but an isolated hamlet; that Holy Island of Glastonbury, perhaps, upon which St Michael once trod, Wayland's Smithy, or sanctified Lindisfarne. All locations from which both native sage, and visiting (even though kinsfolk) scholar, would find freedom to follow our trustworthy paths towards an unprecedented edification! And, in so far as Ludwig Wittgenstein (1889-1951) personally adhered to the analyses of "logical atomism," even he could be characterised as a metaphysician, albeit of a rather typically Germanic sort.

In which case, to British writers, mountains were not so much ugly protuberances which disfigured nature and threatened the symmetry of earth: symbols of God's blameless wrath, or places of dangerous splendour where glorious heights stirred their souls to divine ecstasy; although, admittedly, few were the mountains in our homelands. Instead, for Romantic authors—and also for the critic Marjorie Hope Nicholson (1894-1981)—our British intellectual renaissance at the close of the seventeenth century caused a cultural shift from mountains as places of anguish, to mountains as hazardous battlegrounds of potential jubilation. A development of seismic magnitude demonstrating, as it did, either a recovery of our wildest ways, or an evolution into a more unified aesthetic position. As such, she even traces the literary motivations birthing the process of this drastic change in English fictional narrative.

Before examining claims surrounding tales for an Anglo-Saxon Athos, however, we need to clarify the importance of the novel as a genre. Framed thuswise, a novel is a long prose narrative that describes fictional events and characters, usually in the form of an openly sequential story. Without doubt, this genre has its historical roots in the fields of medieval and early modern romance, as well as in the tradition of the novella. The latter, an Italian word used to describe brief stories, supplying the present generic British term from the eighteenth century onwards. Yet, any extra definition of the genre is historically difficult. Indeed, the overall construction of a narrative, the relation of the novel to experienced reality, the plot, let alone characterisation and the stylised use of language, are "normally" analysed in terms of a novel's internal artistic merits. That uncontested, most of these formal and academic requirements were introduced to literary prose in the sixteenth and seventeenth centuries, in order to give fiction a cultural justification outside the field of factual historiography. Therefore, fictional narrative, the novel's distinct "literary" prose, and choice of subject matter, (creating psychological intimacy), along with the expected length of a text can be seen as features that developed with the Western market for fiction. Furthermore, the nearly complete separation of historical narrative from the field of literary fiction has fuelled this creative adaptation over the last 400 years.

Traditionally, critics cite fictionality as the most common feature distinguishing a novel from historical composition: a perfect specimen being narrative set in the future, like *Ethan of Athos*, an English language science fiction novel by American author Lois McMaster Bujold (born 1949). Some claim this is an unusual book in that the name "Athos"—for the main character's home planet—may actually be a reference to Mount Athos in Greece, while other reviewers have alternatively argued it is an indirect tribute to the English actor Oliver Reed (1938-1999), whom Bujold is known to admire (she has cited him as a model for the protagonist's father Aral Vorkosigan). Risking a detour, Reed played the role of Athos in the 1973 film version of *The Three Musketeers*, the famed tale by Alexandre Dumas (1802-1870). Nonetheless, fictionality can prove to be something of a problematic criterion. Certainly, throughout the early modern period, authors of historical accounts in narrative form would frequently include inventions, which were rooted in folk tradition in order to add credibility to an opinion, or stylistically embellish a passage of text. Trained historians would thus invent, or construct, speeches for didactic purposes: a habit raising a multiplicity of questions regarding the authenticity of even carefully recorded materials. Conversely, novels can capture the personal, social and political realities of a period, or place, with a precision and detail historians would never dare to explore. Hence, the supposed line between writing history and authoring a novel demands clarification in aesthetic terms. Novels, after all, are supposed to show qualities of literature and art, whereas historical accounts are penned with the intention of firing public debate about political issues. So, while a novel can deal with history it is more apposite to approach its formation as a timeless work of art.

In these terms, so-called literary value is a source of constant debate between writers and reviewers. Does, for instance, a specific novel possess either the "deeper meaning" revealed by poetic interpretation, or the "eternal qualities" required of art? In itself, this discussion has allowed critics to develop both the interpretive meaning and cogent investigation of texts marked as "fiction."

Discerned so, a novel nearly always differentiates itself from the philosophical category of "forgery" through an honest announcement of its aim and author. Thence, the word *novel* can appear on title pages and book covers, or just be a theoretical "given." At the same time, any extra artistic efforts on the part of a writer may be advertised in a blurb or preface. On this level, once it is stated whose craftsmanship has produced a text, we, as readers, along with a veritable plethora of contemporary reviewers and critics will quickly become responsible for qualitative debate on the work. In origin, this new critical responsibility (historians were the only qualified reviewers up to the 1750s) made it possible to publicly disqualify many previous fictional outpourings as in any way factual. Clearly, the early eighteenth-century *roman-à-clef* and its fashionable counterpart, the *nouvelle historique*, had presented narrative to their audiences with—by and large—scandalous social implications: although, those literary reviewers who became interested in such fictions during the 1750s offered a less outraged series of critical estimations. For the majority of them, a work is "literature," or in other words, literary art, if it has personal heroes or villains to identify, a continuous narrative with fictional inventions, and a recognisable structure including a climax, sense of suspense, and an unclouded conclusion. Little else, in their view, passes muster. It may relate facts with calumnious accuracy, or singularly distort them: yet critically one cannot ignore any work of this kind as worthless unless it lacks insight, style, or refuses to achieve internal resolution within its own frame of reference. Moreover, it has to compete with other works of invention and art of the same genus, not merely with factual accounts of history. Weirdly, this left those with an "historical" bent to relinquish their previous assessments respecting "medieval" and "early modern" authorship to the evaluation of "professional" literary reviewers. What is more, writing these "fictions," allegedly a private, subjective, enterprise, turned into a flood of Text demanding public interpretation. In book form, these narrations developed a recognisable market of ideological importance to be explored with a didactic (in the school system) and critical temperament on the part of other writers as well as their readers. Thusly, in an anecdotal mood, P. G. Wodehouse

(1881-1975) drolly commented that following his translation into more than thirty languages, he was even being analysed by a Russian monk living in a hermit's cell on Mount Athos.[1]

Somewhat more seriously, this may account for the reasons why C. S. Lewis, as an author, appears to be the perfect litmus test for relations between successful (not to mention well written) books, Christian Orthodoxy, English literary scholarship, and Anglicanism. Undoubtedly, his straddling of these mammoth fields, along with his own meditations on Metaphysics, Holy Mountains and Sin, in works like *The Great Divorce* have provoked many Orthodox readers to raise the question, "Was Lewis an anonymous Orthodox?" Well, Lewis' view of Atonement Theology and Soteriology, not to avoid his public understandings of Heaven and Hell, are compatible with Orthodox notions of the same: standing as they do in transparent opposition to avowed Protestant and Roman Catholic apprehensions of these weighty matters. As such, we may read,

> "Son," he said, "ye cannot in your present state understand eternity ... That is what mortals misunderstand. They say of some temporal suffering, 'No future bliss can make up for it,' not knowing that Heaven, once attained, will work backwards and turn even that agony into a glory. And of some sinful pleasure they say 'Let me have but this and I'll take the consequences:' little dreaming how damnation will spread back and back into their past and contaminate the pleasure of the sin. Both processes begin even before death. The good man's past begins to change so that his forgiven sins and remembered sorrows take on the quality of Heaven: the bad man's past already conforms to his badness and is filled only with dreariness. And that is why ... the Blessed will say 'We have never lived anywhere except in Heaven,': and the Lost, 'We were always in Hell.'" And both will speak truly.

As a matter of recorded biography, that carefully noted, Lewis remained an Anglican. However, it is pertinent to observe that for more than a century, and all through Lewis' adult life, the Anglican and Orthodox Churches were actively engaged with possibilities of union. Unfortunately, from the Orthodox side, this search was surrendered in the late 1960s, when it became increasingly apparent that modernist liberalism, and not mystical theology, would prevail in the Church of England. So recalled, it is very fair to describe Lewis as an "Anonymous Orthodox" – much beloved by readers of Orthodox faith, but officially, with a clear allegiance to the Anglican Communion. In which case, the most sensitive study of Lewis' relationship to Orthodoxy, in all probability, was written by Bishop Kallistos Ware (born 1934) of Diokleia, who additionally taught at Oxford. In an article published in *Sobornost* (an Anglican-Orthodox Ecumenical magazine) entitled, *C.S. Lewis, an 'Anonymous Orthodox'?*, Bishop Ware explores this fascinating question: insightfully relating to his readers that Lewis had a tendency to "idealise Orthodox" tradition and affirms that "even though C.S. Lewis' personal contacts with the Orthodox Church were not extensive, at the same time his thinking is often profoundly in harmony with the Orthodox standpoint."

Said differently, even though Lewis can't be looked upon as an Orthodox writer, pure and simple, his consistent sympathy for Orthodox theology continues to be considered as germane. Undoubtedly so, to the extent of making one of Lewis' biographers comment (in *C.S. Lewis and His Times*, by George Sayer), that after a holiday spent in Greece, together with Lewis and his wife, the author told him of all the liturgies he'd ever attended, he preferred the Greek Orthodox liturgy to anything he had seen in the West, be it Roman Catholic or Protestant. Lewis then went on to say that of all the priests and monks he had ever had the opportunity to meet personally, Orthodox clergy were the holiest; the most spiritual. Apparently, Lewis even referred to a certain innate look they had: a gravitas, a religious dignity. Further, Lewis himself, in one of his letters, speaks of having been at an Orthodox liturgy, which he found uncannily compelling on a deeply subconscious level. As Lewis records, "some stood, some sat, some knelt and one old man crawled around the floor like a caterpillar," meaning, "He absolutely loved it." Of course, on the level of card-carrying membership, critics are aware that C.S. Lewis never took any practical steps towards Orthodoxy, even though professional colleagues felt he worked behind the scenes for a finer sense of mutuality between these twin communions.

Maybe this is partially the reason behind why, in addition to his career as an English literature professor, not to forget a popular author of fiction, Lewis is regarded by many reviewers as one of the most influential Christian apologists of his age. Without reservation, *Mere Christianity* was voted best book of the twentieth century by *Christianity Today* in 2000. Moreover, due to Lewis' initial approach to religious belief as a sceptic, and his subsequent conversion, he has been rightfully dubbed "Apostle to the Sceptics." Undoubtedly, this remembered, Lewis was interested in presenting a reasonable argument for Christian faith. Consequently, books like *Miracles* and *The Problem of Pain* were all concerned, to one degree or another, with refuting apocryphal objections to Christian belief, along the lines of "How could a good God allow pain to exist in the world?" and so on! Lewis additionally became known as a popular public lecturer and media broadcaster, some of his writings originating as scripts for radio talks or speaking engagements. Unquestionably, his autobiography, titled *Surprised by Joy*, (named after the first line of a poem by William Wordsworth, 1770-1850) places special emphasis on the perceived meaning behind his own, individual, conversion. Furthermore, his speeches and essays on Christian Doctrine, many of which were collected in *God in the Dock* and *The Weight of Glory and Other Addresses*, remain well read to this day.

A number of reviewers have attested that Lewis' work has an entirely different atmosphere from that of his good friend and colleague Tolkien: reflective, possibly, of the distinct periods in English literary history they both taught. Instead of the heavy Germanic layering found in Tolkien's corpus, Lewis has a lightness of touch, which owes more to the French. Readers of Lewis almost have similar sensations, some say, to those early audiences of verse epics in the Romance language of southern France. Reminding us all that prose only became the standard form of composition for modern novels over a lengthy period of time: and then, simply thanks to the number of advantages it was said to have over verse as the carrier-medium of communication. On top of this, prose is easier to translate. In point of fact, as Lewis was fully aware, prose dominated the market for European fiction from its inception. Thenceforth, as the majority of scholars have recorded, the development of a distinct fictional language was crucial for this genre type: on top of accessible themes for general consumption.

From that time to this, controversy has raged among novelists, publishers, and critics, regarding the correct aesthetic and literary length for a full novel – especially in English, as the emergent global language, with, arguably, a greater adaptability than other languages. Hitherto, this storm continued unabated! Nowadays, it has become a tempestuous row resting, in measurable part, on the consensus that a novel is, by definition, the longest genre in narrative prose (followed by the novella, the novelette, the short story, the mini-saga etc), although this sequence has also been unstable in terms of word count and page number. By convention, of course, expectations of "something sizey" have been connected with the notion that epic drama, the very lifeblood of a meaty novel, tries to emulate the "totality of life," whereas a novella merely focuses on a single issue. It has been additionally claimed that the short story only looks at a situation whose full dimensions the reader has to grasp in a complex process of imaginative interpretation outside of Text. Either way, whether in eleventh-century Japan or fifteenth-century Europe, or for that matter contemporary America today, prose fiction tended to evolve a unique reading experience matching a readerships' expectations in terms of length.

Recollected thuswise, a widespread knowledge of previously secret anxieties, individualistic fashions, personal opinions, correct "conduct" and behaving "gallantly" spread with voraciously digested English language novels. Love, of the sentimental sort, became the typical field of these romances, whereby novelists scrutinised satirical adventures played out in drawing rooms and boudoirs across the land in devastating detail. Readers, from their side, were invited to personally identify with the novel's characters. All of which meant the very act of reviewing fiction started to change conditions within this rapidly progressing industry: creating on the one hand a public discussion about the suitability of content, whilst on the other, allowing the conscious indignities of trivia to predominate authorial production. Hardly a coincidence, the subcultures of superficial and highly exploitative fiction, along with pornography sold under the counter, became widely available following, perhaps coincidentally, the arrival of professional literary criticism in the 1740s and 1750s. Contrarily, in this expansive period, close literary connections arose with the emergence of "elegance" in *belles-lettres*. These curiously antagonistic trends, however, proved responsible, in the sixteenth century, for a printed market entirely created to publish books without pretentions to art. So, as is the way of the world, the cultivation of *belles-lettres* soon devolved into a compound of genres devoted to personal memoirs, nationalist history and popular science: all written in the everyday vernaculars. Thus, prose fiction became the driving force behind these populist productions, allowing the occasional rarefied masterpiece to slip through, no doubt, but more often than not, tending to concentrate on lucrative, as well as obviously debased, fancies.

As the eighteenth century trundled on, English authors gradually abandoned French ideals of "elegance" and a less aristocratic style of language positioned itself as a happy sales medium. Again, the requirements of style changed as more commonplace themes (opening with legal statements regarding their fictionality), appealed to a taste for intimate "true histories" with an extra touch of spice. That acknowledged, novels in the 1760s, like Lawrence Sterne's (1713-1768) justly famous *Tristram Shandy* started to explore the potentials of prose fiction as saucy psychodrama and bracing tale, even though they invited less than edifying imitations. Novels, moreover, in the ensuing Romantic period conjured a sensation of open-endedness as well as "fragmentary" situations. Besides this, "good taste" (in late-nineteenth-century and early-twentieth-century fiction), witnessed a furthering of deconstructive (in the pejorative sense) attacks on serious English literature through attempts to demolish author-reader intercommunication, thereby permitting models of printed text to be evaluated accordingly. Therefrom reducing, this noted, modern literary criticism to act as a commentator on possible literary structures: the halcyon era of William Hazlitt (1778-1830) having turned into little more, these days, than an academic resource regurgitated at university. Understood so, contemporary authors who write fiction usually gain critical attention almost as soon as they establish their position in the market: whether as traditionalists, or alleged innovators! Hope springs Eternal, nevertheless, since current trends are encouraging an awareness of our British tradition through the publication of bestselling narratives with a recognisable storyline.

Occasionally then, whether a literary Techno Viking, or not, voices from our Orthodox past guide the hand of an English author, more or less after the manner of automatic writing. Unlike anything experienced by the Athonites, sudden spasms jerk the hand as a recipient is overcome by pre-conquest longings and nearly unrecognisable feelings of national, ethnic, unity. Keyboards are seen to move of their own accord in response to old, and largely forgotten, tribal entities that exist between our physical plane and the outer reaches of energised symbol. Pencils, papers, and ink, a la the Inklings, are visibly observed to take on a bizarre similitude to life, as they jostle to give expression to these powers of the dead. All being characteristics, figuratively speaking, of workings by John Cowper Powys (1872-1963). It may equally help to explain why some readers praise his penmanship to the hilt, whilst others remain harrowingly contemptuous towards his books. As a controversial writer from the start, it has been argued that Powys' approach to the novel, is as "alien to the temper of the age as to be impossible for many people to take seriously." The critic Annie Dillard, nevertheless, views things quite differently and has chosen to go on public record saying: "John Cowper Powys is a powerful genius, whose novels stir us deeply." So attested, it may be more than merely noteworthy to observe that throughout his career Powys consistently gained the admiration of fellow novelists as diverse in style as Iris Murdoch (1919-1999), Henry Miller (1891-1980) and James Otis Purdy (1914-2009), along with academic critics such as George Steiner (born 1929), G. Wilson

Knight (1897-1985) and Jerome McGann (born 1937). Interestingly, in his autobiography, film director John Boorman (born 1933) even wrote that he contemplated a movie adaptation of *A Glastonbury Romance* quite early on in his career.

For his advocates, Powys found fame in his first collections of poems published in 1896 and 1899, but these, and three subsequent volumes in 1915, 1916 and 1923, are generally regarded as of minor importance. Against collective opinion, this stated, the Welsh poet and critic Roland Mathias (1915-2007) thought this side of Powys' outpourings decidedly worthy of critical study, going on to write *The Hollowed-Out Elder Stalk: John Cowper Powys as Poet*. Still, it was not until 1915 that Powys published his first serious novel by prevailing critical standards with the teasingly Quagan title, *Wood and Stone*: which attentive readers will notice was dedicated to Thomas Hardy. Atypically, even though Powys enjoyed the status of being a famous lecturer, publishing in both non-fiction and fiction from about 1915, it was not until he was in his early fifties, with the publication of *Wolf Solent*, that he achieved critical and financial success as a novelist. Irrefutably, this novel was reprinted several times in Britain as well as the USA during his lifetime. That same year *The Meaning of Culture* was published, and it too was frequently reprinted. What is more, *In Defence of Sensuality*, published at the end of the following year, was yet another best seller. Naytheless, widespread fame only came with the Wessex novels, which include *A Glastonbury Romance*, *Weymouth Sands* and *Maiden Castle* – even though the latter is set in Dorchester. Precedents notwithstanding, Powys' indebtedness to the Victorian novel as a text type, accompanied by his enthusiasm for Sir Walter Scott, caused many to miss the fact he was obviously influenced by some of the better theoretical influences within modernism. So, affinities between his oeuvre and that of Fyodor Dostoyevsky (1821-1881), Marcel Proust (1871-1922), D. H. Lawrence (1885-1930), the T. S. Eliot (1888-1965) of *The Waste Land* and Chinghiz Aitmatov (1928-2008) in *The Days Lasts More Than a Hundred Years*, have been successfully upheld.

Plaudits, I would contend extremely well-deserved, although for devoted lovers of Mount Athos, it is *A Glastonbury Romance*, that should capture our attention. In Powys' own words, this novel's heroine "is the Grail" whilst its central concern is with the innumerable legends, myths and histories associated with Glastonbury. Furthermore, through this divulging node it is possible to envisage most of the main characters, John Geard, Sam Dekker, John Crow, and Owen Evans as participants in a Grail quest. As such, *A Glastonbury Romance* is not only concerned with the legend that Joseph of Arimathea brought the Holy Grail (a vessel containing the blood of Christ) to England, but with further age-old traditions which tell us that King Arthur was buried there. On top of this, one of the novel's main characters, the mysterious Welshman Owen Evans, introduces readers to the idea that the Grail had a Welsh (Celtic), Gnostic, origin. In this, Powys appears to have used reputable sources on Grail legend and mythology like Sir John Rhys' (1840-1915) *Studies in the Arthurian Legend*, R. S. Loomis' (1887-1966) *Celtic Myth and Arthurian Romance*, and the works of Jessie L. Weston, (1850-1928) including *From Ritual to Romance*. Accordingly, a central narration in *A Glastonbury Romance* is the attempt by John Geard (an ex-minister and now the mayor of Glastonbury) to restore Glastonbury to its former medieval glory as a place of religious pilgrimage: similar concerns consistently mirrored in the minds of the Athonites. His plan, that understood, has its bitter opponents, who actively stand against this upsurge of tradition: particularly the brooding figure of the local industrialist Philip Crow. Supported, as this character is, by darkly corrupted associates like John and Mary Crow, as well as Tom Barter (hailing from Norfolk) who simply sees the legends and myths of the town as anything apart from contemptuous! Unashamedly, Philip's vision of the future is one of more factories, unfettered commerce, and exploitable mines. Unsurprisingly, given the context of this tale, these struggles awaken mystical forces from out of their timeworn slumber, helping to inspire an unexpected alliance between Anarchists and Jacobins, who try to turn Glastonbury into a commune, while John Crow, since he is a pauper, takes on the task of organising a pageant for Geard.

Beyond comment, the spirit of Orthodoxy haunts page after page of this astonishing story. Atop this, Powys' novel reflects the actual burdens posed by a rich cultural inheritance (experienced as an everyday reality by the Athonites, never forgetting the problems faced on Mount Athos in the wake of contemporary incomprehension regarding its true spiritual status) within modern society. In mirrored consequence, Powys' narrative is starkly illustrative, in a number of ways, regarding the legacy of English Orthodoxy, because it blends greed, sanctity, identifiable as well as strong characters, and a deep love of geographical location, with genuine moral concerns from the world around us. His readers, for their part, also discover a wealth of meticulously drawn sequential-plots, accompanied by an ageless Gnostic wisdom, conjoined to a highly charged Christian Perennialism. Without doubt, certain sections stagger under the weight of Athonite mysticism; every paragraph reeling with the knowledge that our actions have consequences above this temporary lifetime. As we may read,

> And as these tides came in, over the brown desolate mudflats, they awoke strange legends and wild half-forgotten memories along that coast. Ancient prophecies seemed to awake and flicker again, prophecies that had perished long ago, like blown-out candles in gusty windows, cold as the torch-flames by which they were chanted and the extinct fires by which they were conceived.

Powys even goes on to name the Blessed Peninsula itself:

> Curiously enough it was the eastern-European visitors—or pilgrims, if you will—and indeed there were many of both types, who seemed most impressed by these discourses of the head of the new commune; and among these none were more affected than certain monastic wayfarers from the slopes of Mount Athos. There was no lack of scribes taking serious notes of all the man said; and although the London papers had grown weary of him, "Gerard of Glastonbury" was already a legendary figure in Bulgaria, in Bessarabia, and in many a remote religious retreat along the Black Sea. The main drift of Gerard's singular Gospel was that an actual new Revelation had been made in Glastonbury.

Structurally, *A Glastonbury Romance* has several climactic moments, before a final major scene. First, there is Sam Dekker's decision, following his Grail vision, to relent of his adulterous affair with Nell Zoyland, and lead a monk-like existence. Secondly, we learn of Evans' failed attempt to control his sadistic urge, by playing the part of Christ on the Cross during the Easter Pageant. Thirdly, the attempted murder of John Crow is coequally climatic. Involving, as it does, Tom Barter's death, when he saves his friend, who is actually Mad Bet's intended victim! Lastly, the novel concludes with a flooding of the low-lying country surrounding Glastonbury, making it once again a Holy Island: the fabled Avalon; our own indigenous Mount Athos.

Tellingly, this causes the death of Geard, along with the end of his ambitious plans for Glastonbury. But, the finale Powys gives to this mammoth tale is strangely more akin to metaphysical ambiguity than tragedy, since just before he dies, Geard asks John Crow, "Do you suppose anyone's ever committed suicide out of an *excess of life*, simply to enjoy the last experience in full consciousness?" Sentiments positing assertions, which raise Athonite questions! Partly, this is why the Grail in Powys' novel is depicted in its Christian form, but also melded with Quagan beliefs and local folklore. Drawing on twentieth-century scholarships intent on finding an origin for the Grail beyond medieval romance, Powys' novel plays up associations between Glastonbury as Everlasting Avalon and the place of King Arthur's promised return! Accorded so, at the closing of its pages a drowning John Geard looks to Glastonbury Tor (itself repeatedly referred to as the domain of the Welsh underworld spirit Gwyn-ap-Nudd) hoping to see this blessed vessel. Followed, as this is, by a short, haunting, enigmatic, passage, which compares the tower on St Michaels's Tor, and Glastonbury Abbey itself, to the unending persistence of the mystic and mythic in everyday life! Fascinatingly, *A Glastonbury Romance* contains numerous examples of Quaganry reflecting Powys' belief that even inanimate objects possess Soul: a notion dating back to the dawn of time throughout Europe. This is why the Sun is described as an "enemy" to the vicar Mat Dekker, whilst different trees are spoken of as listening to a romantic liaison between John Crow and Mary. Other passages refer to the spiritual extension of a characters' "will" existing outside their bodies: especially in the chapter "Nature Seems Dead" where a number of sleeping disembodied personae, or "spirits," move about the town. The novel, in addition, repeatedly refers to a Manichean dualism in the nature of the Divine First Cause, the nearest equivalent to a Judeo-Christian understanding of God in this text. Claimed so, this dualism is seen as tied in with all of existence by Powys, even though, in terms of narrative, it is most strongly present in the character of Owen Evans. Captivatingly, these Gnostic traits are found, perhaps, more strongly in A Glastonbury Romance than any of Powys' other novels, though his works are imbued with the author's mystical attitudes as described in his personal letters and autobiography.

Any adherent of Orthodoxy will instantly recognise the author's love of this luminous landscape and the sensation of an all-pervading Life, along with the intimate relationship that his characters enjoy with the Family-of-Life in its abundant diversity including: animals, the Sky Father, restless wind-gods, chlorophyll-heavy plants, feathery song-birds, our moist Earth Mother, neon-bright insects, and so on. All such having a huge meaningful significance in Powys' works: linking, yet again, to another major influence on Powys: British Romanticism. Especially of the sort detailed by Wordsworth and writers influenced by Wordsworth, like Walter Pater (1839-1894). Confessedly, words such as "pantheist" and "mysticism" are frequently used when discussing Powys's attitude to nature: although deeper inspection reveals that his literary thrust was to encourage an ecstatic response to the natural order! Transparently, epiphanies such as Wordsworth relates in his Ode: Intimations of Immortality worked on the level of a credo for Powys—but with one important difference—Powys believed the ecstasy experienced by a young child can be retained by any adult who sincerely cultivates the power of the imagination. Some reviewers have compared this attitude to Zen, stating that for Powys, as well as the protagonists of his novels (who typically resemble him in any case) the nurturing of these psycho-sensuous philosophies is as important as the Christian religion was for an earlier generation. And in this vital sense, we have reached a point of recurrence.

This is not written to disparage Christian theology, which has a long history of attempting to reconcile the revelation of Providential Spirit in Jesus Christ, Nature, and human reason. Orthodox theology, in particular, stressing the special quality of salvation found through the unique experience of God in Christ-Nature: while at the same time holding human beings responsible for responding to God's Grace: or not as the case may be. Holy Athonites, at this stage of deliberation, thinking, one imagines, of the Blessed (Swedenborgian) Mountain to be climbed within us all, may ponder on the *Gospel of Luke*, 9:28, wherein we read:

> Jesus took with him Peter and John and James, and went up on the mountain to pray. And while he was praying, the appearance of his face changed, and his clothes became dazzling white. Suddenly, they saw two men, Moses and Elijah, talking with him. They appeared in glory and were speaking of his departure, which he was about to accomplish at Jerusalem. Now Peter and his companions were weighed down with sleep; but since they had stayed awake, they saw his glory and the two men who stood with him.

In short, revelation, if we are to bear its potent implications, must be negotiated through a watchful attitude in both Life and the Arts. Among the many attempts that have been made to reconcile this natural theology with Christian faith were those undertaken by the Angelic Doctor, Thomas Aquinas (c. 1225-1274), and that colossus of philosophical inquiry, Immanuel Kant (1724-1804). For many people, this recognised, science and the scientific method seem to complement any true religious understanding. What is more, by adopting paradigms such as these, the physicist and theologian John Polkinghorne (born 1930) found himself empowered to write, "It is the desire for ontological knowledge, and not mere functional success, which motivates the labour of scientists." (*Belief in God in an Age of Science*, 30) In different words, any modern view of natural theology suggests that reason doesn't just seek to supply a proof for the existence of God as much as provide a coherent, intellectual, background, against which the insights of religion may pull together the best of human knowledge: from all areas of Quagan activity. Demonstrably, natural theology attempts to relate literature, science, history, morality and the arts into an integrated vision of our human condition in the universe: traditionally a religious undertaking, to the extent that it refers to an encompassing reality that is Immanent in power and value. Consequently, natural theology is not a prelude to faith or religious experience, but a general worldview within which an experiential faith can have an intelligible place.

Stated thus, our Ancestral Faith supplies answers as readily as it poses new questions! When historically based narratives, sacred myths and literary folklore are gathered together with surviving customs, each provides a unique insight into the long history of the British peoples. In this manner, they represent the cultural recovery of ancient hopes, fears, dreams, lost genealogies, as well as the spiritual expectations of the numberless generations preceding us. Allied to all these remembrances are the robust, yet portentous, oral texts claiming we British may have descended from the ten lost tribes of Israel: an idea recurrent in fable and fairy story. Far from irrelevant, and decidedly powerful as a view in Victorian England, adherents of this alleged "Israelism" even claimed that early medieval sources-stories continue, despite deliberate oppression, to prove such contentions: defenders of this fascinating stance being Adriaan van der Schrieck (1560-1621), a renowned Flemish scholar; and the mysterious English antiquarian Henry Spelman (1562-1641). Beyond dispute, some modern scholars have proposed that British Israelism grew out of earlier schools of thought, especially academies of "Phoenicianism" or "Orientalism" which developed in the eighteenth century. Complimenting this, during the early twentieth century, archaeologists like R. A. Stewart Macalister (1870-1950) said that it was "very popular" for past writers to ascribe a Middle Eastern, or Central Asian, genealogy to the peoples of Ireland as well as Britain. Charles Vallancey (1721-1812), as a case in point, published a work in 1772 attempting to demonstrate that the Irish language was Phoenician, whilst John Pinkerton's (1758-1826) *A Dissertation on the Origin and Progress of the Scythians or Goths* (1787) tried to show that the Scots were in actual fact Scythians: themselves having originated in Central Asia. Progressing further, the historian Sharon Turner (1768-1847) later used Pinkerton's research to identify the Saxons as also being of Scythian descent. Other works, like the *Eastern Origin of Celtic Nations* by James Cowles Prichard (1786-1848), even attempted to demonstrate a Far Eastern origin for the Celts! In Ireland, there additionally emerged a popular school of "Phoenicianism" within which some historians, such as Joaquín Lorenzo Villanueva (1757-1837) sought to link the Irish to ancient Phoenician settlement in these lands. Recognised so, British Israelites have frequently relied on these literatures as historical evidence, besides using the Holy Bible to support their argument. In spite of repeated agitation at Scriptural excursions into twilight geopolitical realms, where very little can be known for sure.

References, allusions, stories, and great quantities of indigenous ink, were joyously spilt in the service of this type of theological reasoning, along with the penning of circuitous comparisons between our Great British topography and sacred cities, holy mountains, as well as royal parks, in the Middle East. Undertaken by questing souls, nearly undiminished reverence was given to those places held as Sacred to Jews, Christians, and Muslims alike: especially domed Jerusalem, the Garden of Gethsemane, and blessed Mount Sinai. Every historic brick, Biblical herb, and inch of glorious rock being held up to the deepest scrutiny, including a carefully sculpted pilgrim route called the "Steps of Repentance," which is composed of 3000 steps dutifully carved into the Sinai mountainside, by an anonymous monk, who aimed to unleash the religious power of these bhakti devotions.[2] Atop of this, innumerable sites of every possible description mentioned in the Old Testament were annotated; particularly those areas that can be seen from the Sinai mountains breathtaking summit, along with the enclosures where Moses "sheltered from the total glory of God." By this, the folklore of hills, legendary temples, and otherworldly centres of the omphalos, were understood to be the physical and textual prototypes of later,

European, earthworks: constructed as these were to be maps and memory aids for those tribes migrating westwards: sites, in the most telling of senses, where further revelation, advanced literature, and speculative inspiration could be actively induced. Beyond question, Mount Sinai proving an obvious exemplar for these undertakings, because this mountain is said to be where the Covenant was struck between Israel and God Almighty.[3] Rival locations of devotion, that acknowledged, were discovered. Mount Tabor, for example, upon which Jesus is supposed to have first revealed himself as the Son of God bore the test of comparison. Moreover, the escarpments of Mount Hira, upon which the Prophet Muhammed is said to have received his initial Vision of the Angel Gabriel stood up to the mark. Such ruminations, in themselves, told traditionally-minded British authors that mountains have always played an essential role as transducers of psychic transformation: that they act in a similar way to Mount Athos for the Orthodox; a profession usually serving to attract tepid tourists, whether welcome or not, as much as it does serious religious pilgrims. Undeniably, in Victorian cases, the financial revenue so generated became important for conservation, even though Sacred Mountains, then as now, should never be reduced to areas of well-funded, but idle curiosity!

As for narratorial comparisons of ancient Mount Athos, as that other mystical Jerusalem, to Middle Eastern religious sites, few and far between are the instances: perhaps showing the innate sanctity of this Greek region. Writers did tell the very occasional tale of monks being in residence since the fourth century, and quite possibly from the third in recognisable communities. Furthermore, during Constantine I's reign (324-337), it was noted that both Christians and Pagans were living on its slopes. Even though by the time of Julian the Apostate (361-363), authors tended to focus their attentions on the graphic destruction of churches on Mount Athos. Christians, it is written, hid in the woods as well as inaccessible places in their attempts to survive persecution. Contrariwise, commentators during the reign of Theodosius I (383-395), told of Pagan temples being destroyed and the Old Ways becoming disparaged: Hesychius of Alexandria (fifth century AD), the lexicographer, reminding his readers that in the fifth century there was still a temple and statue of "Zeus Athonite" on the Mount in spite of everything the Christians could do. However, less of a textual battle and more a matter of divergent histories: after the Islamic conquest of Egypt in the seventh century, many Orthodox monks from the Egyptian desert were documented as trying to find an alternative geographical haven; some of them coming to the Greek peninsula. Ancient scribes stating that these monks built little huts of wood with roofs of straw, collecting fruit from the wild trees to provide themselves with improvised meals!

For we Britons, all of the aforementioned noted, any sense of a possible break in historical continuity with previous generations, or literary tradition, remains unthinkable to this day. Ours is a United Kingdom, after all, where written precedent is manifestly respected and previously recorded practice duly honoured. Guilty attitudes, haunted by a collective confusion regarding the appropriate character of indigenous faith, has enabled people to dimly recall that before the Body of Christ was separated into a number of antagonistic limbs, Britain had only been accustomed to the healthy clash of teachers and missions, not geomantic turmoil. From its very inception, scholars contended, the Church in England has housed three radically different forms of witness. The preaching of St Augustine of Canterbury (died 604) and his successors formed one powerful grouping. Celtic priests coming down from Scotland and associated with figures like St Aidan (died 651), as well as St Cuthbert (634-687), configured another! Remnants of the old Romano-British confession counted as the final factor: divisions obviously reflecting a variety of theological positions at a profound level. Still, within their respective ranks, each of these assemblies accepted the same geographical landmarks, mounds, and Churches, as holy, some using the world-affirming Aristotle as their guide when taking steps towards spiritual authenticity in either word, or deed.

Dwelling inside these apparently ephemeral literary contortions, of course, were rampant fears concerning the relationship between mythic significance, geomantic symbol, and religious truth. Expressly, the Absolute can be viewed from an infinite number of angles. The immortal part of us can additionally be articulated in an endless variety of ways. But, the nature and purpose of storytelling troubled some of our forebears. Geopolitical Myth, perhaps particularly when it is seen as archetypal storytelling, allowing complex metaphysical realities to be explained, worried those few who always wanted to control the many. They were aware that sacred maps of this kind depict the unity within collective folkish ties and act as a way to strengthen clan bonding. As such, they found tampering with this machine code useful for their vested interests. Without too many surprises then, this band of brigands equally realised that deconstruction was intimately related to sacred processes in Literature. It is a means by which ethnic stories can be unearthed in all of their original glory, along with ways to recover the primordial strength built into communal joy. This too they found threatening in terms of commerce. Regardless of their phobias, when disagreement is done, geomantic myth rather like prose literature, may be seen to grow from a people. It has nothing to do with random caprice; still less the wilful assertions of an isolated misfit, but proves a mechanism to make us strong. Unsettlingly for some, it correspondingly makes us righteously rebellious.

Acknowledging this, foreign Churchmen in ages past have been known to audibly bemoan that we Britons are, by nature, Quagans. Overall, they were correct since Quaganry is not a counter-religion, but a mode of Being. On one level, it is an attitude. On another, it is a practical means by which a human being may embrace the Processes-of-Life. On the surface, at least, just such a view has been expounded at the University of Cambridge from its inception. Explaining why the prose originating from this august institution never ran the risk of either textual triviality, or simple memorabilia. Rather, those authors sharing this literary stable found themselves adapting timeless themes into contemporised forms. Scandal, some mean-minded critics penned, configuring the "real" bread and butter of their creative discourse. Nonetheless, escaping from the heavy atmosphere of Queen Victoria's oppressive Empire and reaching out into the dawn of a qualified modernity, Edwardian tattle and hypocrisy became a light-hearted backdrop against which to conduct affairs: literary conditions birthing the emergence of the Bloomsbury Group.[4]

As unlikely interlocutors with Mount Athos, even though it seems to have surfaced in a number of their discussions—Virginia Wolfe (1882-1941) manifestly mentioning it in her influential novel *Orlando: A Biography*, not to mention the comedic reflections made by Ralph H. Brewster (1930-1997) in a detailed memoir entitled, *The Six Thousand Beards of Mount Athos*—these bright, young, albeit mostly secularised things, retained indigenous Quagan traits. Abnormally so, since they hailed from mainstream professional, families. E. M. Forster (1879- 1970), for example, along with Vanessa Bell (1879-1961) had modest independent incomes, whilst others like Lytton Strachey (1880-1932), Leonard Wolfe (1880-1969), Duncan Grant (1885-1978) and Roger Fry (1866-1934), needed to work for their living. Overall, that said, only Clive Bell (1881-1964) could really be called wealthy. Critics additionally observed that all-male members of the early group (except Duncan Grant), were educated at either an increasingly radicalised Trinity College, or Kings College, Cambridge: bastions of freethinking from time immemorial. Without doubt, it was during their time at Trinity in 1899, that Stretchy, Wolfe, Bell, and Saxon Arnold Sydney-Turner (1880-1962) became friends with Thoby Stephen (1880-1906), aka The Goth, who in turn, introduced them to his sisters Vanessa and Virginia in London. All in all, it was through this web of relationships that Bloomsbury as an authorial circle slowly came into concretised being. Serendipitously, perhaps, all the Cambridge men except Clive Bell were members of a semi-secret undergraduate society known as The Cambridge Apostles.

Unquestionably, nearly everything about the Bloomsbury Group seems to be controversial. Most pundits agreeing that this loose collective of extremely gifted friends, partners (in every sense), and relatives, lived, wrote, and studied, in this geographical hothouse for London's literati during the first half of the twentieth century. Ostensibly, their outpourings deeply influencing the course of English Literature, Aesthetic theory, Criticism and the new Economics, in conjunction with contemporary attitudes towards sexuality and pacifism. Contrarily, it is important to recall that formal discussions, concerning these issues, were hardly ever undertaken by its members, even though their conversations, informal or otherwise, continually revolved around these themes. Duly commented, the lives, along with the works of the Group, show an overlapping, almost interconnected similarity between avant-garde ideas and Quagan attitudes. Their conviction about the nature of consciousness and its relation to external nature, the fundamental separateness of individuals involving concepts of both isolation and love, the inhuman realities of Time and Death and interpretations of Truth and Beauty, were shared as a response to essential dissatisfactions regarding Capitalism and its endless wars of Imperialism. These "Bloomsbury Assumptions" are also reflected in its members' criticism of Materialistic Realism (especially in painting and fiction), never underestimating their attacks on the repressive policies of sexual discrimination. Undoubtedly, they hoped to argue for the inauguration of a liberated social order, which was free of established, repressive, Church norms. Rather love (an inner state) was to be held in higher esteem than monogamy (a demonstrable behaviour), despite potential subsequent complications. An avowedly Quagan stance enabling several members of the Group to have more than one serious relationship at the same time, and casting aside as this unmistakably did, accepted cultural practices in the spirit of a rosy-cheeked polyfidelity.

Superficially, the Bloomsbury Group rejected tradition. But, this depends on the mode within which tradition is to be interpreted. In the broadest sense, they were trying to recapture a predilection towards Life easily predating their own Edwardian era, Victorian social coercion, and the narrow "nationalist" confines uncharacteristic of this Island of adventurers, within which they themselves had been raised. In their cultural experiments, aiming at a recovery of British authenticity, they used modernist vocabularies to reform timeworn words and notions. Only the benefit of hindsight finally allowing their readers to see behind the intense hyperbole of deeply animated debate! At their point in history, as is the case now, literature was awash with competing theories – Psychoanalysis, Marxism, Proto-Feminist Theory, and the like: each one of which, to a greater or lesser extent, became part of a particular hermeneutic, often socio-political in its nature. That contended, the Bloomsbury Group were far ahead of their time in realising every reader of Text brings something with them that further informs the reading. Put alternately, the way a reader interprets what is read will, to a significant extent, be shaped by what he, or she, is in themselves: the same holding true for compositional writers as well. Markedly, any literary sensibility worthy of the name must always be mindful of the influences and experience brought to the table. Our native state of Being, more Cavalier than Roundhead, with its full-blooded devil-may-care demeanour, nevertheless respecting the endless interweave of radical freedom with inherited custom. And in this, the Bloomsbury Group stood against the intolerant homogeneity of "Modernist Society."

Thenceforth, in the spirit of Bloomsbury I would like to wax lyrical about British literary landscapes and their timeless geomantic wonders. Unreservedly, the Group intuited, along with our remote ancestors, that the Soul of Nature has many spirits. They understood that both you and I are some of the celestial cells in its Substance, which is why indigenous Sages have always said our European bodies collectively form the Holy Grail. We cup, when all said and done, inside our sacred pale flesh, the divine blood promising eventual salvation for the whole of humankind: a redemption gifted to all who have been touched by Albion's Gnosticism. In this sense, we are not just British men and women with the genetic force of evolution raging inside our ivory skins, but kith to the gods themselves. Each one of us a veritable cornucopia of chemical potentials gifted by ancient and wonderful Identities. Sons are we, and daughters, of this *Theotokos*.

For some, such a Celestial Chalice is actually a Horn, calling Doomsday. For others, without this sanguine structure, there is nothing on this earth except the hell of DNA junk and Information impurity. A netherworld compounded by various pollutions of physique, as well as the brain – desperately spread by our sworn enemies: or in other words those who simply cannot embrace their destiny with delight: some of them noticeably cowering like curs before the vistas of perfection. Unashamedly, these geomantic others, who invariably prove true cowards, condemn themselves to judgement in the long run. Particularly when presented with the possibility of an unlimited freedom. The moral choice is theirs, no doubt, because we are all free to be Serfs of the Psyche, or Spiritual Aristocrats recognising history itself as our bondsman! Nonetheless, time is running short and our current decisions will unfurl across generations to come.

This is why we urgently need a gathering of all the disparate Clans. Once more, our Afghan and Russian cousins must join with Iranian and Serb in order to bless the staggering achievements of our martial past – as we stride into a scientific future crowned by muscular genius. Peoples of intimately related plasma, we need to congregate again: especially with the unsuspected Azeri; a tribe, which continues to embrace the delights embodied in Reading, Art and Drama. Above question, it is their mission to remind us Westerners that literature once stood as the redemptive cultural energy within our inherently progressive Communities. Unequivocally so, when opposed to the loud rhetorical components inside established, lazy, Churches and redundant liberal institutions!

By analogy, in a state of inspired consciousness, William Blake (1557-1827) once asked us, his native countrymen, "And was Jerusalem builded here, Among these dark Satanic Mills?" His intention, of course, being mnemonic. He hoped, generally speaking, to remind us all that we Islanders are in a constant state of challenge: owing to migration, half-forgotten inheritances, along with deeply misunderstood religious treasures. With these influences on his mind, Blake seems to have felt that we British Israelites are far from being a fully Christianised people. In our hearts, according to this Bard, we never really were anything of the sort in any case. Emphatically, every attempted, but unsuccessful invasion, by welcomed refugee and invited settler has only added to our confusion in terms of diluted literature, dried water meadow, levelled mound, and obscured folklore. But now is the era, Blake intuited, to seize this bull by its horns. Out of surviving cultural memory, our novels, our traditions of tolerance and respect, we Britons need to recover the meaning embedded within our earthworks. Only then will Glastonbury once again become the blessed Isle of Avalon and our own sweetly-indigenous Mount Athos, whereon the power of long lost Priests and Kings can uplift our descendants into a vision of better tomorrows.

SELECTED ENDNOTES

1. Similarly, humorous comments related to Mount Athos as a place of naive otherworldliness continue in contemporary works, such as *Edward Trencom's Nose*; a novel by Giles Milton. Therein, we may read that the monks diagnosed the protagonist as having suffered from a stroke, although in fact he was merely at a loss for words.

2. Bhakti devotional worship is a Hindu term outlining a purely emotional path to Deity through whose receptive Grace salvation may be attained by all, regardless of sex or class.

3. One of the many recent examples of this type of literary recreation being Keith Ward's *The Promise*, wherein the *Pentateuch*, or the opening five books of the Old Testament, is rewritten as prose fiction in an attempt to explain its message in geographical context.

4. This even includes its membership and name. Alternative critics have contended that the word "group" better classifies this gathering of writers, artists and intellectuals, while others have objected that the social cohesion implied by the term "set," describes the actual nature of their meetings.

"Our peace shall stand as firm as rocky mountains."

– *William Shakespeare*

Problem VI.
Behind Open Doors

O NLY TWO TYPES OF PEOPLE INHABIT THIS EARTH: onlookers and actors. The former simply live their undemanding lives within the carefully defined boundaries of a specific auditorium: never daring, of course, to venture forth into the mysterious balconies beyond. The latter, however, expend unbelievable amounts of personal energy, both participating in the mysterious events taking place in these largely unknown territories, as well as trying to meticulously explain their dramatic wonders to sadly uncomprehending viewers. Perhaps only other actors truly understand the significance of such amazing dramas; stimulated as they are by the dazzling evidence of heavily scarred limbs. Although, on reflection, the very recounting of past (character-driven) performances may actually lose more wisdom than is gained by a raconteur! After all, every theatre likes to tacitly keep its most inhuman secrets behind heavily draped stages, while the very process of articulating the meaning behind these boards, more often than not, bewilders everybody.

Atop of this, actors are occasionally forced to hide behind the open doors of criticism. Having all of the features, physical or otherwise, associated with an Island adventurer, they find, nevertheless – when asked to play affront the luxuriant canopies backstage, that skill is never enough to silence their critics' potential tempest. Neither is a deep knowledge of distant lighting alignments, as they dance across constellations of personal experience. Without doubt, such, terrible contortions, so witnessed, should provide banquets of thought among the onlookers in the Stalls below, but that would necessitate them waking to the sumptuous facts effectively fencing the economic realities of their seating.

Another reason for such profound confusion is that some actors, having climbed on top of the multileveled rigging, feel the burning compulsion to testify to the Marvellous upon their return to the stage. After all, they claim witness to the distant clash of worlds, whilst half whispering of Spirits and Light. Thus humbled, they wisely pursue non-speaking roles before the onlookers, or write scripts for a profession in the hope that circuitous enactments will help to elucidate their account. So planned, they remain fully aware that such terrible Enlightenments should provide extra feasts for exuberant reflection among even slightly somnambulant spectators. Yet, at the midnight of the day, those riding the chariot of Thespis (sixteenth century BC) in this specific manner tend to consist of deeply disappointed hacks.

If therefore, along with Shakespeare, one wishes to ascend this noble vehicle—agreeing all of our Earth is a stage—it should hardly come as a surprise to discover resonant undercurrents like despair, *áskēsis*, or unnamed dread, often surfacing in our day-to-day Text! Certainly, in terms of *áskēsis*, this ascetic practice is usually seen as far removed from the spheres of Anglo-Saxon, Middle-English, or Modern authorship: whether biographical (as in writing hagiographies) or historical; let alone within novels, plays and theatre. Further, metaphysical arguments underpinning a lifestyle bounded by self-imposed constraints on material appetites in the pursuit of religious goals, are generally understood as remote from all of these aforementioned worlds. Additionally, if *áskēsis* is tangentially interpreted as either bodily "training" for acts of service, or cerebral "exercise" designed to clarify our human grasp of the innately conflicted natures inside us, only pictures of penitent Desert Fathers, isolated hermits, or present day Holy Athonites, come to mind. Still, as someone who is also writing about the stormy perceptions mastered by Henrik Ibsen, not to forget having had a teaching career coloured by Western Personalist authors, such as

Samuel Beckett (1906-1989), and Norman Mailer (1923-2007), I have started to wonder if there actually is such a vast, unbridgeable chasm between the ideological rigours of the ascetics and the brooding anxieties upon contemporary life carefully detailed and fully drafted by these ingenious thinkers? As Mailer commented in *Cannibals and Christians*,

> We live in a time which has created the art of the absurd. It is our art. It contains happenings, Pop art, camp, a theater of the absurd ... Do we have the art because the absurd is the patina of waste ...? Or are we face to face with a desperate or most rational effort from the deepest resources of the unconscious of us all to rescue civilization from the pit and plague of its bedding?

His sense of genuine spiritual urgency mirroring those sensations of "sickness" experienced during the sleepless nights of the ascetics.

Observations such as these should hardly shock. Basically, even though Orthodoxy in its Western form was virtually extinguished in the British Isles following the Norman Invasion, there had already been centuries of literary tradition framed by this genre-context. Once conceded, however, that the Orthodox religious impulse is not confined to either Monastery, geographical territory, or Church denomination, but clearly seen in other cultural spheres, like English literature, it becomes easy to understand that we are dealing with the true stuff of drama: especially when contemporary attempts to "detox the soul" are placed in a secular, although not necessarily irreligious, substructure. At this juncture, Sacred and Absurdist Theatre find commonality. Even though much maligned by its critical opponents, this solidity detected, and frequently misunderstood as an artistic Movement generally, Absurdism must be interpreted in one of two principle ways. Firstly, as the spiritually humbling admission that this world is far too complex for a human brain to comprehend: mammalian intelligence being designed to uncover survival strategies in a jungle and not to solve the "riddle of the Universe." Also, secondly, in the sense that some adherents of Absurdism have argued human beings create, or reveal, emotional contradictions above and beyond the bewilderingly intricate moral entanglements concomitant with human life: albeit, as human beings, we lack the skills required to extricate ourselves from the ensuing practical consequences. Perhaps this is why Albert Camus (1913-1960) states in *The Myth of Sisyphus and Other Essays*:

> Man stands face to face with the irrational. He feels within him his longing for happiness and for reason. The absurd is born of this confrontation between the human need and the unreasonable silence of the world.

All of which implies, as Camus was fully aware, humanity is thrown back into an encounter with radical Faith. Henceforth, Olympic athletes undergoing physical privation to prepare for contest, or the lifestyle adopted by a starving artist consciously undertaken for Art, are equally attempts to rise above immediate constraints in a manner (indirectly) analogous to the unending prayers of the Athonites. They are all attempts to attain Transcendence. Understood so, Beckett's play, *Waiting for Godot* is best elucidated as "meaningfully absurd." This is not to claim that Beckett secretly believed in God, or at least the (debatably) crude God of classical Theism, but instead, as an atheist, was fully aware of the implied value behind conscious denial, inner-struggle, frustrated labour, and a potentially redemptive, even though irrational, enlightenment. As one of the vagrant's muses:

> The tears of the world are a constant quantity. For each one who begins to weep somewhere else another stops. The same is true of the laugh. Let us not then speak ill of our generation, it is not any unhappier than its predecessors. Let us not speak well of it either. Let us not speak of it at all. It is true the population has increased.

In which case, it is far from paradoxical that Beckett's characters, Estragon and Vladimir, continually reflect on religious despair and Quagan repentance. Assuredly, they are even conscious that since only one of the thieves crucified alongside Jesus will be saved, the Evangelists themselves are struggling with similar Mysteries of Faith.

At the risk of contradicting Martin Heidegger (1889-1976), human beings are not merely "thrown into the world" as abstract phenomena. Neither do we simply wander in a sphere we did not ourselves create. Our condition, in fact, is that of intimacy with a thriving continuum. Thus grasped, it is incontestable Holy Athonites suffer few of the infirmities either Vladimir, or Estragon, experience in Beckett's play. Instead, these competitors of the soul cultivate ascetic rigours as an aid to metaphysical, as well as bodily, health. Without contradiction, those practising *áskēsis* challenge their physical circumstances by acting against Nature in a quest for Absolute Context. Rarely falling victim before the Existential, or surrendering to the grim vicissitudes of base-materiality, men such as these find Hope beyond frail, human, flesh. At this point, Swedenborg's penmanship, Orthodoxy Theology, Quaganry and Absurdist Theatre seem strangely reconciled: whilst apparently ironic statements by August Strindberg (1849-1912) take on a new light. As he pithily comments in *The Ghost Sonata*, "There are poisons that blind you, and poisons that open your eyes." Argued so, Tradition may indeed be the next artistic revolution in literature, as well as on the boards. Its themes, after all, such as religious *Áskēsis* and experiential *Theosis* (whereby the frequently unsolicited activities of Divine Grace slowly deify the recipient), reach above Modernist one-dimensional objectivity, and gift us with a concrete hermeneutic offering Personalist insights. At this point, the existential becomes the humane and individual Mystery leads to feelings of qualitative orientation: along with a revived appreciation that Beauty is not a philosophical irrelevancy lurking beneath script, verse, and story.

An interesting parallel example from antiquity to that of Beckett's play may serve to elucidate my point. St Genesius (286-303) was a gifted playwright, actor, comedian, as well as being the leader of a troupe of actors, in Ancient Rome. When the Emperor Diocletian (244-311) initiated his great persecution of Christians, Genesius, who was a Pagan, hatched a grand scheme to construct a play parodying the Christian Sacraments: to expose them, as it were, to the ridicule of an educated audience. Thusly, he resolved, one day, to represent Baptism, with all its attendant ceremonies, as ludicrously as possible.

To this effect he became well acquainted with all that takes place during the service of holy immersion. He then cast the various parts for the play and instructed the actors in what they were to do.

On the day of the performance, the Emperor Diocletian and his entire Court were present. Thereafter, the comedy, after due preparation, began with Genesius acting in the principal role. Feigning to be sick, he lay wearily down, calling to his friends to bring him something to relieve his torment. When they had done this, he said that he felt he was soon to die, and wanted to become a Christian – and that they should "baptise" him. Everything was brought upon the podium that was used during actual services of baptism, and an actor playing a priest came on stage in order to "baptise" the ailing catechumen. All of the necessary questions were put to him, which are asked of those who are to be accepted into the Church. Then, the ceremony was performed in such an obviously ludicrous manner, that the Emperor and all the people surrounding him shouted with laughter.

Nonetheless, at the very moment when these Pagan actors scoffed and blasphemed against the Holy Sacrament of our true Church, and as his supporting player poured water over the head of Genesius, the Almighty touched his heart and illumined it with Divine Grace. Suddenly, as well as unexpectedly, seeing the truth of Christianity, an entire change took place in the performer, and he loudly and earnestly proclaimed his faith in Jesus Christ. For their part, his companions, not knowing what had happened, continued in their blasphemous mockery. Moreover, once the whole ceremony had been performed, they threw a white robe over Genesius in derision of the garment usually given to the newly converted and baptised; so clothed, they presented him to the people amidst considerable uproar. But Genesius, already an authentic believer in Christ, turned to the Emperor and confessed to him, with great dignity, what had taken place. Genesius declared solemnly that until that day, blinded by idolatry, he had scoffed and derided Christianity, which was the main reason why he had proposed to represent baptism on the stage for the amusement of the populace. Yet, during this sacrilegious performance, his heart had changed and he desired to become a believer. He even said he had seen the heavens open, and perceived a hand touching him, when the baptismal water was poured over him. He further stated that before they had baptised him, he had even seen an Angel with a book in which all his past, grievous, iniquities, had been recorded – who despite this, assured him his sins would all be washed away by this sacred ceremony. After relating his experience, he added he renounced idolatry, accepted Jesus Christ as the Son of God, and embraced this Saviour of the world. Thenceforth, he Genesius, would live, and eventually die, as a Christian! By conclusion, he exhorted the Emperor and all those present to follow his example and worship the Highest God. Without realising what he had done, feasibly, Genesius had discovered that Quaganry is the single solution to Existential questions.

Undoubtedly, students of Sacred Drama (burlesque or otherwise) nearly always seem to start their studies from the wrong position. They seldom enquire into the way within which a production starts its life: all too few of them ever investigating the nature of those spirits moulding the meaning of such manifestations. To be fair, perhaps these things are simply inscrutable, whilst their actual performance is invariably "all right on the night." With such theatrical notions in mind, playfulness as an activity standing in direct contrast to work, holds a number of unsuspected psychodynamic propositions. It is intimately linked, when all voiced and effectuated, with the struggle to attain personal freedom, along with the comforts of pleasurable gratification. Related to the Greek conceptual cluster, hedone, best elucidated as "enjoyment" or "delight," the felicities of play have often been seen as the end goal of Existence-in-Itself, or at the very least a primary trait built into the bedrock of human nature. Some scholars have even stated that in the form of qualified bliss, our play "instinct" is the ultimate value, standing in direct contrast to pain as the final disvalue. These commentators further their arguments by claiming we should shun the grim tutorial vicissitudes of the latter and only seek the obvious satisfactions of the former. Curiously, no less of an authority than the majestic Aristotle (384-322 BC) regarded pleasure as the successful concomitant of skilful living. And penetrating thinkers like the "God-intoxicated" Benedict Spinoza (1632-1677) came to look upon pleasuring intimacies as the resultant feeling of having passed from a lesser degree of perfection to a greater summit of excellence. All allowing, that said, certain moribund moderns with immense clinical expertise to postulate, a la Sigmund Freud (1856-1939), a "pleasure principle" operative in all of our daily affairs.

Traditionally, this acknowledged, mirth and frolic have been predicated as essential human attributes inclusive of intelligence and will. What is more, anyone with a religious disposition tended to additionally see these qualities as close to the core of the human Self; endowments, some claim, only perceptible when Spirit acts with a completely human face. Whether or not these facades have the extreme features of demons, or gods, inscribed upon them! This is not said as a quasi-reductive manoeuvre fallaciously shrinking metaphysics into a series of interlocking natural phenomena. Rather, it is to look for a basis upon which our comprehension of the uniquely human condition may rest. Broadly speaking, it is always unwise to discard notions of Quaganry, which, at this juncture, prophetically come to the fore once again. All be they remembered as theological planks taking human selfdom as the superstructure of all conceivable interpretation. What else, when all appointed and cast, apart from Human Identity gifts us with the means to recognise objects in the world around us? The fact that this so-called "school" only appeared in the latter half of the nineteenth century is neither here nor there. The importance of Quaganry, as an enduring philosophy, is located in its adherent's stand against populist notions of Pantheism, as well as with any view advocating crude nuts and bolts materialism. Perhaps the writings of Friedrich Schleiermacher (1768-1834) in 1799 first allude to this momentous insight? Then again, perhaps not! Put in other words, abstracted principles of "personhood" permit the recognition of intelligibility. In this regard, the American poet, Walt Whitman (1819-1892), published a somewhat prickly essay on Personalism in 1868, whilst Amos Bronson Alcott (1799-1888) may have initially borrowed this telling urgency from him. Fascinatingly,

Alcott himself used this complex of ideas to argue that Reality is a Divine Person who sustains the Universe by a continual act of will. In this cogent sense, the vast majority of writers may be historically divided into two camps; Quagans, who find their explanatory principles in human nature itself and Impersonalists who develop their explanations from a sense of outer objective attachments.

This tends to be why serious critics maintain Theatre starts with the Existential: always a good place to formulate theses, all be they a denuded territory from which to draw conclusions. So postulated, it must never be forgotten that contemporary Quaganry focuses on a human being's motivations, physical actions, acknowledged responsibilities, and innermost experiences. Proceeding further, writers associated with this genre are intent on discerning the meaning, or purpose, of an individual life. Using Theatre, thuswise, as an imager for broader explorations, Quagan-galvanised playwrights typically concentrate on what they believe to be supremely Subjective. Core aspects of our composition, for instance, like consciousness, spirituality and religious conviction, allied with related intensely "psychic" states such as freedom, guilt, and regret. Digging a little deeper, modern Quagans have contended that Western scientific thought largely concerns itself with the experiential study of physical-objects-in-space along with the academic categories it finds necessary for this classification of descriptive procedure. These systems, all the same, prove dramatically limited, not to mention impoverished, in terms of qualitative analysis. Principally, this is for two reasons: firstly, because the exploration of physical-objects-in-space has tended to minimise both the Meaning and Value of a truly individual Being. Secondly, in so far as this method has attempted to grasp the intrinsically value-laden human condition (through frameworks only applicable to objects), these techniques have overlooked the immense qualitative differences between human and non-human Being. This is why the majority of Quagan writers radically disagree with any form of positivism, when this type of thinking declares that only the tools of the empirical sciences can supply us with accurate knowledge. As a "stable," Quagans counterclaim that in order to grasp our unique qualities as Human Being, much more adept techniques are required to construct the holistic theoretical models necessary to outline our multi-levelled lives.

By this, it should not be assumed that playwrights and poets have denied that technically precise, and highly penetrating observations, are possible with regard to the world of phenomena. Nor should it be assumed this type of scientific scrutiny was felt to be pointless. Quagans, that maintained, strongly assent to a position, which holds every human person, unlike objects-in-space, or organisms-in-general, lacks an essential nature given at birth as an already completed Selfhood. Contrarily, we tend to argue that every human being's essential nature is peculiarly separated from their physical existence, because it is never completed in-itself. Once realised, a fully developed human essence can only be envisaged as a possible future event. Our existence, recognised so, is always tragically estranged from genuine and authentic modes of expression and in this sense we are never ourselves enough to truly experience the world around us in a thoroughly meaningful way. A painful paradox! Consequently, Quagans would add these are the real reasons why the vast majority of people flee from their spiritual responsibilities, preferring to sink into the average and the expected; even though such intended diminutions fall devastatingly short of a truly fulfilling religious target. A goal, dare I suggest, challenging each individual's psychic slumber, by stressing the vital significance of subjective states of awareness and shedding an unheralded brilliancy on distinctively human qualities. It is our playful appetites alone, they would conclude, that tell us Art, Culture, Theatre, and Ethics, reveal the potential freedom in our emergent selves.

In a nutshell, Quagan-energised Theatre continually aims to interpret this subject-object encounter in witnessable miniature. To achieve this, it seeks to express the flow of Becoming into Being as (literally) a stage for possible "states" of Being. Incontrovertibly, although in retrospect, a vast number of serious writers have implicitly discussed these Quagan themes throughout the history of Theatre and Criticism. All of which implies certain extremely general descriptions of human Being are not entirely out of the question at this moment in time. Overall then, those influenced by Quagan notions of Dramatisation, whilst tacitly agreeing with Jean-Paul Sartre's (1905-1980) declaration, "existence precedes essence," would, conversely, speak of the transition from false to genuine modes of Personhood. In terms of performance, they would ascribe to the cognitive value of particularly affective dispositions and moods. Beyond doubt, they would additionally reject that these kinds of feeling-states are merely subjective, or arbitrary. Contending instead these qualities indicate dimensions of Being that might otherwise be ignored or overlooked. Here the stage value of "anxiety" might be cited, due to the fact this condition is not called forth by either objects, or scenarios, but arises as a disclosure of dissatisfaction. It is the sudden flood of tragic freedom within a character, along with the recognised irresponsibility surrounding an empirical self's manifold imperfections. A situation aggravated by blinding intuitions regarding potentially qualitative existential modes. Understanding such dislocation, as well as the roots of compulsion associated with these affective-cognitive states, seems to be twofold. Firstly, the idealisation of "Mass Society" with its almost demonic desire to either obscure, or deny, the necessary reality of personal existence has been convincingly pinpointed by such commentators – and rightfully vilified in a "Swedenborgian" sense. Secondly, in similar vein, Quagan playwrights have railed against modern society's fearful abuse of mass-communications, not to exclude its over-employment of depersonalised, machine-minding, industrial settings, as deliberate desensitisation. They have even laid bare the conformist anonymity required by city life, while warning of the grave dangers posed to humanity by both collectivist and totalitarian social orders. Perils always made manifest through the Arts well before other creative, or political, spheres. Stated so, in terms of theatre-making, Quagans continue to protest against the genuinely sinister, intellectually limiting, and avowedly presumptuous claims of "scientism," that seem to be sweeping across the entire Western world. This reductive attitude, they argue, is actually an idolisation (in every sense) of technical procedures as the main (or the only) source of knowledge about our inmost lives. Atop this, it is an attitude, which blithely chooses to overlook the facts of personal Being within our sphere as an entirety. In this respect, Heidegger's masterly *Being and Time* can aptly be given a fruitful context as the critique of especially insidious intellectual errors implicit in this area of twenty-first-century thought.

For all that, the debate concerning any relationship between Theology and Drama is highly complex. In many ways, it is a field bristling with lexical dissonance and forthright disagreements. The nature of the obvious theoretical ties, that agreed, becomes privy to investigation once their motivation-contexts are pinned down. Possibly confusing for each side, is the occasional argument claiming that in the specific context of drama a person may playfully define himself, or herself, as anything he, or she, "wishes" to be—a bird, for example—and then, to become it on some imaginative level or other. All of which removes the innate sanctity of intended liturgical enactment. Until now, this tentatively mooted, most Quagan playwrights would readily concur such choices can only constitute fantasy, along with a tellingly inauthentic existence: adding that such "wishes" should be understood against a background that states a person is a) defined only insofar as he or she acts and b) that he or she is responsible for his or her actions as a human being. For instance, someone who acts cruelly towards other people is, by that act, defined as a cruel person. Further, by this action of cruelty such persons are themselves responsible for their new identity (a cruel person, a beast). Still, people are people, and theatrical processes neither advocate irresponsibility, nor remove limitation (internally or externally), for their actions, private "wishes" etc. And overall, those who participate in theatrical expression, be it as Liturgy or Theatre, need to remain fully aware of the distinctions between these staged events as palpable.

Besides this, any expression of liturgical practice is never merely theatrical. Demonstrably, on this level, they are not the same experience. Without any doubt, Liturgy (Greek: λειτουργία) is the customary public worship offered by a specific religious group in honour of Higher Principles; according to their own particular traditions. As an undertaking, therefore, Liturgy is sometimes rendered in English translation as an act of "service," referring to an elaborate, edifying, and formal religious ritual such as the Eastern Orthodox Divine Liturgy (Greek: Θεία Λειτουργία) and Catholic Mass, or daily observances like the Muslim Salah or Jewish domestic offices. As a well attested religious outpouring, Liturgy is, additionally, a communal response to the Sacred, through a wide variety of previously rehearsed activities reflective of thanksgiving, repentance, praise, or supplication. Ritualisation may occur in both camps, no doubt, yet liturgically it is customarily associated with landmark life-events like birth, the coming of age, marriage and death. In addition, the religious rites marking these events form the basis for establishing a relationship with Divine Agencies – never to forget other participants in the Liturgy. Methods of dress, the preparation of food, as well as other hygienic practices, are all considered liturgical activities in their own staged arena.

Thus argued, traditional English "miracle plays" sometimes cross these boundaries, having arisen from chanted responses and simple religious pageantry in the early Medieval Church. Scripted "revelations" being re-enacted through the stressed delivery of spoken words, silence and stagecraft; all of which remained uneasy, although on occasion essential, bedfellows. Symbolic characters, like "Judgement," or "Mercy," talked on stage with a self-realising efficacy; as the Hebrew Prophets themselves are said to have done outside of the auditorium. Such dramaturgical invention, furthermore, seems to have been scripted in order that the "revelatory" Word was made much more potent to untutored folk through the medium of dramatised engagement. Perhaps this is why the time and place of each performance became a matter of careful calculation. For the Craft Guilds of the fourteenth century (as in the Bible itself), "revelation" formed part of a spiritually instructive sequence, whereby the world found both order and redemption; again and again. In this way, entertainment was put in the service of Christian ideas and a new Theatre developed directly from religious ritual;

rather than prayerful reflection. It was not, of course, denied that similar types of theatre had existed in ancient Pagan days, merely that laymen would find this form of instruction particularly felicitous when participating in the Mass. With this liturgical claim in the collective mind, it is merely a matter of investigation to locate records affirming the recitation of Miracle dramas across medieval Europe.

Having debated thus, contemporary Europeans need to recall that these aids to a Christian experience of "revelation" became progressively opulent, despite the understandable reservations of some ecclesiastical critics. Arising from manifestly humble origins in Anglo-Norman French, for example, *The Harrowing of Hell* had its place as the earliest documented "performance piece" in England, towards the end of the thirteenth century. But, when historians of drama trace the steps of its subsequent dramatisations they find this show swiftly evolved through performed tableau and responsorial psalm into a much more complex enactment; perhaps especially in Northern Europe. By the same token, the emergence of movable stages and identifiable scenarios delighted audiences from the fourteenth century onwards. Eventually, the comic byplay, the narration of an off-stage moral observer and the spoken recognition that life, even in matters of worship, can occasionally be light-hearted, all assisted theatrical managers, along with aspiring playwrights, to take their rightful social positions during the extraordinary cultural developments of the sixteenth century. Either way, the actual authorship of these carefully constructed, latter day "mystery plays" is still as much a matter of heated discussion in academic circles as is the precise design and theological import of these spectacles.

Considered from a Quagan perspective, there is an existential interiority, as well as a humanising objectivity, to all things in Being and, by refraction, on the stage. Even simple retellings of legend stir ethnic recollections within our Folk-Soul, whilst serious drama awakens our sense of elation into an experience of the Beautiful. Among the giants of philosophy it was Friedrich Schiller (1759-1805) who found this fact overwhelmingly pertinent.[1] Indeed, in a stream of breathtakingly intelligent letters, this German thinker explains that elation stems from the "play impulse," which establishes the bedrock of aesthetic sensibilities in humans. It is an impulse, moreover, allowing morality and irrepressible feeling to coexist. As a dramatist and poet, Schiller coequally maps a "formal impulse," along with a "material impulse" as the arches of a viaduct built between effective living and the necessities of nature. Thusly, he reasons that play is free and spontaneous; combining, as it does with conscience, to project the ideal of perfection. In none of these cases, however, did Schiller claim our human construction of events was the primary factor in stagecraft. Put otherwise, he contended that Being constantly shines through appearance. As a far from obvious Quagan, Schiller, nevertheless, posits play as a proof of the macrocosmic design radiating within microcosmic form. For him, everything is truly a "Lila"[2] of the Lord. In order to illustrate this point, he discusses the notion of tragedy. Initially, Schiller interpreted tragedy as a display of suffering, intended to arouse pity in observers. He ends up, per contra, by concluding that tragedy is actually "moral resistance against suffering;" – a position leading him to place poets as the providers to philosophy of First Principles and never vice versa.

Reminiscent of these postulations, in our own time, Tom Stoppard's (born 1937) *Rosencrantz and Guildenstern Are Dead* was staged at the Edinburgh Festival Fringe as an Absurdist tragicomedy in 1966. His play expanding upon the exploits of two minor characters from Shakespeare's grim masterpiece *Hamlet*! Comparisons were quickly, and correctly, drawn to Samuel Beckett's *Waiting for Godot*, due to the presence of two central characters, who almost appear to be twin halves of a single, desperate, man. Unarguably, many of Stoppard's plot features are similar: the characters pass time by playing questions and answers, impersonating off-stage personae, and remaining silent, or interrupting each other for long periods of time. Evidentially, his twin characters are portrayed as two fools, or clowns, in a world completely beyond their understanding. And as such, they stumble through philosophical arguments, while proving incapable of realising their intellectual implications: all making them muse on the randomness and irrationality of the world around them. Ironically, they even present arguments founded on existentialist ideas between themselves as a means for Stoppard to demonstrate to his audience that there are obvious limits to human capacity. Contextualised so, British Theatre may usually be divided into two broad categories: large-scale commercial productions that are designed to have widespread popular appeal, and small scale "Art" centred productions aimed at specifically targeted audiences. In which case, the place and purpose of "Fringe Drama," as an essential part of the world theatre process is the last remaining arena of imaginative revolt. Remaining, at the end of the evening, (potentially) lucrative in its own right, socially challenging and unrepentantly innovative as a dramaturgical form.

With the gift of hindsight, arguably, miracle and mystery plays inherited from the Middle Ages still connote the highest point attained by Fringe Drama. This is for three reasons, which need to be considered together. Firstly, these productions were extremely successful combinations of art—poetry, drama, costume, instrumental music, dance, song—and as such embodied genuine communal attempts to embrace cohesive social symbols. Secondly, they took their subject matter from Myth; best understood during this era as stylised imagistic narrative illuminating human experience at depth, in openly Universalist terms. Undoubtedly, the unique property of sacred storytelling is that such performances express Quagan insight into the human condition for every man, woman and child, in every age. Also, these realisations, no matter how terse or compact, proved inexhaustible at all times. Thirdly, each occasion for the performance had religious significance. In actual fact, they were staged by the Craft Guilds in order to display both their skills, as well as their status, on culturally significant occasions. Therefore, over time, traditions like these became crystallised folk memory, preserving the struggles, along with the aspirations of a specific community through changing interpretation and redirected emphasis within such productions. Perhaps that is why mystery plays remain an important seasonal element of local festivals to this day.

However, with the emergence of spiritual radicalism, wherein individual narrative began to replace collective performance, the entire notion of Community Theatre gradually came into question. Theatre, it was argued, should be in a particular place where plays were performed, and that whilst tangential issues, like cultural education, outreach and social engagement were undeniably important, they should not be at the expense of this fundamental rule. In a similar vein, pundits continued, theatres must be administered in order for actors to perform effectively, even though it was stressed by these very same commentators that actors do not perform for the upkeep of theatres. By the 1800s then, recognised critics had become correct, when complaining that funds were too often spent on paying down deficits, on better management, on marketing, and on vaguely ironic projects seeking to make theatres more accessible. Nonetheless, they seem to have felt the very purpose of Theatre was found purely in self-expression as catharsis: coupled with the repeated enactment of social psychodrama. Manifestly, Fringe as a distinct theatrical endeavour starts to splinter from these allegedly normative processes during this period, because it proclaimed the necessity of preserving performance as a multi-layered dramatic engagement with an audience; an engagement, which cannot be limited to the simplistic demands of entertainment.

Modern Fringe, revolutionised by the likes of Stoppard, has inherited this mercurial stance from the great dramaturges of that era. It is experimentalist to the core. It even acts as a creative counterbalance to West End and Broadway productions. Likewise, contemporary Fringe embraces the cultural realities of an ethnically diverse Theatre scene. Yet, this adaptability has proved a curse as well as a blessing. On one hand, British Fringe is undergoing an atavistic renewal by going back to its localising origins. Conversely, the near disintegration of a single, coherent national symbolic narrative, has simply managed to bewilder modern audiences by forcing them to choose between overly esoteric productions, or technically sophisticated trivia. In this sense, British Fringe Theatre has truly emerged as a functional folk laboratory.

Incontrovertibly, Fringe represents a lively alternative to the dreary consumer-oriented soap drama offered by companies afraid to take artistic risks, or stretch the mindsets of their potential audiences. Above this, anyone experienced in Fringe has learnt that people fully appreciate quality over spectacle, and normally resent the condescending attitudes of well-known impresarios towards public taste. Our proof is found in the fact that Fringe shows often become hits via word-of-mouth recommendation, as well as in evidence which demonstrates that audiences repeatedly return to our gigs once a reputation has been established. This is not to agree with contemporary reviewers when they claim all of these carefully rehearsed ensemble pieces are synonymous (even though their aesthetic value is genuinely elative and not merely an amusement) with deeply philosophical stage introspection, but to assert their, often reflexive, relationship. One of the factual demonstrations of this dramaturgical assertion is to be found in the nature of the intended audience. Religious scenarios, for example, form part of Worship. They aim to achieve Communion with higher levels of Being. So contextualised, even monastic performers seek audience-participation with Being in-and-of-itself. Elevation, not entertainment, is the agreed spiritual goal. Hence, their performances, in spite of superficial similarities to communal play, are undertaken to achieve psychophysical objectives internally—as well as externally surrounding—the person of the esoteric engineer: clearly so, if one considers the wiltingly beautiful Easter celebrations of the Greek Orthodox Church in this respect.

Performance events such as these equally have a trickledown effect in terms of Folk production. Without risking misrepresentation, I conjecture that for his part my colleague Elchin Afandiyev (born 1943), would cite the endurance of Azerbaijani village Folk drama, along with medieval European stagecraft, as educative public entertainments in this regard.[3] Unreservedly, my dear friend is mindful that the sources of human significance may be experienced through symbol as well as the implements of working men. He would point to everyday artefacts such as embroidered aprons, hammers and plumb-bobs as the potential props of Meaning. Undoubtedly, he would also argue that inherited village spectacles, like Novruz,[4] were ways to express collective creativity, even though it was actually the marshalled artillery of serious modern theatre, which produces the best potential means of extending consciousness. As a playwright revelling in subversion, Elchin wants to focus on entertaining immediacy in his work and remains cautious towards any notion of a boundless transcendence as described by Schiller. Each would surprisingly agree, that contested, on the role of Silence and Revelation as important dramaturgical devices in theatre production: dramaturgical tools, that may be seen as a structural means to uncover the hidden power gifted by any journey into the divinising human Self.

At this point, we have squared the circle by being awake to the fact semantic frames built around these seemingly well-understood lexical items continually prove instructive, although inexhaustible. Clarifying, perhaps, why most scholars, without question, would agree that the common coinage of "Revelation" is to be found in the New Testament. Once this is conceded, it becomes clear that words such as "Reveal" and "Revelation" cannot have been used in the everyday sense of the verb "to disclose." Probing further, anyone reading Biblical extracts is suddenly confronted by the previously unsuspected presence of a sophisticated theological vocabulary. Unequivocally then, philologists studying New Testament lexicography tell us that this word item must be interpreted as entirely eschatological.[5] When speaking of "revelation," Christian writers are talking about a final unveiling of Divine Intention at the end of this age. Still, the implication is not that revelation only takes place as a concluding scene in the unsettlingly brief drama of Salvation, but that it will be an actual series of supernatural events rooted in a future mystery. When all determined and undertaken, overtly religious words such as "revelation" need to be understood in an atmosphere of spiritual "encounter;" a process easily lending itself to exploration within a theatrical environment.

In our dreams we can study Silence, even though not really in the turbulent day. Unquestionably, it seems to be a far more impenetrable problem. In its hyper-dimensionality it moves like a frilled ballerina's tutu, implying overall communication through graceful gestures and magnetising smiles; albeit never verbally. Slowly understood, Silence is even, beyond Metatext: it is neither a refusal to speak, or the absence of sound, nor a failure to inform. Silence, in itself, is qualitative endeavour. This may be why in the seventh century St Maximus the Confessor talked about a "mystical silence of inspired experience." By this, the holy man appeared to be drawing on Desert Traditions far older than Buddhism, whereby the Fathers described three types of Silence: of words, of desires and of thoughts. On close inspection, they are stunningly positing Quagan ideas, which include the notion of an "enlightened recollection" intimately bonded to Pure Consciousness. Each concept explaining why these interior explorers looked towards levels of perfection above quantitative adjectives and strangely suggestive metaphors. They stood firm in their experience that quietude, stillness, never forgetting our uniquely reverberating individuality, is to be discovered in the meandering "articulations" of Silence. Expressed elseways, the lack of audible, or indeed subjective sound, according to these expert "psychonauts" never ever quashes higher order communication.

Taken together, Revelation, as well as Silence, have always proved fruitful theatrical devices in staged attempts to recreate human interaction with the unarguably metaphysical. Maybe it is also fructifying to note these superficially basic techniques additionally formed part of the burial rites of our Viking ancestors. According to Professor Neil Price of the University of Aberdeen, in saying that the Vikings had "no defined religion," we moderns tend to miss the ways their spirituality found expression. Silent, yet intensely elative reflection, along with an epiphanous relationship with the living forces of Fire and Ice, all formed part of the Viking lifestyle. As a matter of fact, these warriors acted out their basic beliefs and abstract intuitions at the graveside of fallen comrades. In the case of a vanquished Hero, especially elaborate rites of passage seem to have been performed by the entire community. Eventually, Price continues, these Scenarios became a form of village Theatre, easily predating the Sagas and may have contained within them the very origins of Norse Mythology as a genre. With the passage of years, tribal bards sang of powerful giants, valiant Princes and Heavenly Intelligences within the complex web of the Wyrd, whilst mothers and farmers talked of Fairies and Wizards. From those Quagan days to these, it seems as if ritual found expression before either Myth, or Folktale, fully formulated. Using such delightful and poignant rubrics, it is easy to see how playfulness may be experienced as both idle fun, on one side, or as the acquiring of intricate life-skills on the other. Once settled upon, these guidelines equally tell us that there really is no greater tragic poet, than the Norwegian Henrik Ibsen. Without doubt, he stands shoulder to shoulder with Shakespeare as a Master of his craft. Moreover, he was a man with uncompromisingly clear eyes for social trauma. It is, indeed, telling that Ibsen's allegedly Modernist plays abound with talk upon the icy ferocity of nature and the lingering legacy of Viking heroism. Stated thus, at every turn of the plot in his disturbingly provocative play *The Master Builder,* obstructive powers are seen to be at work in the lives of his characters; principalities referred to by the language of Nordic folklore. In addition, his verse drama *Brand*, presents his audience with an unsparing vision of a Christian Minister driven by his soul-numbing faith to risk the deaths of his wife and child, in order to prove his Bible-based convictions: actions, of course, witnessed by a chorus of spirits. Inherited genre restrictions are not, that acknowledged, the real literary issue in these plays, but the perennial appeal of revealed Being. As humans, we need to mouth this Absolute through the figures of Elves when young, and as stifling moments of elative significance when we become adults. Beyond dispute, in this process of articulation, Theatre remains the premier medium of such a playful and yet deadly serious confrontation, since nowhere else may Silence as well as Revelation be applied with this aesthetic effect.

We Britons are equally the sons of Vikings. Exactly as our Russian cousins assuredly are – following recent research. This appears to be why, in the land of Shakespeare, we have an easily attuned ear towards the drama of life on all of its various planes of concretisation: a natural faculty provoking poets such as Blake, probably in a characteristic fit of consternation, to tempestuously declare, "What is a wife and what is a harlot? What is a church and what is a theatre? Are they two and not one? Can they exist separate? Are not religion and politics the same thing? Brotherhood is religion. O demonstrations of reason dividing families in cruelty and pride!" Without a second thought on any Briton's part, Blake was certainly not barking about either Orthodoxy, or the Athonites. If Theatre, that illuminated, be merely a place where people idle their precious leisure hours in entertainment, then let's set alight these completely redundant venues with incendiaries. Let's do it this very moment! Burn, dynamite and bury these buildings beneath the accusatory earth. Transparently, multimedia venues already exist which are far better equipped for having fun: as well as locations more aesthetically pleasing to the eye than these typically antique auditoria, where aficionados can experience their own, private, cathartic release! A side street Bordello bathed in lascivious red light, or a gamer's messy, even though hi-tech bedroom, or local widescreen cinema, would provide this necessary outlet on a more equitable basis. Lessons antagonistically learnt from August Strindberg, that most uneasy, experimental, and groundbreaking, of Swedish souls. Assuredly, in a manner uncannily reflective of the Athonites, both as a person and through his magnificent brainchild, the Theatre of Revolt, Strindberg stood firm in his cavalier dismissal of mediocrity, by focusing on the small, expressive, "chamber" production.

When reflecting on overtly Quagan themes like these, be it in an Athonite cloister, or among the gods in a theatre, it is useful to dust off the records of nineteenth-century Europe. Especially noting that among the subculture examining esoteric ideologies (along with concomitant spheres of experimental Performance) actors interacted with the politically rebellious as an essential artistic response to the cultural zeitgeist. In Continental provinces, Puppet Theatre, village tent entertainments and pantomime remained equivalently influenced by the villainy of Punch and the traditional sparkle of a Fairy Godmother's wings. But in Blighty the research of Orientalists, allied to the brazen literary outrages of explorers such as Sir Richard Burton, allowed for the introduction of innovative and exotic themes in the Capital. During the period of Occult Revival in Symbolist Theatre, moreover, openly Hermetic, Arabic Sufi and Chinese Buddhist imagery emerged on stage.[6] This led several conservative critics to denounce such styles of theatrical production as little other than a series of flirtations with Evil. With hindsight, it is difficult to see the wickedness behind heavily patterned flying carpets and the silken turbans of golden Genii, or the lavish re-constructions of Egyptian civic ceremony; yet, unarguably, audiences did sense a threat to their political conditioning on a fundamental level. Once viewed from this seditious perspective, Symbolist playwrights like Maurice Maeterlinck (1862-1949), or slightly later, crazed albeit ingenious dramaturges like Antonin Artaud (1869-1948), may be seen as dangerous, ungovernable revolutionaries in their attempts to dramatise the effects of invisible forces on everyday life. A century, or so, later, at least according to Dr Edmund B. Lingam's essay, *Contemporary Forms of Occult Theatre*, it also explains the professional resistance encountered by a young Sir Peter Brook (born 1925) when he consulted the magician Aleister Crowley (1874-1947) on the conjuring scenes in Brook's revolutionary production of Christopher Marlowe's (1564-1693) masterpiece, *Dr. Faustus*.

In rebuttal, many critics insisted that the tone of the pulpit was tangential to Theatre: not irrelevant, but merely off the mark. Ergo, *Magic* as G.K. Chesterton's (1874-1936) first play met little opposition from clergy in any denomination. Correspondingly, its exploration of Occult Theatre seemed tame as well as predictable to insiders. In any case, when it appeared, his reputation had already been made and his occasionally ramshackled brilliance could easily pen illuminating essays (*The Defendant*), novels (*The Napoleon of Notting Hill*, *The Man Who Was Thursday*), criticism (*Robert Browning*, *Charles Dickens*), philosophy (*Orthodoxy*), detective stories (*The Innocence of Father Brown*), and verse (*The Ballad of the White Horse*), as the compulsive hallmarks of a genuine writer. Since, however, drama was absent from this list of literary attributes Chesterton's sparring-partner, George Bernard Shaw (1856-1950), demanded he write a play. A 1908 letter even threatens: "I shall repeat my public challenge to you; vaunt my superiority; insult your corpulence; torture Belloc; if necessary, call on you and steal your wife's affections by intellectual and athletic displays, until you contribute something to the British drama." Shaw went on to offer Chesterton a plot: about the horrified return of St Augustine to an England he dimly remembered converting. Unfortunately, this particular play was never written, even though Shaw's ultimatum did indirectly result in *Magic*. For all that, Shaw's wanting of "a religious harlequinade" proved, more or less, fertile. Illustrating why, quite possibly, Chesterton gave him a fantastic comedy with the singular force of a parable. Now, admittedly, the stagecraft is overtly creaky by modern standards, and some of the extravagantly rhetorical lines must have been nigh on impossible to deliver without that between-the-teeth laugh used by actors to cope with contemporary verbosity. Anyway, for each of its faults, *Magic* continues to read well and hits home with important facts about contemporary ethical attitudes tainting society at large.

To be Chestertonian for a moment, this play became topical in its day precisely because it had ceased to be pertinent. Centring, as it does, on the psychological impact of the protagonist's paranormal gift, it is difficult to believe that we, as "desensitised" modern audiences, would accept, rhetorically speaking, that the conjuror's tiny miracle would even come close to breaking a man's mind: especially after the endless moral affronts relayed by our international news services on a day-by-day basis. Alternatively, these supernormal effects are unlikely to raise any agonising theological crisis in our souls, generating instead, a reaction more akin to disconcerted confusion. Undoubtedly, Chesterton's official conversion to Roman Catholicism didn't occur until 1922, yet his views on such issues were already known and remarkably lucid. To his mind, God doesn't mess around with paltry miracles on the verge of simple affectations within the natural order. Maybe the conjuror, that argued, thinks that he knows too much, and, as such, sees his abilities as demonic, or harmful for the spirit. Or those secondary personae in the play are too prone to scepticism and superstition to achieve spiritual balance. At any rate, in matters of ultimate Truth, religion or no religion, Chesterton, as playwright, seems to contend that nowadays we Britons speak with the ethically relativist voice of the Duke in his performance piece: our consciences blunted by the "banana madness" induced through too many pointless choices. In attempting, this confessed, to stage the consequences of freedom, Chesterton can only be applauded, although it is difficult to see how his usually potent creative powers have been stretched. Anyhow, he only wrote two more plays: a period piece entitled *The Judgment of Dr. Johnson* (1927) and another parable, *The Surprise* (posthumously published, 1952). Justifiably in terms of stagecraft, this conceded, *Magic* remains his best theatrical venture.

Infinitely more fruitful than Chesterton in these fecund matters is the mind-boggling Absurdist ingenuity of Eugène Ionesco (1909-1994). Born in the beauteous wilds of Romania, circumstance soon moved Ionesco to France. In fact, Gallic affairs generally played a huge part in Ionesco's life, gifting him again and again with the inner resolve to never hide behind any of the open doors guarded by overly professional churchmen, politicians, or career-centred theatre critics. His position, furthermore, as one of the foremost figures in the Theatre of the Absurd is due to Ionesco's shameless continuation of Quagan themes with "blunted" metaphysical implications. So, beyond repeatedly ridiculing the most banal situations, Ionesco's dramas depict in a tangible way the solitude and insignificance of human existence—as one object—among others. In a similar fashion to Samuel Beckett, although arguably much more philosophically astute, Ionesco felt this type of theme was linked to his personal theatrical vocation starting late in life. Chronologically, he did not write his first play until 1948 (*La Cantatrice Chauve*, which was initially performed in 1950) with the English title *The Bald Soprano*. Certainly, anecdotal evidence respecting the origin of this masterpiece, has it that by the age of 40 Ionesco decided to learn English using the Assimil method: a technique insisting whole sentences are copied into a student's notebook in order to memorise them efficiently. Yet, when re-reading his work, Ionesco began to feel he was not learning English, but rather rediscovering some astonishing truths – such as there being seven days in a week and that ceilings were spatially above us in a room. Things he already knew, no doubt, but which struck him as stupefying, since they were indisputably true. For Ionesco, the truisms and clichés of this conversation primer disintegrated into comedic caricature and empty parody, whereby language itself disintegrated into fragments of words. That said, original theatrical performances were magically instigated.

Looking behind, family resemblances to Genesius abound in the life, testimonies and works of Ionesco. Each understood the idiocy of trying to find Essential Value in a world made up from objects-in-space. Furthermore, both of them realised that on the basis of organisms-in-general, ridicule and even blasphemy were rational reactions to the vacuity surrounding them. This may be why Ionesco takes great pride in attributing the subsequent success of this production to accidental occurrence. What else could it be in a world composed of objects-in-space? Additionally, if extra proof were needed, when first performed *The Bald Soprano* was largely unnoticed, until a few established writers and critics, among them Jean Anouilh (1910-1987), championed the play, thereby enabling Ionesco to develop his most innovative one-act "nonsense" plays: another demonstration that this world of organisms-in-general cannot yield its real Meaning to the physical sciences. Daring to speak for him, the emergence of these absurdist sketches, within which Ionesco termed phrases like "anti-play" (*anti-pièce* in French), express ennui and futility with surreal comic force – precisely because they parody the conformism of the bourgeoisie so precisely, along with conventional theatrical norms. In these enactments of pure nonsense, Ionesco rejects conventional storylines as their basis, instead taking their dramatic structure from accelerating rhythms and cyclical coincidences: in psychodynamic words, irrational and Quagan intuitions of individual redemption. Through this, Ionesco disregards liberal psychology and materialistic forms of dialogue, which can only ever produce a dehumanised culture with mechanical, puppet-like characters who speak in endless non-sequiturs: the implication being that if drama only looks through the secularised eyes of objects-in-space, or organisms-in-general, the Meaningful Essence of life is lost to human understanding.

Overtly, Absurdist theatre, like Athonite views *sub specie aeternitatis*, or the everyday wonderworking of traditional dramaturgy, uncovers a cultural mirror reflecting the truly spiritual. Theatre is, consequently, an artifice by which audiences observe a little of their own moral worth as individuals, or their lack of honest, humane, values as a social grouping. In recent decades, productions such as the genuinely subversive *Shockheaded Peter*[7] have even sought to revive something of this staged encounter with Being to theatre-goers of all ages, through Fairy tale mixed with Quagan realities; a surprisingly traditionalist admixture. But, the importance of this specific type of production is found neither in acts of quasi-religious mimicry, albeit instructive, nor in the ultimately trivial accomplishments of mere cultural empowerment. Rather, the enduring necessity of Sacred Theatre is rediscovered in its detailed revelation of human selfhood, on a psychological, moral, political and fundamentally religious level. Whether or not this narration takes the form of insights into criminal irresponsibility, the observation that our world is peopled with powerful and inhuman forces, or the iconic life and wisdom of an ethical giant living on Holy Mount Athos! That way or this, these performances bestow a typically obscure and largely hidden knowledge of our spiritual selves.

SELECTED ENDNOTES

1. Schiller is not usually seen as a Quagan, but a close reading of his work reveals a number of compelling reasons for this reinterpretation.

2. A "Lila" is a concept within Hinduism which literally means a Divine "sport," "pastime" or "play." It is common to both non-dualistic and dualistic philosophical schools, but has a markedly different significance in each.

3. For a more in-depth view of "Elchin Theatre" see Appendix 2.

4. Novruz is the Islamic Easter. A seasonal celebration of Spring.

5. Alan Richardson (ed.), *A Dictionary of Christian Theology* (London, 1969).

6. Edmund B. Lingan, *Beyond the Occult Revival: Contemporary Forms of Occult Theatre*, PAJ: A Journal of Performance and Art (Volume 28, Number 3, September 2006).

7. *Shockheaded Peter* was a 1998 musical based on the popular German children's book *Der Struwwelpeter* (1845) by Heinrich Hoffmann. Created by Julian Bleach, Anthony Cairns, Julian Crouch, Graeme Gilmour, Tamzin Griffin, Jo Pocock, Phelim McDermott, Michael Morris, with musical accompaniment by The Tiger Lillies (Martyn Jacques, Adrian Huge and Adrian Stout) their production combined elements of puppetry and pantomime. Commissioned by the West Yorkshire Playhouse in Leeds and the Lyric Hammersmith in West London, the show debuted in Leeds before moving to London and subsequently on to world tours.

"Climb every mountain, ford every stream, follow every rainbow, 'til you find your dream."

– From *Sound of Music*

Problem VII.
Theology on the Toilet

O
NCE UPON A TIME IN AMERICA, A VOCAL GROUP CALLED THE
Four Seasons sang "Silence is Golden." A sentiment Philips
Records certainly seemed to agree with in 1964. After all,
they released this track in the hope listeners would not only agree,
but also purchase the vinyl. And as such, it is common knowledge
this song went on to receive rave reviews worldwide. All proving,
quite possibly, that it was a shared sentiment across our Earth. Yet,
peace and quiet appear to be disappearing in our time. Nowhere
is really silent nowadays. Indeed, it is as though each and every
opportunity to "take stock" diminishes in direct proportion to the
preponderance of "time-saving" technology in our homes. Overall,
a dubious "advance" slowly abolishing every single distinction
betwixt "public" and "private" space. An unspoken revolution, dare
I suggest, of externalised interiors, wherein the psyche is turned into
a perpetual performer. Almost, a transhumanist subversion, I am
horrified to add, recasting human affairs in the superficial mould of
continual entertainment – staged before an audience of surveillance
cameras and mobile phones. Inert mechanisms, in themselves, which
nevertheless have reduced the entire Western sphere to a third-rate
melodrama. Converting, thereby, our neighbourhoods into endlessly
enticing green rooms that never close their doors. Concomitantly
explaining, at least in part, why privacy is such a major legal problem
in the United States – as well as our United Kingdom. But, when all
discussed and debated, this myriad of artificial eyes remains blind to
one uniquely private area – our restrooms.

Observed so, every convenience has developed into a veritable safe-haven from everyone else's prying lens. In this sense, the "dunny" has become a place of recovery and theological reflection: a tiny oasis of integrity and inspiration. Thus, without irony, I can honestly say these tiny, isolating, cubicles are now sanctuaries of solitude, placid reading areas, and semi-fortified refuges against unnecessary intrusions into our individual affairs. Interestingly, even before the Findhorn Foundation was fixed as a concept to its founders, the modern mystic Eileen Caddy used to channel Higher Energies as she sat in the calm of a Scottish loo.[1] Proving beyond all question that communication with supernormal realms is equally made comfortable in these confines. Thence, by extension, both the executive elite, along with our most humble citizens, can thankfully catch their breath in these truly solicitous domains. Demonstrating, thereby, that in the midst of a planet on the verge of exhausted collapse, each one of these tiny nooks offer restoration to our common humanity – albeit temporarily.

So, somewhat uncharacteristically, I recall once returning from the safety of a toilet seat to an argument about Swedenborg, Art, Quaganry and Mount Athos. To be honest, it had been brewing all morning in a French Café near my flat in Clapham, London. Provoked, quite possibly, by my defence of Modalist theology to an Anglo-Catholic friend. At which point, let me speedily contextualise that I, myself, am a British Quagan, not an Anglo-Catholic.[2] To be completely honest, I am a Free Church priest – even though I confess to being deeply influenced by Swedenborg and Oneness Pentecostals in my theological outlook. Each a factor causing some to say I am actually a Protestant with a sacramental theology. Conversely, my confrère was a staunch Church of England traditionalist; not to ignore the fact he is additionally the Assistant Editor of The Church Times. I could sense, thenceforth, dark accusations of "flirting with heresy" on the conversational horizon. This firmly intuited, we talked about Swedenborg's remark, "..... the Bible has an inner, spiritual meaning for angels and an outer, material-level meaning for people on earth"[3] in an atmosphere making me feel any repetition of these materials would simply throw extra fuel on an already burning fire. As it was, I found myself fighting a rearguard action, whilst waiting to be denounced as an anti-Trinitarian. Naytheless, my friend took another tack by suddenly holding up his cup and challenging, "Is this God?" Exasperated, I found myself desperately bellowing "yes, yes, yes ..... and no" in the sure and certain knowledge my point had already been completely misunderstood.

With a backward glance, this particular coffee morning initiated regular and highly enjoyable weekly sessions, wherein the relentless conditions of life in our tough city could be discussed, alongside relationships, culture, celebrity gossip and religious convictions. Moreover, I often introduced Swedenborgian aphorisms on these occasions like, "A life of kindness is the primary meaning of divine worship," as genuine food for speculative investigation.[4] Conjectures, eventually developing into (at St Peters Anglo-Catholic Church) a monthly Quagan depth meditation and prayer circle designed to examine these weighty topics. Phrased in a different manner, notions picturing our Heavenly Mother-Father, Hir Resurrected Son, and our Holy Comforter as aspects, or a modus, of the One Monadic Deity, became regularly debated subjects. Each meetup, hopefully, transforming into a loving exploration of essential theological issues; over hot, very sweet, tea and chocolate biscuits – whilst attendees held their Bibles in-hand. As a consequence, these tasty encounters with dogmatics allowed everyone present to understand Salvation as far more than a collection of ideas in the head. Instead, living authentic lives mirroring Apostolic compassion was understood to be paramount. Guided, when everything is dusted and done, by wise, inherited, customs, and a received spiritual praxis.

Strangely, Swedenborg's visionary light on these undertakings didn't stop glimmering. Ultimately, his experience-based annotations (secondarily) implied a number of para-physical facts – like the need to consciously cultivate stillness. Accompanied, as these insights were, by subtle injunctions suggesting a mind made silent to the onslaught of crushing anxiety, disabling paranoia, pointless triviality and numbing materialism, quickly renews its strength when completely quiet. Simultaneously advancing, it must be emphasised, resistance to the narrow parameters generated by largely misunderstood doctrines. Undoubtedly, inner-solicitude isn't simply the absence of psychological thunder, but rather an opportunity to synchronise with the Glorious Absolute; or one's own True Self. In this respect, many religious traditions defend the importance of being "composed" spiritually for personal growth to genuinely begin. For instance, within Islam, blissful Sufi Saints insist on prayerful repose, whereas tranquil Buddhist Lamas explain anyone honestly seeking Enlightenment requires equipoise. Further, teachers of Advaita Vedanta (as do the many schools of yoga), say gentle *Mauna* is essential for soul-expansion. Each religious group framing (in their respective turns), what the Jewish sage Perkey Avot explains through his postulate, "Tradition is a safety fence to Torah, tithing a safety fence to wealth, vows a safety fence for abstinence; a safety fence for wisdom ... is silence." Examples reminiscent, clearly, of communal quietude advocated by some Quaker Meeting Houses, where every worshipper waits in patient expectancy for Providence to speak inside their hearts. A mystical attitude, similarly, shared by metaphysical authorities such as Eckhart Tolle – when he discusses a *via negativa* forming "locations" within which a heavenly hush exists. Taken altogether, every one of these sacred conventions weaves a perennial thread of noiselessness, balance, and calmness, into a Golden Fleece used to restore mind, body, and Spirit, alike.

All a criss-cross, one may add, interlacing untroubled circles, undisturbed spirals, and restful cycles ..... of empowered clans, mighty individuals, as well as political practises! And understood so, one of Merry Old England's Master Poets, William Blake (1757-1827), had hushed, but strong Libertarian tendencies. He lived them. He breathed their uplifting and intoxicating airs. Unmistakably, these gusts of freedom inspired every sentence within Blake's work and encouraged him to ask questions in a fashion similar to the priest and English Lollard, John Ball (1338-1381) when the latter proclaimed: "When Adam delved and Eve span, who was then the gentleman." Unmistakably, during his lifetime, Blake was not particularly politically active in any well-established public party, (something of an oxymoron to a Libertarian in any case) although in his verses, engravings, and personal life, he literally embodied an attitude of "devil-may-care" rebellion. Certainly, that said, Blake loudly decried the abuses of class privilege. He also raged against senseless wars, along with the spiritually blighting effects of an increasingly callous Industrial Revolution: a revolt individually pursued by practicing nudism and crafts, whilst encouraging experimental attitudes towards sex. This is probably why, in a relatively recent study, *William Blake: Visionary Anarchist* by Peter Marshall, our Blake, as well as his contemporary William Godwin (1756-1836) is portrayed as one of the forerunners of modern Libertarianism. Oh, orbits, ages, cycles, circularities and agendas! Without doubt, recurrent social irritations frequently find expression in the Arts, along with dissident religious, and radical philosophical movements. Moreover, such reactions against oppression almost form a "tradition" (from the Peasants Revolt, through to the True Levellers, the Diggers, and dare I suggest the Suffragettes), of established Counter-Culture, wherein alternative images of "nationalism" are explored. Foresights, it may be stated, of an Ideal, local, but evolved landscape. This could be why, to my mind, Blake did not go far enough in his revolutionary zeal: perhaps due to the fact he was a Christian, albeit of a highly unusual type: a man who sought Salvation both inside and beyond this Earth. Hence, his poetic "characters" are weary of linear time, even though vaguely aware that other, not to forget deeper, forms of Earth-based spirituality still haunt any call to genuine revolt. Ah, currents, tides, orbits, and cultural Seasons! Round and around like the stars of Heaven, or the atoms beneath our bodies (each building the very blocks of Life about us), these Ancestral Voices call us all back to our Quagan Heritage. Indeed, every dusk, they mutter questions demanding answers to why we Britons have allowed this land to be furrowed by its mortal enemies? Every nervous ice-pure rivulet of Liberty returning to the surging, salted, political Sea forcing individual examination. Thereby, causing humble earthworms and seasonal Robin Redbreasts to inquire into the reasons why we indigenous folk allow a ruthless exploitation of our homeland to continue? After all, every migrating bird beating its feathery way back to its nest seems to sing melodic queries as to why we natives aren't rising up in open revulsion at our incarcerated estate? In part, doubtlessly, these interrogations reveal tendencies whereby Libertarianism may be viewed from two starkly divergent angles: as a search for Eden, or the original conditions of innocence before corrupted secular "history" began. Or conversely, a view wherein a simple, rational, political, rejection of the current tyrannical social order is finally proved unfair and unsustainable!

That stated, either of these interpretations are vital in understanding a Universalist Libertarianism, so-called, or a theoretical National Libertarianism in praxis. Henceforth, we need to probe into the links between these twin ideological streams before examining their English context. Firstly, I suspect most scholars would agree that the idea of Libertarianism, riddled as it is by paradox and confusion, springs nevertheless, from transparent root-perceptions. Rather like a Tree-of-Life, it originated from the Latin lexical item "Libertas" (meaning Freedom) implying, as this does, that any ruling elite usually creates more harm than good, while hereditary Aristocrats, rampant privilege, Royal Families, and embedded financial interests merely desire their own advantage. Contrariwise to this, Libertarianism stands for The People. It proclaims an unapologetically high anthropology and upholds the innate goodness of each human heart: along with the patience required to permit us all to evolve into spiritually mature lives. First mouthed, in this sense, by William Belsham in the context of metaphysics, the word *libertaire*," was later taken up by the French libertarian communist Joseph Déjacque in a letter to Pierre-Joseph Proudhon in 1857. Thereafte, in the mid-1890s, Sébastien Faure began publishing a new *Le Libertaire*, following the Third Republics banning of "anarchist" publications. A move designed to prevent this conceptual cluster of ideas from further condemning the obvious mechanisms of cultural degradation. Prefaced, as such notions are, by suggested strategies for the enforced removal of illegitimate hierarchies – ranging, in their expression, from robust calls to direct, violent, action, all the way to a saintly and educated passive resistance!

I suspect nonetheless, whether consciously acknowledged or not, this twin stream of ideals actually arises from a shared source-intuition that human lives—once more integrated with the environment—can only lead to social betterment. Great Nature, as sentient witness and supreme healer underpinning this type of fundamental discourse: a hidden Hylozoist metaphysic, disappearing into an unspecified antiquity, while being the real author of charming, Edenic, tales. In this sense, ancient religious stories about a lost primordial paradise, State of Innocence, or a Fall from Grace, are very far from naive, or simplistic. Rather, they underscore the manner in which legends of a Golden Age, or Myths describing a vanished Garden of Eden, tend to uncover the very best psychological characteristics of a people. Its viewpoint demonstrating the noblest of its ethnic attitudes!

With this in hand, modern Jewish eschatology holds that history will complete itself by coming full circle: to its ultimate, original, destination – when all humankind will return to the Garden of Eden, as outlined in the Old Testament. So observed, in Jewish Kabbalah as well as the Talmud, Hebrew scholars contend there are two types of hallowed location for the dimensions of Heaven. The first is terrestrial: a place of abundant fertility and luxuriant vegetation, known as the "lower Gan Eden." Although, there is also a second oasis of perfection, which is envisioned as being celestial: a "higher Gan Eden," or the habitation of moral principle, where justified Jewish, and non-Jewish, immortal souls will gather together on the Day of Glory. Manifestly, the Rabbanim differentiate between *Gan Eden* and this more bounded material Eden: teaching that Adam dwelt purely in Eden, whereas Gan has never been witnessed by any mortal eye. What is more, according to serious Jewish scholars, the higher Gan Eden should correctly be called the "Garden of Righteousness." It was created, they say, since the beginning of the world, and will appear again at the end of time. Those dwelling therein will be "clothed with garments of light and eternal life, and eat of the tree of life" (Enoch 58,3) as co-habitants with God and His anointed ones. Thence, this Jewish rabbinical concept of a superior Gan Eden, largely unknown in our gentile sphere, is opposed by the words *gehinnom* and *sheol* -

figurative names for the abode of spiritual imperfection and forced purification for the wicked dead: places seen as being at the greatest possible distance from celestial liberation.

Unquestionably, the Biblical "garden of God," described most notably in the Book of Genesis (Genesis 2-3), and additionally mentioned, indirectly, by the Prophets Ezekiel, as well as Isaiah, is also found in Global Text as the Akkadian *edinnuz*: itself derived from a Sumerian appellation meaning "steppe" or "plain." Orientalists agreeing that after 500 BC, Persian uses of the term "paradise," usually meaning a royal garden or hunting-park, gradually became a synonym for Eden. Undoubtedly then, the word *pardes* occurs three times in the Old Testament, even though always in contexts other than a connection to an earthly spiritual haven. In the Song of Solomon iv. 13, for instance, we may read: "Thy plants are an orchard (*pardes*) of pomegranates, with pleasant fruits; camphor, with spikenard." In this, and accompanying Biblical examples, *pardes* manifestly means "orchard" or "park," even though in apocalyptic literature (and in the Talmud,) "paradise" gains its associations with Eden as a heavenly prototype for a physical encampment of the Blessed: often stylised after literary Hellenistic influences.

Awkwardly, the Sumerian concept of Dilmun, sometimes described as "the place where the sun rises" and "the Land of the Living," is the scene for some versions of their creation Myth, not to forget being the place where the semi-divine Sumerian hero of the flood, Utnapishtim (Ziusudra), was taken by the gods to live forever. Beyond debate, Thorkild Jacobsen's translation of the *Eridu Genesis* calls it "Mount Dilmun," which he locates as a "faraway, half-mythical place." In this respect, Dilmun is additionally described in the epic story of Enki and Ninhursag, as a site where the construction of our world transpired. The promise of Enki to Ninhursag, our Earth Mother, is narrated as: "The land of my lady's heart, I will create long waterways, rivers and canals, whereby water will flow to quench the thirst of all beings and bring abundance to all that lives." So, Ninlil, the Sumerian goddess of air and south wind had her home in Dilmun. Atop this, these territories are featured in the grand *Epic of Gilgamesh*.

But, in the earlier epic *Enmerkar and the Lord of Aratta,* the main sequence of events—which centre on Enmerkar's construction of the ziggurats in Uruk and Eridu—are outlined as happening in a place "before Dilmun had yet been settled."

In the case of Islam, the idea of Eden is linked to ethical and merciful themes from the start. In the Koran, Muslims read that the Prophet Adam, whose role is to be the Father of Mankind, is looked upon with continual reverence. Eve, for her part, as the "Mother of Mankind" receives honours unparalleled in the West. Unsurprisingly, therefore, the Garden of Eden is not seen as an entirely earthly place, but more like an archetypal Kingdom. As such, according to the Koran, both Adam and Eve ate the forbidden fruit in a *Heavenly* Eden. The result being that they were both sent down to Earth as God's representatives. Each antagonist dispatched in their turn to a mountain peak: Adam to al-Safa, and Eve to al-Marwah. Islamic tradition, furthermore, tells us that Adam wept 40 days until he repented, after which God sent down the Black Stone and taught him the Hajj. Moreover, according to the Hadith, believers are told Adam and Eve reunited in the plain of Arafat, near Mecca, soon afterwards having two sons, Qabil and Habil. This version of the narrative being more morally consistent with the notion of a merciful God, possibly, than the Old Testament's portrayal. Interestingly, Muslims argue original sin does not exist, due to the fact Adam and Eve were forgiven by God. Explaining, in its turn, why modern liberal movements inside Islam view God's command to His angels to bow down before this post-Edenic Adam, so to speak, as a spiritual exaltation of Humanity: offering in its wake a theological justification for supporting human rights. Others, that observed, understand this Koranic scene as a way to show Adam that the biggest enemy of humankind on earth will be discovered in their own egos.

We British, needless to say, have been heavily influenced by the Abrahamic Faiths for nearly two thousand years. Perhaps a lot longer, if the War poet and historical novelist Robert Graves (1895-1985) is correct in his researches that the Druids themselves debated the religious significance of the Hebrew Prophet Ezekiel's visions.

Either way, we have been imbued for untold centuries with forms of Christianity which seem to have deliberately forgotten how indebted they are to the Paagan world, especially Nordic priests, Gaelic storytellers, and Greek poets, for our understanding of the politically utopian. Indisputably, Celtic stories of the legendary Hy Brazil (a land that may be the Viking Atlantis), as well as Greek concepts surrounding tales about the health-giving golden apples growing in the Garden of the Hesperides, have all helped to mould Christian views of Eden; along with our necessary search for a superior way of conducting social affairs. All motivating us as an Island people to search for, explore, and learn lessons from these less rule-bound, legendary, and carefree lands. Theoretical places, furthermore, which were already in the minds and hearts of the translators of Biblical Hebrew and Christian Greek texts. Thusly, we indigenous folk wrote as we knew, idealised, and remembered. Our own poets and scholars sensing the correct complexion of these paradisial realms in the mode of a material, achievable, bliss!

This helps to explain why Libertarianism and Eden are perennial obsessions inside our English Folk-Soul. It may also elucidate why there appear to be two types of Englishmen: Travellers and Aboriginals – mirroring, potentially, an earlier division betwixt Actors and Onlookers. The former actively examining vistas surrounding the new and marvellous, whilst the latter are rarely brave enough to venture too far beyond the comfortable confines of their domestic compounds. Undoubtedly, in the world of English letters a number of formidable spirits, like Percy Bysche Shelley (1792–1822), Samuel Taylor Coleridge (1772–1834), and Sir Herbert Read (1893–1968), have unrepentantly sallied forth into previously uncharted Libertarian domains that, in ages past, had encouraged foreign Churchmen to audibly bemoan that the British are, by nature, Pagans: an assessment, by and large, verifiably correct if one interprets "Paganism", or "Quaganry" as a modus of Being, but not a counter-religion. On one level, truly, it is a personal attitude. On another, it is a praxis by which means a human being may engage with the Substance-of-Life Herself. Comments implying there may indeed be such a thing as National Libertarianism, since our British search for Eden can take place in the journeys of adventurers, or in the smaller, intrinsically meaningful, everyday battles to be free.

Generally speaking any search for Liberty and tranquil hush is golden. A sentiment, without irony, aligning The Four Seasons to Cunning folk in every age: to Quagan healers, wandering Minstrels, and shamanic therapists. Comparably, it associates these American singers with Seers like Swedenborg who would have immediately extended this keynote into matters of personal regeneration. At which point, coherent links between established mystical paths unexpectedly emerge—especially with regard to intuitive theologians such as Sabellius—himself the Father of Modalist thought, as well as a theological guide to me personally. Above argument, the life and work of this busy 3rd century priest reveal a number of esoteric methodologies whereby stillness is employed to achieve supernal clarity. Even though, in our era, when such a lustrous surcease is more vital than ever, few would deny the lack of suitable venues to attain this goal poses a problem. Sadly, experience shows plain candidates like public parks to be desperately overcrowded, besides libraries being predominately geared towards study. So, in a world actually transforming into a stage, the modest ministrations of our restrooms cannot be overvalued. At the end of the day, there are few other spaces allowing any type of immediate peace. All meaning that theology on the toilet is not as bizarre a claim as it may first appear. On the contrary, our conveniences offer a practical "understructure" from where we can rebalance ourselves, startlingly, while accessing deeper resources leading to a health-giving pause amid our daily grind.

SELECTED ENDNOTES

1. Eileen Caddy MBE (1917-2006) was a New Age author and spiritual teacher, best known as one of the founders of the Findhorn Ecovillage, near the village of Findhorn, Moray Firth.

2. The term "Quagan" is occasionally divorced from its Free Church origins and applied as a direct synonym of "Christopagan," whereas (a metaphysically sympathetic) Anglo-Catholicism refers to people, beliefs and practices within Anglicanism that emphasise their Catholic heritage and identity.

3. Swedenborg, Emmanuel. *The New Jerusalem*. Section, 252.

4. Swedenborg, Emmanuel. *The Doctrine of the New Jerusalem Concerning Life*, 1.

"Chasing angels or fleeing demons, go to the mountains."

-John Marsden

Problem VIII.
Some Ugly Poets

MY RUSSIAN COLLEAGUES KEEP ASKING ME IF I THINK Moscow is the third Rome. In all probability, I suspect that I do; or at least, it will be. Now, this opinion arose from a conversation I had many years ago with a remarkable Welsh Orthodox monk. His name was Father Barnabus. I met him on a long and enlightening journey from Bridgend in Wales back to Euston Station in London. To this day, I recall that, as I desperately fought my way to a dirty seat on the packed, irregular, service, I saw a man dressed in black robes who looked really interesting. Seizing the moment, therefore, I decided I would ask his permission to sit in the opposite seat. In response, he shook my hand and proceeded to talk about everything under the Celtic Sun: proving to be one of those amazing people having an opinion on every conceivable topic. Beginning with lessons in advanced Welsh pronunciation, he then moved to international affairs. "Was I aware," he asked, "that the Patriarchate of all the Russia's took an ever more belligerent view with non-Byzantines?" Also, he inquired as to whether "I was acquainted with the fact that Muscovite cosmopolitan culture had, at one time, been far ahead of its Western counterparts?" We then proceeded to discuss my obsession with Russian literature, which almost ran on a par with my love of our British letters; although Father Barnabus insisted halfway through our discussion, that he could go no further without a cup of tea and he would buy us both a hot, steaming, "mug" of the said milky liquid. To this day, I vividly remember him as my second teaching-guru: a veritable tour de force – recalling especially the last words he spoke to me were, "We may not meet again in this life." Recently, I heard from a very close friend that Father Barnabus died a year, or so, later. So, all I know from this happy encounter, for certain, is that in Nature's Golden Memory this good man will rest Eternal.

Following this chance meeting – if such things exist, I felt like one of the ugly poets of lore: a bedraggled gnome, or smoke-mantled dwarf, both overweight and cumbersome. Like one of those wandering folkish versifiers who prefer to keep on the move, while writing about their travels and trying to make sense of them all in occasional verses. Indeed, without the handsome face of a classical heroic statue, or the body of an Ancient Greek athlete, I was more like a bulbous grotesque incapable of emulating his political elders and professional betters. In a manner similar, perhaps, to Robert Byron (1905-1941) who wrote *The Road to Oxiana*. Overall, the most graphic travelogue of its period. Certainly, as an Oxbridge tearaway who loved Mount Athos, a confirmed "philhellene" and an art critic of considerable taste, not to mention something of an early authority on Byzantine history, this other Byron's penmanship still serves as a template for such freewheeling authorship.[1] Assuredly, there has always been a close association between travel writing and so-called "outdoor literature," as mastered by Henry David Thoreau's (1817-1862) in *Walden*, whilst in practice these genres have often overlapped due to their being no definite boundaries between them. Unsurprisingly, so observed, fictional travelogues make up a large proportion of this literature; tending to be why critics insist on distinguishing non-fictional from fictional works. A distinction proving notoriously problematic to conclusively ascertain. These are some of the reasons, this recollected, why travel literature is best understood as writing which aspires to classical literary value: its outpourings always veering towards much more than a simply record of the phenomenological experiences undergone by an author when journeying to a place for the pleasure of adventuring, or to expand the psyche with new peoples, experiences, and alternative cultures. With like notions in mind, the composition of even a basic literary travelogue may, sometimes, exhibit a noticeably coherent aesthetic, or narrative structure, beyond the logging of dates and events as found through an airport's online booking system, a ship's log, a personal itinerary, hotel reservations, or a meticulously detailed travel diary.

Qualified so, there are examples of poetry and novels allied to this genre climbing to the very pinnacles of literary excellence, as in Homer's *Odyssey*, as well as Joseph Conrad's (1857-1924) deeply disturbing African voyage *Heart of Darkness*. In addition, other works, though based on philosophical, or admittedly satirical journeying, like *Gulliver's Travels* by Jonathan Swift (1667-1745) or Voltaire's (1649-1778) *Candide*, along with Samuel Johnson's *The History of Rasselas, Prince of Abissinia* may clearly be counted as superlative literary interweaves of fact and pure imagination. The most famous story of this type being found in the writings of Marco Polo (1254-1324) which must be seen as one of the many "fictionalised" works of travel literature actually based on a factual journey. Arguably comparable, this noted, in our modern era, with Jack Kerouac's (1922-1959) *On the Road* and *The Dharma Bums*, wherein the story of Kerouac's physical travels across the United States, during the late 1940s and early 1950s in pursuit of spiritual beatitude (Beat) made such compelling reading for his generation that Kerouac repeatedly found himself on the bestseller list.

Milestones in World Literature all, even though in real terms each of these authors adapted the opulent style, fidgety psychology, deconstructive grammar and exploratory content, of an already rich, but arguably, pedestrian text-type. In eighteenth-century Britain, for example, almost every writer of renown was expected to make a contribution to travel literature as a genre. It had something to do with professional pride, as well as being a way to play to the gallery with respect to cultivated audiences. Thusly, Captain James Cook's (1728-1779) *Diaries* were marketed in an equivalent way to a modern bestseller; only to meet with adulatory reviews. In which case, it may come as a surprise to those outside of the industry that critically systematic studies of travel literature only emerged as a legitimate field of scholarly inquiry in the mid-1990s: developing its own journals, conferences, organisations, anthologies and monographs.[2] Previously to this, professional critics had tended to interpret travel writing as a variety of escapism, exoticism, or downright fantasy. All of which meant that foreign terrains, and their attendant societies, were described in overtly primitivist vocabularies: as a way to entertain, as well as sensually excite, general readers. Unquestionably, even in the otherwise sexually repressive Victorian era, a number of discourses on topographical and bodily difference, normally with a shockingly eroticised literary zest, assisted in the sanitisation and dissemination of their triumphalistic colonial mindset: gifting us moderns with inroads into the zeitgeist of their age. Nowadays, this recognised, the study of travel writing is encouraged through the lens of contemporary academic fashions; as in Foucauldian literary criticism. And in this respect, Edward Said's (1935-2003) book *Orientalism,* rightly or wrongly, has proved a landmark in postcolonial literary interpretation. Further, a burgeoning interdisciplinary preoccupation with present forms of globalisation, migration, and posited cultural diversity, expressed in other fields of literary study, most notably Comparative Literature, has enabled critics to take historical "snapshots" of the way our forebears ideologically envisaged distant domains.

This may be why the vital significance of travel writing, as an uneasy literary genre, only came to my attention following the woefully inadequate BBC bicentennial celebrations of Charles Darwin's (1809-1882) legacy as a Naturalist author: coverage making me realise the fabric of the Good has many weaves and that the glittering powers of the continuum enjoy a multiplicity of forms in their struggle against dark disorder. Once recognising this ageless truth, the impending critical crisis in literature implied by misused "word stratagem" techniques became all the more transparent. Literature, at the end of the day, like reportage, implies some sort of "agreement," or as Swedenborg would have called it, a "moulded form," concerning applied vocabularies. Unless this occurs, readers and viewers need to remain on their guard against academic solipsism, along with a militantly imposed secular disbelief in anything of worth and relevance. All meaning, the fundamental conditions for genuine "communication" cannot have been met. It is all well and good to talk of raising the abstract rungs of common-room debate to the highest possible position on the ladder, in a faculty lounge, yet the contextual quality (not just the analytical quantity) of our linguistic exchanges must remain paramount. Contended so, it would be remiss to forget that Darwin was a de facto travel writer who changed our view of the world: an oversight unworthy of real forgiveness.

Examined thus, Darwin the author, takes his rightful place among the greats of literature: an honoured position reminding readers of the status our literati are supposed to attain. Realised as such, we learn from innumerable biographies that following a rather chequered education, including an abortive attempt to study medicine, Darwin finally graduated at Cambridge in 1831 with a Bachelor of Arts Degree. An achievement seen, back then, as his first step to becoming a Minister of Religion. Soon afterwards, during the December of that same year, we read he began his five-year voyage on HMS Beagle, where his official post was "Ships Naturalist" on this Admiralty surveying vessel! It is well known, on top of this, his particular theory of Evolution emerged from the raw, pregnant, data, collected on this trip and was further stimulated by his reading of Thomas Robert Malthus' (1766-1834) essay, *On Population,* published in 1838. Having annotated this, the influence of his grandfather, Erasmus Darwin (1731-1802), who wrote a series of poetic discourses called *The Botanic Garden* comes into significant focus: legend having it that on Erasmus' desk there was an inscription saying, "everything from shells." This, along with his receipt in 1858 of virtually an abstract of his own corpus from Alfred Wallace (1832-1913), jolted Charles Darwin to apply himself with renewed vigour to complete his own Magnum Opus. As a matter of historical record, they jointly published *On the Origin of Species* in 1859: a text both eloquently structured and engagingly readable.

His basic argument, this ascertained, runs along the lines that every species of living thing is mutable. They come into existence, change, and more often than not, perish altogether. Darwin coupled this to the fact all living creatures increase at such a rate that the offspring of any single pair would eventually crowd the Earth, if their multiplication were to go unchecked. Still, the competitive effort of other creatures to survive, as well as reproduce in their own right, provides a natural balance within and beyond the species. With his additional observation that all creatures slightly vary in limb, organ and life function, a new radiance was shed on fundamental adaptive processes. This was due to Darwin's realisation that variations have a tendency to be passed on from generation to generation by natural inheritance. Taken together, these mercurial life functions provide the necessary conditions for biological selection, whereby unfavourable variations, along with their possessors, are slowly eliminated: thenceforth permitting new species to come into existence. As a point of information, Darwin hardly uses the word "evolution," which in its modern usage appears to have been popularised by George Fredrick Hegel (1770-1831). Possibly, Hegelian metaphysics aside, this is why Darwin held that the history of Humanity was largely explained by his theory. To illustrate this point, he even highlighted the interconnection of all organic things in the Great-Family-of-Life via hand drawn "tree of life" diagrams, whilst graphically documenting the ruthless urges that each and every creature had to ensure its own survival.

Unarguably, there is a position from which Darwin's theories must be seen against prevailing trends in British factual literature. Chiefly, the theoretical frames of native scholarship were built on Empiricist foundations. The French were quite rightly seen as Rationalists, while the Germans (maybe because of Hegel's monumental influence) were largely understood as Idealists. It was attested, moreover, that the most reliable source of human knowledge was experience itself. This is, undeniably, an epistemological argument possibly stretching back to Aristotle himself. Thenceforth, as a specifically British philosophical underpinning, Empiricism (as additionally honed through naturalistic and nominalistic precursors into a movement upholding "direct inspection" as the only trustworthy key to human cognition) arose. An idea sadly limited in our contemporary age, however, to the weighing and measuring of external objects. Above these factors, it is essential to recall that the Darwins, as a family, formed part of the "Intellectual Aristocracy," which, admittedly, transformed this country on a moral, academic, and financial basis: along with the Wedgwoods, the Tates, and the Huxleys etc. Sticking closely together, these families frequently intermarried in order to forge alliances between social progressivists, as well as emergent wealth. Without question, the Darwin-Wedgwood family line can boast of ten Fellows of the Royal Society, not including well-established poets and artists, among its ranks. Even the composer Ralph Vaughan Williams (1872-1958) was a distant Clan member. So recollected, the youthful Darwin was marginalised, at first, in favour of his more freethinking brother, another Erasmus (1804-1881); a man who was invited to became a Cambridge Apostle. By religion, all of this recollected, the Darwins were overwhelmingly Unitarian; especially Free-Church and Non-Conformist. Each theological position, curiously, reflecting their social status. With hindsight, at that stage in British history the educated middle classes were frequently considered dangerous, if not openly antagonistic, towards the traditional social order maintained by the land-owning gentry. Far from irrelevant then, the theology of the Darwins conflicted with the Anglican Church. An institution perceiving itself to be the defender of timeless social truths. Including, of course, a structural hierarchy stretching from the six-winged Cherubim, endlessly floating in an Infinite Sea of Subjective Fluorescence, down through the reigning Monarch, the House of Lords, their extremely trustworthy Yeomanry and eventually to the lowest cultural strata at the basic roots of British communal life!

So, there's the snag. Spiritually, Charles Darwin grew up amid the heady atmosphere of free-thinking libertarianism, unbounded authorship, creative experimentalism, and philosophically untrammelled colleagues: all of whom had a good grasp of ethics and a comparative understanding of inter-religious categories. This is easily exemplified by the fact that the Unitarian writer Harriet Martineau (1802-1876) welcomed Darwin's theory on the transmutation of species as a genuine advance in political understanding. Accompanied, as such praise would have been, by this rather elite subculture's support of radical scholarship; Hindu poetry, vegetarianism, Buddhist Sutras and even notions of a British Druidic revival – being topics of considerable fascination. Incontestably, Harriet's brother the great Unitarian preacher and theologist James Martineau (1805-1900), himself declared that ad hoc miracles did little to expound the Mystery of Mysteries from his very pulpit. Without too many surprises, therefore, some members of Darwin's social circle, such as Professor John Stevens Henslow (1796-1861), publicly spoke of a need to recover the natural religion of our antediluvian ancestors.

Undoubtedly, it would have been intriguing to see what Darwin thought of Mount Athos if he had been a visitor there. Although, no one should assume a negative reaction on his part. As a traveller, after all, captivated by the beauties of Nature, a probable pan-deist, and a young writer exploring human biological interactions with the created sphere, he may have come to speak of this blessed place with sentiments similar to Lord Byron. Understood so, and in terms of unexpected reactions towards the Holy Mount, endless seem the unusual celebrity guests of the Athonites; some of whom have astonishingly complex religious views as opposed to an innocent-minded Quaganry. One such Armenian patron was the esoterically inspired visitor George Ivanovich Gurdjieff (1866-1949), who makes it abundantly clear in his book *Meetings with Remarkable Men* that he was raised as an Orthodox Christian. Supporters and foes alike may also be astonished to read him remark: "I know the rituals of the Greek Church well," adding many years later, "and there, underlying the form and ceremony, there is real meaning." As a matter of record, Gurdjieff's first religious tutor was the seventy-year-old Dean Borsch, the highest spiritual authority of the region. Besides, it is well-known that as Borsch aged, he asked a young priest named Bogachevsky to tutor Gurdjieff and "confess him" every week. Consequently, for two years, Bogachevsky tutored the young Gurdjieff and then, when the priest was posted elsewhere, had Gurdjieff continue his confessions by mail. Regarding Bogachevsky's religious calibre, it is said that he later went to Mount Athos as a chaplain and a monk. Once there, weirdly, he renounced monastic life and journeyed to Jerusalem. According to Gurdjieff, in the long run, Father Bogachevsky joined an extant Essene Brotherhood and was sent to one of its secret monasteries in Egypt. Gurdjieff even stresses that this holy man was given the name Father Evlissi; later becoming a personal assistant to the abbot of its chief monastery! As a book which made a considerable impression on our British readership in its day, this curious, but compelling, story finds a finale when Gurdjieff tells his audience that the Essenes had preserved the original teaching of all Holy Jesus Christ himself, "unchanged" from generation to generation: inspiring some readers to travel to this domed city in order to search for these hidden adepts themselves.

Among other, better known, ugly poets travelling to the Holy Land in quest of the miraculous may be numbered the Magi, commonly referred to as the Three Kings, or Wise Men of the East. On Mount Athos, the Fathers will be quick to explicate Christian tradition, wherein a group of distinguished foreigners who visited Jesus shortly after his birth, bearing gifts of gold, frankincense and myrrh arrived at their intended, sanctifying, goal. In fact, within the Gospel of Matthew, the only one of the four Canonical Gospels to actually mention the Magi, they were the first religious figures to honour Jesus. The Gospel stating "they" came "from the east" to worship the Christ, "born King of the Jews." Still, upon close inspection, the account does not mention the number of people either "the Magi" or "they" refers to. European folklore respecting the three gifts having led to widespread assumptions that there were three men. Have it this way or that, in the East, the Magi were normally said to number twelve – in the manner of a travelling band. Additionally, their identification as kings in later European Christian writings is probably linked to Psalm 72:11, wherein we read, "May all kings fall down before him." In which case, the Magi were popularly referred to as monarchs.

In itself, interestingly, the word *magi* holds a number of conundrums. It is the plural of the Latin word *magus*, borrowed from the Greek *mágos* (μάγος), as used in the original Greek version of the Gospel. Equally, the Greek term *mágos* is itself derived from the Old Persian *magus*, whilst in its turn from the Avestan *magâunô*, i.e. the religious caste into which Zoroaster was born. Addressed differently, "pagan" priests, of the caste of Zoroaster, were the first people to attend the Nativity. Without contradiction, as an integral part of their religion, these priests would have paid detailed attention to the stars. Western historians even recorded them gaining an international reputation for astronomy and astrology both: dual aspects of a once highly regarded science.[3] These religious practices, along with a use of Astro-Theology, caused derivatives of the word *magi* to be applied to the occult overall. Developments eventually leading to the English word *magic*. Analysed so, in the King James Version the term "wise men" is translated in exactly the same way to describe the wise men led by Daniel of earlier Hebrew Scriptures (Daniel 2:48). Thusly, without inherent contradiction, the word may also be rendered as *sorcerer*, such as happens when giving narrative details of "Elymas the sorcerer" in Acts 13:6-11, or Simon Magus: a man considered as heretic by the early Church. Of course, the phrase "from the east," more literally from the rising (of the sun), is the only information St Matthew offers his readers about the region from which they came. Even though, historically, a collective opinion slowly emerged that they were Persians, Babylonians, or Jews from Yemen – because by this time it was more than possible that the kings of Yemen were also Jews: a view held by John Chrysostom (347-407). Armenian tradition, on the other hand, identifies individual "Bethlehem Magi" as Balthasar of Arabia, Melchior of Persia, and Gaspar of India, although the historian John of Hildesheim (1320-1375), re-tells a tradition from the ancient silk road fortification of Taxila that one of the Magi passed through this city on his way to Bethlehem.

As one of the most absorbing traveller's tales from antiquity, we are informed that the Magi found Jesus by "following" a star, which customarily became known as the Star of Bethlehem. Over the years, a huge variety of theories have been presented as to what this skyward phenomenon refers to, since stars do not visibly move and, therefore, cannot be followed. Some commentators, this acknowledged, have come to believe that the Magi pursued a planet, which, without a telescope could easily be mistaken for a star when it slowly moved across the sidereal sky. Yet, upon finding the Christ-Infant through the ministrations of this Star, we are equally told the Wise Men venerated the Son of God by presenting him with his three symbolic gifts. For which they were rewarded by Powers Celestial, through the medium of a dream, with the foreknowledge that Judean king Herod intended to kill everyone associated with this affair: thereby allowing the Magi to return home by a different route. Those inside of the Christian faith may not always realise how strangely all of this reads to the uninitiated. But this is rather the point. Many of those commenting on these stories have felt they were Arcane (or Essence) teaching tales. All meaning, without a fully trained mystagogue to unlock their mysteries, they cannot be forced to yield their secrets. Once fully recognised, hints for this type of interpretation are provided everywhere in-text, along with subliminal messages instructing readers that the greatest journeys are undertaken when a traveller wants to walk within his, or her, own soul.

Unwaveringly, according to courtiers surrounding Pope Gregory the Dialogist (540-604), the Saint frequently eulogised on this theme, commenting that "having come to know Jesus we are forbidden to return by the way we came." A remembrance helping to explain why there are so many traditional stories about the fate to the Magi after these events: one such narrative outlining to readers that, having taken different paths, the eldest King was baptised by St Thomas on his way to India. Another story describes how their collective remains were discovered by St Helena and subsequently brought to Constantinople: only to make their way to Germany and the Shrine of the Three Kings at Cologne Cathedral. A narrative prompting Sebastian Brock (born 1938), an historian of Christianity, to comment in this regard: "It was no doubt among converts from Zoroastrianism that ... certain legends were developed around the Magi of the Gospels." Anyway, Anders Hutgård suggestively concluded that the Gospel story of the Magi was enhanced by an Iranian legend concerning inspired Pagan priests and a star: connected—as this was—to proverbial Persian beliefs claiming the rise of a star predicted the birth of a ruler; along with myths describing the manifestation of a divine figure in fire and light. Such a model for the homage of the Magi might have coequally been provided, it has been mooted, by the journey to Rome of King Tiridates I of Armenia (accompanied by his incumbent magicians), to pay tribute to the Emperor Nero (37-68 AD). All of which took place in 66 AD, a few years before the date typically assigned to the composition of the Gospel in question. Paralleling these theories, the legendary Christian ruler of Central Asia, Prester John was reportedly a descendant of one of these Bethlehem Magi. So, for travel writing aficionados, all things considered, it is not as overwhelmingly of worth that the Magi frequently appear in European art inside scenes of perpetual adoration, as are their depictions of journeying: a popular topos especially in the Middle Ages. Either way, little mention is made of the fact that in Byzantine art, the Three Kings are pictured as Persians, wearing trousers, and crowned with Phrygian caps.

In these Britannic shores, wise men were normally seen as Druids, herbalists, or village healers. And as such, a picture survives on the Franks Casket elucidating our specifically native take on this event. Probably a non-Christian king's hoard-box (an early seventh-century whalebone carving), that had managed to survive Christian attacks on non-Christian art, this casket portrays a courtly scene with the Virgin and Christ facing the spectator, while the Bethlehem Magi devoutly approach from the (left) side. Seen so, the entire imagery is illustrative of scenarios from previous ages when Quagan priests, in mystic trance, foretold momentous events to guide their clan leaders through historical tribal changes! Somewhat instructively, instead of an angel, the casket depicts a (brilliantly) white swan, interpretable as the hero's fylgja (either a protective alter-ego, or shapeshifting spirit) overseeing these proceedings. All validating opinions arguing that among non-Christians, the story of the Magi had always been quite popular due to its theme of exhausted travellers enduring a long journey who were nevertheless still generous to a fault upon arrival.[4]

Art, of course, is bigger than all of us: which is why it is unwise to minimise the power of its plastics. A personal detection reinforced after re-watching the American 60 Minutes programme about Holy Athos and an instinctive compulsion pushing me to voice my conjectures regardless of professional parameters! So, slightly distressed, I caught one of the American Fathers, Maximus, who had formerly been a Professor at the Harvard Divinity School, claiming that nothing on Athos could be described as "Art," even though the camera crew were openly "stunned by the magnificence" surrounding them. Hearing this, from the good Father, I felt immensely disappointed, once again, at dismissive clerical attitudes towards the workings of the Beautiful on human souls. To be honest, I had hoped for a much more enlightened attitude by the Orthodox Community in general concerning the transformative effect of Art on our Human Condition. Above this, these clearly counter-intuitive claims ended up by enfeebling conversation between both parties and eventually producing ridiculous statements from the journalist conducting these interviews – who found himself reduced to commenting "whatever you call it, it is priceless." Forgiven in part, because of the power behind his assertion, Father Maximus nonetheless reminded me of the age-old interrelationship betwixt literature and the plastic arts: a reciprocity demanding a brief textual detour.

Undoubtedly, this bewildering clash started to confirm a chain of suspicions within me. Theories concerning the character of the Beautiful in Art, or in Art and Nature, appear, thus derived, to find their origin in the Greek word *aisthesis*, which may best be understood as "sensation." As such, during the course of the centuries, this term has come to designate those elements of our experience wherein the highly implicative lexical phrase "full of Beauty" seems pregnant with heavenly possibilities. They are literally occasions when the aesthetic sense uplifts and elevates our consciousness. This may additionally be why Arthur Schopenhauer (1778-1860) attests these moments arise from an appreciation of ideas apart from their particularity, by a knower who has been elated beyond the circumstances of his, or her, specific existence. In alternate words, someone recognises the

Numinous in a manner leading to possible moral reintegration. So, the fact Mount Athos has the largest collection of Christian Art in the world takes on different, transfigurative, implications. Pilgrims, scholars, visitors, priests, as well as friends, are invited to participate in a mystery – rather than an academic issue begging exegesis. They are asked to embrace a less scientifically candid, but infinitely richer sense of creative-value in their lives through the ministration of beautiful words, places, objects and people.

To sketch my point a little further, these powerful influences, after all, have come to hint at a suppressed cultural undercurrent in European affairs. In travel literature, for example, cultural pundits like Philip Sherrard (1922-1995), have written about the enduring religious impact of ethnicity, local geologies associated with ideational landscapes, dominant colours, traditional architecture, latent imagery, customary dress, and our sense of communal identity. Arguments touching on essential intuitions within each individual soul and their respective communities: regarding regional politics, agricultural resources, and the encultured interests of self-identified groups. A concept moreover, which may coequally be understood in terms of gender, nationality, history, or any other loosely correlated, yet avowedly fundamental, category. Unreservedly, reading between Sherrard's lines, even minimal group bonds retain visceral importance. In which case, Identity Politics is always just beneath the surface of cultural discourse, and not merely the type of narrative found among postcolonial activists, class warriors, or feminist, gay, and lesbian pressure groups. Exhorted so, by Sherrard himself, his subtly insightful work deserves much closer attention than it has previously received: especially because he was a pioneer of Modern Greek studies in England, along with its subsequent implications for our own indigenous British culture. Particularly believing, as Sherrard did, that "post-Byzantine" life and society in Greece is still organically (if not essentially) related to the spiritual tradition of the Eastern Orthodox Church.

Far from being tangential, or marginal, whole Civilisations, as well as many small-scale artistic and cultural movements within a given Civilisation, have articulated an identity politics of this sort. In recent decades, when Islam started to present itself as a superior alternative to Western Society, this has clearly been in evidence: whilst in reduced measure, the punk subcultures and skinhead gangs within our society appear to have been reactive protests against the secular homogenisation increasingly demanded by dominant "liberal" ideologies. On one level, it is meta-expression among elites of an overall, already existent, Identity: through international seminars, political initiatives, and diplomatic missions. And assuredly, these expressions also find their localised counterpart via film festivals, musical concerts, and dramatised performance. Unswervingly then, ugly wandering poets publishing in English (even though this may not be their native tongue) along with artists from across every part of the United Kingdom, who continually struggle with the universality of their medium, remain transparently energised by the spiritual atmosphere produced in their own indigenous tradition. In additional, across the Continent of Europe this phenomenon equally holds true, because national limits imply meaning: Orthodoxy and the Holy Mount offering a powerful Byzantine frame of aesthetic reference. All betokening that even a cursory list of contributors to this restorative endeavour must number unlikely giants, such as C. P. Cavafy (1863-1933) and Odysseas Elytis (1911-1996) among their ranks! The former penning *A Byzantine Nobleman in Exile Composing Verses* within which we may read:

> The frivolous can call me frivolous.
> I've always taken important things
> Extremely seriously. And I insist that no one knows
> The Holy Fathers, or the Scriptures, or the canons of the Councils
> Better than I do.

Or in a related manner, when Elytis eulogises beatified Quagan attitudes to life in his remarkable *The Axion Esti*: a masterpiece that takes his readers through a "Genesis," "Passion" and "Gloria" as a means to raise mundane awareness into a state of adoration – like the Three Kings of Holy Scripture. As the poet says:

Praised be the cloud on the grass
The swoosh of a lizard on a wet ankle
Mnisareti's deep gaze
Not the lambs yet granting forgiveness
The bell's gold-evoking wind
The rider westbound to his ascension
And that other unseen rider heading
To impale the coming hour of decay

Undeniably, even a superficial reading of these verses testifies to a "remoulded" Byzantine influence on each of the poets, whereas a closer analysis uncovers the presence of a carefully crafted, albeit inherited, form-structure. Perfectly positioning, as this does, an antique, idea-rich, content of subversive relevance in our age! But the real surprise is to find each of these poets contending that once human beings capture this sense of undiminished Beauty in themselves, and in creation generally, then—if so willed—they may recover a full disposition towards harmony within the Self, with others, and with the environment overall: a textual inheritance and aesthetic technique demonstrably stemming from tropism in late Byzantine Orthodox literature.

Extending this theme, Marc Franz (1880-1916) the extremely gifted German painter, occasional printmaker, and sculptor, was said to be "shocked" by his visit to Mount Athos. Through painting, Franz had already started to overcome his personal feeling of spiritual malaise and uncover the subtle mystical forces animating Nature. Still, as his ideas about the Beautiful developed, some critics spoke of an unacknowledged debt to Athonite tradition. Without doubt, his increasingly symbolic use of colour accompanied by simplified non-naturalistic and "rhythmic" shapes, were intended to literally conjure the metaphysical; a creative obsession driving Franz to explore the sphere of Great Nature with fresh, uplifted, eyes. Following one of his habitual outbursts, Franz is quoted as saying, "The ungodly human beings who surrounded me did not arouse my true emotions, whereas the inherent feel for life in animals made all that was good in me come out." Perhaps, as some of his admirers whispered, Franz found his adoration for the glory of Creation impossible to escape. In any case, art historians have never managed to unearth images of the divine within humanity painted by a man more or less openly applying Orthodox conventions to his canvas.

A further indicative example of a man "unconsciously" striving for salvific tradition is to be found in the fascinating figure of Sergei Symeonovich Sakharov (1896-1993), although he seems to have abandoned the practical side of his art just prior to ordination. As a thinker whose works are beginning to have an influence on our British audience, it is interesting to note that as a child, Sakharov would pray for hours each day, recalling that he experienced the *Uncreated Light* when a boy. Atop this, it is common knowledge that Sakharov read widely as a youth; searching through novels by the Russian Greats for answers to his Quagan questions. Known to be extremely talented himself, Sakharov studied at the Academy of Arts between 1915 and 1917, and then at the Moscow School of Painting, Sculpture and Architecture between 1920 and 1921. Observably, Sakharov always contended that he used Art as a "quasi-mystical" means "to discover eternal Beauty," going on to claim he saw creativity "breaking through present reality ... into new horizons of Being." Eventually, however, he felt the profane world sank to its knees before the problem of death, whilst individual frustrations at the perceived inability of modern art to express purity, led him to abandon these pursuits. In the end, Sakharov took his rightful place on Mount Athos as Archimandrite Sophrony, leaving pundits to postulate on the potential artistic marvels a man like this would have produced, if he had continued to be artistically creative inside an Orthodox monastery.

My preference, it must be mentioned, is to comment on the British Arts scene. It goes without saying, I feel a greater critical familiarity with indigenous members of my own Artistic Community. So stated, Sir John Kenneth Tavener (born 1944)—not to be confused with his namesake from previous periods—offers the best example of my emergent thesis: that there has been a continuous Orthodox cultural undercurrent in British society for hundreds of years. Hence, as a native composer known for his religious "minimalist" works, such as

The Whale, and *Funeral Ikos*, Tavener nonetheless joined the Russian Orthodox Church in 1977 – intuiting that Orthodox theology and Orthodox liturgical traditions were already creative influences on his output. Beyond debate, his explorations of Russian and Greek culture, as shown in Akhmatova's *Requiem* and *Sixteen Haiku of Seferis* boldly reveal far earlier inspirations. What is more, works like the *Akathist of Thanksgiving* (1987, written in celebration of the millennium of the Russian Orthodox Church); *The Protecting Veil* (first performed by cellist Steven Isserlis and the London Symphony Orchestra at the 1989 Proms); and *Song for Athene* (1993, performed at the funeral of Diana), *Princess of Wales* (1997) all evolve unrepentantly Orthodox themes. Flowering, some would suggest, in the composition *Eternity's Sunrise* after Princess Diana's death. Now, it has been alleged in the British press, that Tavener left Orthodox Christianity to explore a number of other religious paths. Hinduism and Islam have been mentioned in this respect, as well as influences from the writings of the mystical philosopher Frithjof Schuon (1907-1998). Yet, from his side, Tavener apparently remains stalwartly Orthodox: arguing that its elative effect in the Arts remains without compare. For him, Orthodox Art is unrepentantly traditionalist in both an individual's sacred journeying and a collective call to deeper mysteries beyond time. It is a revelation of the ever-thrilling Absolute in our overly mobile lives: through poetry, paint, music, performance and metal.

Tartishly perhaps, at the end of the evening, I tend to agree with Father Maximus when he remarks that Mount Athos is neither a library, or a museum, nor an Art gallery! Said differently, it is not a riddle needing resolution, a place to be entertained, or just an UNESCO World Heritage Centre to be visited. Instead, the Holy Mountain is a place where radical encounters with the Beautiful oppose existential drudgery by offering genuine glimpses of the Divine. An aesthetic possibility encouraged and sustained in radically traditional Arts, even though rarely realised in the random experiments of contemporary craftsmanship. So contended, the influence of Mount Athos in the Arts is sensually-elative. Perpetually fuelled, as this is, by the continuing splendour of Orthodox

Culture! And as such, European Society can do little apart from benefit when this spiritual opulence is taken beyond the monastery walls, or attained within them: a realisation made by some of the Fathers themselves and one of the reasons that Jade Music/Milan Entertainment Inc. released the album *Hymns of Mount Athos* sung by a Choir of Monks from the Monastery of Simonos Petra: a recording that proves the enduring adaptability of the Orthodox view.

In this respect Johan Wolfgang von Goethe (1749-1832) similarly talks of Beauty as a path to the Absolute. Undeniably, as one of the last organic intellectuals in our Society, he remains convinced that Beauty sets us free. Concurred so, and as a man of nothing but goodwill towards Holy Athos, the most intriguing observation, arguably, made by the *60 Minutes* film crew nearly slips past inattentive audiences. Watching carefully, the American reporter attending early morning liturgical prayer, comments that there were "flashes of ecstasy" in the monks: a secular admission that Holy Athos is not so much a fun place to visit, but rather the first vital step on a journey leading to destinations which demand spiritual reverence upon arrival. Spirit, at the end of the day, must dominate matter. Our human spirit! This is the very reason that every successful act of surgery, each newly discovered fact and all the voyages of Island adventurers manage to demonstrate the potential divinity of our human race: an Orthodox postulate claiming we will be born again into the light of our better selves, once we have taken initial, tentative steps, into their secret majesty. The only drawback being that this previously unsuspected common ground with Humanists obscures everyday evidence demonstrating they are normally "inhuman" in their view of worldly conditions! Usually, they choose to sanitise, disturbingly reduce, and then arbitrarily legislate about the rights and wrongs of traditional belief as it suits them.

By contrast, Orthodoxy's pragmatic viewpoint tended to settle well with our British attitude towards life until recent times. Beforehand, perhaps, we really were intent on the preservation of spiritual freedom as a good in its own right: a passionate belief motivating us to continually explore this Earth and to locate a new and better Britannia: be it physical, psychological, or magical. Like children, we listened to the first account of such a fantastic country in the *Chronicon Universale Anonymi Laudunensis*. Written, so scholars tell us, by an English monk at the Premonstratensian monastery in Laon, Picardy; its pages said to cover the history of the world until 1219! Indeed, surviving in two thirteenth-century manuscripts, (one in the *Bibliothèque nationale de France*, Paris, and the other in the *Staatsbibliothek*, Berlin) the *Chronicon* is a rare literary treasure even by contemporary standards. Hardly unique, however, because there is a second text known as the *Játvarðar Saga* (*Saga Játvarðar konungs hins helga*): an Icelandic tale about the life of Edward the Confessor, King of England (1042-1066) quilled along similar lines. Now, this latter volume – compiled in the fourteenth century, in Iceland itself, probably using the *Chronicon Universale Anonymi Laudunensis* (or a common ancestor) as its source, easily rivals the former. Cleverly, therefore, the *Játvarðar Saga* relates that when English rebels, fighting against William the Conqueror (1028-1087), became sure that the Danish king Sveinn Ástríðarson would not help them any further, they agreed to leave England for Constantinople (*Miklagarðr*): all of which is possible with regard to factual history. In addition, readers are told that this English force consisted of about 350 ships, a "great host" and "three earls and eight barons," all led by one "Siward Earl of Gloucester" (*Sigurðr jarl af Glocestr*). So constituted, they sailed past Pointe Saint-Mathieu (*Matheus-nes*), Galicia (*Galizuland*), through the Straits of Gibraltar (*Nörvasundz*) to Ceuta (*Septem*). Once there, they captured Ceuta, killed its Muslim defenders, and plundered its gold and silver. After Ceuta, they seized Majorca and Minorca, before embarking for Sicily, where they heard that Constantinople was itself being besieged. Beyond that stage of the account, details of any "New England" discovered on their journey became impossible to realistically verify. Ultimately, the sources in question are late, whilst many of the elements are, in the words of one historian, "unreasonable." Anyhow, all that can be attested is, in geographical terms, our other homeland seems to rest somewhere over the rainbow.

Commonly neglected, this literature of fabulous journeys and incredible lands brings to our table a wholly different set of literary issues. Markedly so, once we realise we have returned to that place where there are hard and fast divisions between travellers and aboriginals. Only this time, such demarcations are much more difficult to draw. This is because locations of these types are couched in the vocabulary of creative possibility more than a merely physical journey. After all, it is the storytelling of Celestial Mechanics and infinitely parallel worlds. So, with this in mind, I would like to describe a pathworking to Mount Athos I myself undertook many years ago when I first started to delve into the mysteries of ancestry. Please don't misunderstand my intentions. I am not saying such contemplative practices are merely probabilistic invention, but that the imagination has potentials barely glimpsed at present; whether it is a form of play or not. A psychological truth, moreover, garnered when I encountered the Image of Hiram Abiff as in a dream: like an unexpected gauntlet thrown down by the energies of the Collective Unconsciousness. Weirdly, this happened a few hours before I was going to swear a Quagan pledge. All I recall for certain is that I found my route barred by this living Freemasonry archetype. He stood in front of me, an elderly, tall, and lightly bearded man blocking my way forward. Inexplicably, I instantly knew who he was, whilst the vision was extremely clear in its choreographed message – this far and no further along such a path. Astonishingly, his figure was so detailed that I noticed he wore a classical Egyptian headcover of white cloth, covered with silver stars, whereas his thin body was adorned in the blackest of robes. Anyone who understands the initiatory process must immediately recognise this kind of iconic encounter, as well as its terrifying significance. During the third initiation, as usually explained, a candidate must force his, or her, way beyond their judge. Fortunately, I was already aware of this and, a few days later, I took the Oath regardless. Nevertheless, I remained fully aware this kind of experience did not contradict my unquestioning devotion to the Eternal Spirits of Mount Athos. In fact, I felt vindicated in my efforts, since they are the true architects of Space, Time and Causation. They themselves are the secret eyes of the Holiest Triangle.

In myself, I felt this inner quest went further. Now, I was free to witness scenes of our earthly Paradise and arrive on the slopes of an inner Athos recognisable to Swedenborg: either that, or undeservedly discover cataclysmic horrors similar to inaccessible polar-regions at a magnitude quite unbearable to even "Viking Man." Undoubtedly, the terrors of these chilling lands will always be outside of physical endurance; taking place between blood-curdling temperatures that none but the strongest can survive: and inhabited, as they are, by openly crushed creatures next to blinded by the incessant storm of colossal hurricanes and surreal terraqueous distortions! All life, at this height and depth, seemingly frozen! Somehow alive, yet frigid to the core, while retaining (to their own detriment), an expression of feature that these conditions have engraved on their bodies! Conversely, this understood, I knew that once beyond the self-contempt imposed by liberal modernity, and cleansed by the blue baptismal seas surrounding this hallowed peninsula, I would step ashore onto the sentient marbles, which paved my way into the perfumed Garden of Heaven's Queen. Warmed and uniformly welcomed by the Fathers, the dazzling radiance of domed Russian monasteries – along with their silvered perfections, amid rapturous song, awaiting us all at this blessed Mountains' peak continually beckoning. Maybe one day, as a self-confessed ugly poet, I will try to write this psychodynamic travelogue in greater depth – who can tell?

SELECTED ENDNOTES

1. As an acquaintance from early days, Evelyn Waugh noted Byron's native adventurism. In 1928 he wrote in a letter to Henry Yorke "I hear Robert has beaten us all by going to India in an aeroplane which is the sort of success which I call tangible."

2. The first international travel writing conference, "Snapshots from Abroad," organised by Donald Ross at the University of Minnesota in 1997, attracted over one hundred scholars and led to the foundation of the International Society for Travel Writing.

3. For a closer examination of Astro-Theology see Appendix III.

4. More generally they appear in popular Nativity scenes and other Christmas decorations that have their origins in the Neapolitan variety of the Italian presepio or Nativity crèche.

"It's impossible to fall on mountains you fool!"

- Jack Kerouac

An Optimistic Epilogue

YEARS BACK YONDER, FOLLOWING MY INITIAL READING OF Swedenborg's *Arcana Celestia* I decided to climb atop the literature of Holy Athos. To ascend this creative hillock of poetry, prose and indirect theatrical works – as a transformative site of the scared in British Letters. At which point, my enthusiasm discovered I was far from alone in undertaking such a challenge. Indeed, once was a time when an equally equipped scrambler, Søren Kierkegaard, had similarly scaled the slopes of Hegelianism, since he felt that an honest consideration of simple and obvious fact brought speculation back to spiritual truth. This is why he compared Hegel's philosophy to a steeply situated palace, adding that humankind was expected to live in the Porters Lodge outside of this stately (intellectual) residence. Anyway, I surmise Kierkegaard felt stimulated by this expedition into abstract altitudes. Likewise, speaking personally, the Norwegian playwright Ibsen has proved to be the natural theatrical heir to our own, beloved, Shakespeare, by scampering (Alpine style) across the presumptions of stagecraft, in order to demonstrate that contemporary audiences need cultural immediacy to grasp religious issues. As such, it is fascinating to observe that Ibsen's piercing thespianism regarding "what one is doing now" is readily understandable. Moreover, his intuited grasp of "what one is going to do in the future" is coequally comprehensible, even though, by definition, less certain.

Correspondingly then, any discussion concerning the future presence of Mount Athos in English arts must be tentative as well as individual. What else could it be? Upon critical inspection, after all, this captivating image of the sacred has already been seen as either an uncomfortable reminder of our ancestral Orthodoxy, a danger to piety, a pleasant place to visit while travelling through Greece, an escape from the grinding demands of the Capitalist world order, an immortal witness to human folly, a treasure-trove of ageless lore, a unique cultural force, and even a lens through which we can glimpse Eternity: all views handling a number of pertinent cultural aspects of the Beauteous Peninsula, whilst still falling short of its real enigma. Hence, it took a military man to ascertain the essence of the problem. Accordingly, for Sir Patrick Leigh Fermor, the impact of Mount Athos on the world of British creatives is discernible in its ageless lesson of vigorous endurance. As this man of action reminds us, it is a blessed symbol of unchanging, but Radical Tradition. Neither a half-forgotten hostel for the socially inept, nor a meaningless aesthetic meme belonging to previous Byzantine glories, Mount Athos is a highly charged metaphysical engine. Lastly it is, as Paddy redolently states, one of the principle spiritual tutors of a continuous European identity.

Geopolitical attestations, I should nevertheless confess, usually leave me in a state of deep ethical paralysis. Frankly, if the truth be known, we all embody a number of identities. In myself, I confess to being staunchly British, as well as proudly European. By the same token, Tradition (literary or otherwise), may be seen from a huge number of differing perspectives. As occasioning remembrance on the joys and sorrows of previous ages, or as a stabilising force strengthening us to embrace futurity. Keeping this in mind, Anglo-Saxon festivals have always enchanted me: especially during times of Harvest and Repose. Furthermore, whatever epithets we use to signify these ancient, hallowed, celebrations, a fair percentage of our indigenous customs were undoubtedly born from Orthodoxy, along with that intriguing Quagan faith characteristic of these shores. Long ago, such celebrations marked the key dates of that communal year; the day when planting crops began, or farm animals were herded, or when winter foods were carefully stored. As Islanders, we were additionally mindful of Life days, like the Spring Equinox, and Death days like the Winter Solstice, when we honoured the struggles of our forebears. To boot, it is no accident that we pay our respects to the soldiers of two World Wars around the time of All Souls Day or Halloween. This in itself exemplifying a profound awareness on the part of the early Church that seasonal rites proved impossible to purge. Such authorities could mould or distort them, but to defy these living connections betwixt human communities and our sentient continuum courted disaster. An obvious irony, some said, considering that so many Christian rituals had their origin in Hebraic celebrations of the very same events. Nevertheless, as post-conquest Church institutions gained in political power, they did their best to cut people off from their Quagan cultural heritage: a process ending up with a puritanical suspicion of the festive calendar altogether, and an explanation for the increasingly dark connotations nowadays given to festivals like Halloween. But, we Britons are by nature Quagan. This is why we have always found it easy to enjoy the stuff of life with our songs, our drinking lifestyle, our folk-rituals and our dances. Rather, like the Orthodox, we have continually felt Nature Spirits to be both Immanent, as well as Transcendent, in our acts of Worship. After all, these ceremonial affirmations of Identity and Meaning assisted participants to assert their place in the spirals of Creation; blessed circles wherein human beings discover their relationship with starlight, blood, bone and air.

Please do not misunderstand my literary purpose. I have nothing against the largely plastic trivialities surrounding modern day Halloween parties. Come Jack-o-lantern, or green-faced Witch, we all need to adapt to changing cultural circumstances. Even Americanisations like the vaguely annoying "trick or treat" games played by children in their neighbours need to be encouraged as ways to let off some "communal steam." At the evening's end, there has never been anything wrong with high spirits, or those intermittently visceral activities, which prepare younger generations for the inevitable knocks they will experience in life. All I am saying is that we mustn't forget our native British traditions. Tied, as they are, to the endlessly wheeling seasons! Undeniably, this recalled, Anglo-

Saxon spirit lore is still preserved in our inherited social activities. All meaning, conker fights, raging autumnal bonfires, and Bramley-apple bobbing, have a history that stretches back into the long nights of native antiquity. On a slightly more serious note, it was whispered that particularly at this time of year the spirits foretold someone's death through small, yet noticeable, interruptions in domestic patterns. The cries and movements of a startled bird, flowers blooming out of season, any clock striking thirteen times, or pictures suddenly falling from a wall—even the persistent appearance in ironed linen of the diamond-shaped crease known as a "coffin"—have all been cited as death omens. It was also a British custom to tell local rooks of an ageing landowner's death. A courtesy paid to birds associated with Woden by new proprietors standing under a canopy of trees to give this sombre news to the assembled birds, whilst adding a promise that only "he" and his "friends" would be allowed to hunt fowl in the future. Local pundits even claimed that if this ceremony were to be neglected, village Rookeries would be abandoned; a sure sign of communal misfortune. Synonymously, the lore surrounding rooks and ravens is surprisingly rich. If rooks flew away from their nests for no reason, it forecast the loss of land and the downfall of a Noble Family through poverty. Such sympathies, shared between men and other living creatures demonstrating the interconnection between all things in the Orlog.

More disturbingly, autumnal events like the startling appearance of corpse candles were held to be infallible warnings of death sent by our spirit ancestors. Indeed, these lights are lambent flames, which are frequently seen to float over the ground between a Parish Churchyard and the home of the doomed person. This is because their path indicated the route that the funeral procession was most likely to take – or so it was hinted. Now, if the spirits were foretelling the death of a child, the flame would burn blue in colour; in the case of an adult, its flame would be yellow. What is more, the body of a deceased Kinsman usually needed to be examined for the signs and portents of future fatal incidents. Therefore, the mature matrons of a British village would frequently say that if rigour mortis was atypically slow to set in, then the spirits were announcing another death in the same household before too long. On top of this, keeping a corpse in the family house through an entire Sunday, or leaving a grave open during the Sun's golden midday, provoked protective spirits into giving extra indications of impending violent death. Thus, the annual Armistice Evening in November—a modern survival of the ancient Wodenist Einheriar or Heroes Day—commemorates those brave warriors who have given their lives in the service of our nation through relighting the flame of valour. It is, however, a double-edged act of remembrance in that our communities attempt to welcome the shades of the departed back home, at the same time as being an expression of our guilt. In previous centuries, it was argued that only Great Souls found the level of individuation necessary to be received into Valhalla's High, whereas those who had never fought in Holy Battles (demanded by Quagan struggle) went to the gloomy realm of the faceless goddess Hel. That is why her "piebald" character was described by the poets as both black, like our fertile Earth-Mother, whilst, simultaneously, unsettlingly pale in her corpse-like complexion. Adding a reason why Saxon Sages taught that the hard-won wisdom gathered over centuries of strife showed us an ever pregnant end to every season.

In a similar manner, Harvest, the Saxon *hlaf-mas* or loaf-mass (known nowadays to some Quagans as Lammas-tide), was the culmination to our English festival of fruits, or in other words, that occasion on which the first corn was ground and made into loaves. This ritual marked the end of the ripening season, lasting from May until October. In addition, this communal rite saw Corn Dollies woven into arcane shape and distributed as gifts, inspiring some folklorists to comment that rural celebrations of Harvest Home were seen as a mixed blessing. Unquestionably, none of the reapers wished to cut down the last sheaf of corn for a variety of reasons. Consequently, they threw their sickles at the last stand of corn in an attempt to decide who would get this solemn duty. The sheaf was then plaited into a female form and given a place of honour at the subsequent supper. This reflected, Quagans don't believe in

Conclusion. Unlike the desert religions of Christianity, Judaism or Islam, our dogmas proclaim Process: a veritable metempsychosis of possibilities. Also, as seekers after Continuity, Quagans embrace every level of existence in all of its complexity and dynamism. Our view is that Spirits are archetypal forces in the starry continuum; powers within which every other environmental process operates. Energies creating, one might state, the basic structures of the Cosmos. Call them Quintessence, thenceforth, or by whatever name you will, their strength is their Presence. As such, they are the Identities who govern a magical "Becoming" rather than a merely static "Being." They are the Divine Causes, after all, as well as the Holy Effects of all things. To an extent, this is seen in our forefather's attitude to fertility and sex, along with the acts of fleshly Worship our kinsfolk practised. Ergo, we Quagans still stress the bipolar or experimental: the actualisation of every potential. To illustrate this point, our allies only need is examine ancestral attitudes to British soil as a substance to nurture and venerate; it was the conscious embodiment of all edible things, as well as being the final resting place of all material objects.

Beyond question, Harvest is a time of abundance and celebration, not an occasion for malicious tricks, or drunken aggression. Across the globe, similar seasonal festivals have marked the repose of the previous cycle, along with a charged expectancy for the next. This is one of the ways we all find a sense of orientation in our lives. Above doubt, in Europe, the latter Church has done its damnedest to accentuate the ambiguous side of these celebrations and highlight the uncertainties, which accompany the start of any rebirth. Adopting this plan of ideological attack, they have steadily assaulted our righteous gratitude to the Nature Spirits by turning children's minds to mischief and more mature folk to simple abandon. But, as Quagans, it is our duty to oppose these dislocations in our ageless tradition and dance to the rhythms of a resurrected tune. In this, we feel nothing but brotherhood towards the Athonites and their resolute stand against the false ephemera of an enforced Global Society. Proclaimed so, history is once again turning in favour of a healthy Tradition, finally understood as the steady basis of all cultural adaptation.

Admittedly, far too many British Quagans as well as their Orthodox brothers and sisters, appear unconcerned about what is going to happen in the future. Nostalgia is our mutual problem. This is sadly pellucid in our overly wistful tracts, leaflets, and books, with either an openly romantic religious gloss, or a longing for better times in the past. For all that, following the acuity of Swedenborg, it is nearly beyond belief that our religious Ministers waste so much of their valuable time addressing the clod-like assertions of an obviously career-based scepticism, when spirits are now openly at war around us. Unrepentantly, some members of the younger generation have sensed that a call-to-arms has been sounded. They seem to perceive dark, destructive forces remaining dangerously unchallenged in our society and, quite justifiably, are starting to accuse their more mature neighbours of a bewildering spiritual narcolepsy. Many of them even feel that these devious shades are threatening the fecund environment; gathering a hellish, technocratic, momentum, against our Mother the Earth. All of which makes it truly astonishing that— as twin movements—we have done so little to support their spiritual concerns. Perhaps especially so, once we remember how few other Churches uphold the Sanctity-of-Life on any level as intrinsically worthy of respect! In fairness, a number of factors hide these mighty battles from general view: most notably the fact that their outward form is usually disguised by pious political hyperbole and marketing misinformation. Moreover, militant commerce has an uncanny way of silencing spiritual reflection, along with the moral implications of industrial procedures. So sensed, contemporary Youth is again proving far ahead of their strangely disconnected elders, because they remain alert to the observation that nothing is religiously neutral in an age where complex agricultural techniques, coupled to ethical complacency, are effectively manufacturing a brand new branch of the Black Arts. Arguably then, from the legendary Dr Faustus, to the fictional Victor Frankenstein, the same charge against modernity has echoed across the centuries. A warning continually voiced by the Athonites and recalled in Francois Rabelais' (1494-1553) famous saying that "science without a conscience is the ruin of the soul." This coequally explains why some reviewers can't help feeling the ingenious Pythagorean himself would have been shocked at the depths to which people sink when science becomes a slave to corporate business ventures. And indicative, some may add, of why Monsanto's representations to the media always seem to have a Faustian atmosphere about them. Time and again, the smell of sulphur seems to choke their official pronouncements: at least to my mind. Hence, it is unwise to ignore these historic meditations as "simply" subjective, whilst such a company openly wages a campaign to genetically modify our very food with apparently minimal public consent. So much for contemporary liberal politics!

Unfortunately, vulnerable Third World countries appear to be the ecological "No Man's Land" betwixt sustainable progress and veritable demonic, global, manipulations; an example being easily discerned when appraising Monsanto's "Terminator" technology. Asking, of course, why any decent-minded company would patent the genetic engineering of otherwise healthy plants to produce sterile seeds is unsettling enough. But the projection that this plan, if implemented, would reduce African and Indian farmers to a kind of credit dependency (whereby they are obliged to buy replacement seeds every year, rather than use existing stocks), is undeniably sinister. Without doubt, those that unclean spirits would destroy, first they make servile. In addition to this death-dealing research, commentators have pointed out that future environmental effects of genetically modified crops are, at present, unknown. Apart from steadily increasing evidence, which demonstrates that processes of cross pollination can actually spread herbicidal tolerance to wild plants in a manner similar to a virus. Long term, this means that instead of reducing the amount of chemicals applied in farming, some producers are becoming locked like junkies into chemical slavery, just to defend their perfectly natural crops. What else can be said, except that the striking hubris underlying these commercial decisions is staggering; a sin the spirits are ominously threatening to punish in this life.

Partly, the problem is caused by a global free-for-all to maximise profits for irresponsible shareholders, at the expense of Fertility and Freedom. These transparently wicked designs are further linked to a weakening of our British borders as obvious defences against corporate insanity. Perhaps surprisingly, nationalist politics have proved to hold more substance than merely old-fashioned xenophobia, despite the calculated slanders mouthed by politicians associated with multinational business executives. Accompanied as these improprieties always are by a crippling lack of religious perspective concerning the environment from their side! In which case, we Quagans need to be more mindful of forests and foliage as our other ancestors in a way similar to those who have already passed into Spirit! We know, without question, once there our friends and family will be One with the vast continuum. It can even be said that our loved ones have joined with these archetypal energies in the sacred process of unending creation and thereby deserve our unending respect.

Radical Tradition is our primary weapon in this struggle: although "tradition" appears to summon a series of textual contentions regarding its own ideological status: causing authors themselves to exhibit reservations about an unfettered use of the term. Frithjof Schuon, for instance, shows an interest in these issues when he writes:

> "traditionalism," like "esoterism," [...] has nothing pejorative about it in itself and one might even say that it is less open to argument and a far broader term, in any case, than the latter; in fact, however, [...] it has been associated with an idea which inevitably devalues its meaning, namely the idea of "nostalgia for the past."[1]

Likewise, Schuon is quite correct to distinguish between those aspects of our cultural inheritance, which empower the future and a simple yearning for the theoretical certainties that may, or may not, have characterised a long lost cultural childhood. With this indisputably on the table, Schuon nonetheless goes on to contend "it is quite clearly a crime or a disgrace not to feel this nostalgia," albeit recognising that the power within his first theoretical thrust has already proved extremely successful. Possibly, it was with parallel thoughts in his psyche that Percy Bysshe Shelley once wrote: "if only the past would die at last." As a Romantic poet, in the end, who adhered to the passionate ideologies of revolt in its attempt to strike against the relentless linear flow of "progress" eulogised by the Enlightenment, he recognised the need to recover ancient wisdoms. Noticeably, atop this, each of these men refused to turn their back on the vital significance of Radical Tradition in the captivating sense of a qualitative social current containing spiritual experiences from the past, which both energise and mould the continuity within our affairs. Comparable in perception, that is, to Rene Guénon (1886-1951) in their objection to the type of cultural inertia discrediting future organic advancements. Thusly, it could be argued that Radical Traditionalism and Perennialism are directly synonymous.

Even here, however, critics need to exercise caution. This is because Guénon himself tended to dismiss any application of the epithet "traditionalist" since it implies, in his view, a kind of sentimental attachment to customs that—most of the time—have lost their metaphysical foundation. Yet, on this point the Athonites can stand firm and proud. Without any confusion, the spiritual bedrock of a living Orthodoxy underpins each and every day on blessed Mount Athos and the word "traditionalist" is demonstrably appropriate in this thriving case. So, with the Holy Mountain as our acid test, metaphysical "philosophy" can rightly be designated "perennial" due to its durability, universality, and immutability; it is, as St Augustine (354-430) of Hippo reminds us,

> The letter takes figurative expressions as though they were literal and does not refer the things signified to anything else ... There is a miserable servitude of the spirit in this habit of taking signs for things, so that one is not able to raise the eye of the mind above things that are corporal and created to drink in eternal light.[2]

It remains a shame after agreeing with the Saint on so much, that Augustine doesn't seem interested in admitting this blade cuts two ways. If, on the first swing, Christianity is merely the present dominant form of an ageless perennial Faith, then by the second swing, every other form of this same Faith is equivalently valid as a spiritual path to the Blessed Absolute. The unravelling of these comments, this duly jotted, needs to be explored in a different work.

All that can be said at the moment is we prodigal sons of Anglo-Saxon Orthodoxy are no strangers to Radical Tradition in any of its senses. This is why London can offer few pleasures greater than a church crawl. Most assuredly, following a fortifying glass of Port in a nearby pub, both the art and architecture of untold centuries are gifted to native and tourist alike. Indubitably, most of the historically significant churches are found to be within easy walking distance of the centre; while the City's lesser-known ecclesiastical trove is often secreted in the dingy alleys surrounding it. Furthermore, wisdom awaits a seasoned church crawler in the nascent form of local folklore. To this day, rumours decanted around the weather-vane roofed on the Banqueting Hall in Whitehall, claim it was actually erected by James II (1633-1701) in 1688, so that he could tell at a glance whether the wind was blowing "Protestant or Popish." As a practising Roman Catholic, James knew that many of his own people were praying for a favourable breeze to bring the Protestant Prince (William of Orange), into a Devonshire Harbour and end his reign as Monarch. Of course, there are but few contemporary church crawlers' who can honestly savour the activities of our Folk-Soul through the medium of such minute talismanic devices.

Incontestably, this stated, legend, the clash of dynasties, and a natural struggle for indigenous Faith, additionally fermented in other lands. Put analogously, even at the London Book Fair 2011, in Olympia, such recognisable battles seemed to be silently raging: especially once the presence of Russian Orthodox clergy had gathered to announce the launch of Patriarch Kirill's (born 1946) new, as well as thought-provoking book *Freedom and Responsibility: A Search for Harmony, Personal Rights and Human Dignity* – making such celebrations appear more like the salutation of a Church militantly recapturing its traditional grounds, than an enfeebled call to a largely pointless ecumenism. Observed so, it was nevertheless cheering to see this refreshing revival of inherited custom in these clearly incongruous surroundings.

Upon taking my seat, therefore, as a guest of the organisers, I felt comfortable in the knowledge that Radical Traditionalism stood firm against the so-called "liberal" elite. Directly contrasting, as this philosophy does, life-affirming spiritual values against a heavily mechanised and openly inhuman urban conformity: the latter disguising toxic social views in the guise of communal promotion! Undoubtedly then, as a useful epithet for a variety of allied cultural groups, Radical Traditionalism demands a healthy veneration of our ancestors and the earth, along with a respect for small-scale, native, political organisations. As activists, its supporters personify a positive parochial diversity, whereby the full Company-of-Life is honoured. Perhaps it is only this revolutionary sense of Tradition, which can deliver us, nowadays, from the insidious poisons of global monoculture.

With these thoughts in mind, I listened to the stirring, and suitably brief, words of the Anglican Bishop, Richard Chartres (born 1947) of London, as well as Metropolitan Hilarion (born 1966) of Volokolamsk as they joined forces to extol the virtues in this first-ever English language volume of documents by His Holiness. Still, following the welcome receipt of my complimentary edition, and quickly skimming the dust jacket, confusion began to set in. It was not the inspiring notion of an ethical "multi-polarity"—alluded to in the publisher's blurb—that unsettled my sense of occasion. Neither was it the delightful fact that this official soiree was held amid disconcertingly narrow tables endlessly replenished by very pleasant wines. Instead, it was the complete lack of engagement by non-Orthodox participants, which aroused my literary suspicions.

Returning home, I rushed to read the book so as to decipher these bewildering reactions. A second scan simply reminded me that other places had suffered the consequent burdens of Empire. A third, and more careful perusal, brought me back to ethnic base, whereby the remembrance that we are related (albeit distantly) as kith to the Russians was brought manifestly home – with strikingly familial features, some have contended, in the best of possible psychological terms and the worst. That recollected, on the level of theological discourse, each chapter of Patriarch Kirill's text revealed a cluster of religious concerns only partially experienced by the West. Truly, Patriarch Kirill reflects upon issues recently debated by Pope Benedict (born 1927) himself, including the so-called problem of homosexuality and the dangers of totalitarianism. Still and all, it is difficult to resist interpreting the Patriarchs' grip on ethnic dispute and social disintegration as anything other than stronger than the Pontiff's; coupled as it is by his piercing analysis and a refreshing political realism. Maybe, the tacit problem with this event was that the text in question appeared too far ahead of its theological time for slumbering European congregations.

This is not to say that there are no flaws in his book. His concept of Liberalism, for example, seems to be genuinely clouded by a pragmatic American sense of "anything goes;" rather than a healthy British "hands on" approach to economic structure and social organisation. Moreover, despite Orthodox disputation to the contrary, Liberal authors hold a variety of views on the relationship between Church and State; particularly in Nordic countries. Atop this, the Patriarch seems unaware that discordant pastoral Courts have already deviated in their decisions, showing, therefrom, little commonality of Christian opinion. Arguments surrounding the ordination of women priests act as a case in point; although it is actually the installation of female Bishops, which will disassemble two thousand years of "Catholicity" on a symbolic, not to forget morphological, level. Fashionable issues notwithstanding, the launch of this book heartened an otherwise materialistic and largely fruitless meeting of the business classes, in their shameless profiteering from the ingenious labours of other people. In which case, we need to raise a glass of champagne in celebration of a revived and increasingly empowered Christian Orthodoxy as it takes its rightful place on the world stage: an undertaking that must include Athonite public witness.

All in all, this may be the time for toasting! Towards the end of the day, these mountain men are a blessing to European Culture, East and West. Are they perfect some may ask, well no! To be human is to waver from the bull's eye of perfection on a regular basis. Conceded so, the legacy concretised by the Holy Mount is staggering: motivating some Orthodox commentators to declare that the next twenty years will see an inevitable revival in Church fortunes. Instead of trailing behind topical social discussions concerning business ethics, they argue, Orthodoxy will, once again, capture public ground. And if this proved true, vocations would explode anew, whilst potent re-articulations of Orthodoxy could only reinforce the word "Tradition," at the same time as forging additional dimensions for the Radical Traditionalist "School," above, but still inclusive, of its present activities protecting nationalist folklore. Contrarily, Radical Traditionalists, textually resting on centres of excellence like Mount Athos, would be able to point to "Integral Tradition" as a truly profound application for this type of endeavour. Those so inspired, explaining that Tradition equally consists of eternal principles bearing Divine origin, which call humankind back into a relationship, described by Schuon, as one of "transcendent unity." Against the "modern error" Radical Tradition would come to increasingly propose a "Primordial Tradition," transmitted from the very origin of humanity and partially restored by each genuine founder of a new religion. Supported therein, by such assertions, spiritual as well as literary cultures could recover their prominence in a similar way to any other creative environment. What is more, these demonstrations of intent would uphold literary endeavours as intrinsically valuable for the wider community: forming their own distinct cultural complex, as undertakings both inevitable and necessary to human wellbeing.

Neither are we Britons afraid of radicalism. In itself, the term "radical" is derived from the Latin word *radix* meaning "root," referring, in these cases, to the need for perpetual reorientation towards the root truths of Faith. One way Christians achieve this is to revisit the Sermon on the Mount, or the Gospel of Mark; the earliest of the canonical gospels. Conversely, this reorientation may comprise of Christians rediscovering an anti-imperialist heritage within their own traditions, such as Methodists studying John

Wesley (1703-1791), Baptists remembering the Anabaptists, and Roman Catholics recovering Francis of Assisi (1182-1226) as central to witness. Contemporary Christian activists, for their part, could equally grapple with Capitalist Church assemblies by restoring the core teachings and practices of Christ Jesus; like turning the other cheek and rejecting materialism in the name of Spirit. Radical discipleship, then, appears to call Christians to follow the Will of God through personal action and instance. This may encompass literary productions, that may be seen as either subversive, albeit clearly centred experimentalism – or understood as the joyful recovery of vibrant energies at the base of their inheritance.

With these healing reflections in mind, any serious literary enterprise must encapsulate the dream of transcendence through endlessly suggestive tiers of visionary penmanship. It must, at least in these Islands, give textual expression to this cultural Holy Grail – realising that such a quest, once commenced, cannot be relinquished, whilst simultaneously offering jewel-like glimpses (as our native writing does), of Holy gardens, and paradisial elation. In this respect our literary ancestors, in a manner reminiscent of Swedenborg, Arthurian Knights and Holy Athonites, are not simply our loved ones from the past. Nor are they the originators of humanity in all of our multidimensional effulgence! Rather, our ancestors are also the trees, grass, and flowers surrounding us. They are the hills we walk upon, as well as the archetypal processes, which gave them birth. Undoubtedly, they are coequal to those natural-miracles we look upon from afar, like Mount Athos. This is why our Mountain Queen,[3] like that of the Athonites, is the All-Encompassing-Monas. English novelists say She is the Triple Mother of Destiny! British journalists claim that She is Truth! Those poets who know Her best, however, hint that She is the Light of Magical Reconstruction. Maybe that is why in ages long past, She was seen as the ever-pregnant Mother of Mighty Powers! Nowadays, of course, She is depicted as a Virgin Mother, whose footstool is the Crescent Moon, while Her halo is composed of twelve sacred Stars. So revered, She remains in every epoch, the dazzling Empress of all things living and dead! The very Mother of Salvation, and the Sister of authorship! As such, even the Angels, old British men murmur, approach Her with the utmost caution, because the literature she inspires may turn the world upon its head with sheer adventurous delight, whether it be sung by a mature soul in deepest monastic retreat, depressing urban jungle, or delightful village green.

SELECTED ENDNOTES

1. This quote is taken from Schuon's masterpiece *From the Divine to the Human*, page 8.

2. St Augustine needs to be read with much greater attention than is usually given by doctrinaire divinity students. Maybe particularly when reading his *The Four Books of St Augustine on Christian Doctrine*.

3. The World War 1 poet, Robert Graves (1895-1985), gives a series of references to the Sacred Feminine as a "Mountain Mother" in his remarkable book, *The White Goddess*.

Appendix I.
Listening to Ismail Kadare in English

Some reflections after his talk in London at the French Institute (2006)

THE ALMOST UNBEARABLE SIGNIFICANCE OF CONTEMPORARY Spiritualism often finds relief in twenty-first-century literature. Indeed, during the last couple of years the best poetry and prose have consciously touched the supernal in order to gift otherwise oppressive political regimes with a healing contextual balm. It was therefore a delight when the Albanian author Ismail Kadare (born 1936) recently spoke so openly concerning these complex textual uncertainties. Rather like Desiderius Erasmus (1455-1536) arguing in praise of human folly, Kadare's November interview at the French Institute allowed him to attack militant literary reductionism as a marketing deception. No doubt, Kadare conceded, it was possible to lie concerning his inscrutable inspiration, but this would simply waste everyone's time. After all, poets themselves didn't really understand the process; they just needed to sing. Kadare's disarming candour may, however, offer us an insight into his mystery. It may even partly reveal the symbols as well as the injuries moulding his personal laments.

Let me elaborate this comment. As a master of International Letters, Kadare continues to weave historic events around disenfranchised characters. He seems obsessed by the dialectical position occupied by allegedly liberated men. The obvious vacuity of rekindled vendettas, the alarming distortion of social freedoms, along with the tragic strategy adopted by Albanian youth in retreating from transcendent possibilities – are all set against a guarded optimism borne of ethnic survival. This indirectly suggests that Kadare (the novelist), senses a sterility within imposed literary customs that, sooner or later, become their own antithesis. For him, culture appears analogous to a natural habitat wherein human beings are both nurtured and restricted, yet outside of which they wither. By extension, a foreign literary habitat cannot develop conditions necessary for a previously established group to truly thrive. Kadare's confession to suffering from this problem has always risked ridicule, or a dangerous vulnerability. Moreover, to challenge his Countrymen to wrestle with these issues demands a sensitivity (on their part) that can either inadvertently offend, or invoke national rejection. What else can be said? Kadare may reside in France, but I heard the voice of an Albanian soul singing with pride that evening.

Appendix II.
The Theatre of Genius

Examining the Life and Work of Elchin Afandiyev – A talk by David Parry sponsored by The European Azerbaijan Society and delivered at Pushkin House, London, on 21st November 2011

1. *Thanking Mr Julian Gallant.*
2. *Equally thanking The European Azerbaijan Society as sponsors for this talk.*
3. *Opening comments on Gruntlers' Theatre and Elchin's work.*

Perhaps Gruntlers' Theatre is best described as an experimental Arts group holding regular events across London. Each month we celebrate poetry, drama, music and film with an Internationalist flavour. We are committed to the promotion of groundbreaking Symbolist performance as a means to attract new audiences to radical High Arts. Gruntlers' also embrace the mind-opening aesthetics of Radical Traditionalist consciousness. New talents are encouraged and established talents showcased. Our belief is in Beauty, Truth and Freedom.

4. *Introduction:*

There is nothing more serious than fun. According to Friedrich Schiller playfulness, in all of its manifestations, is as vital to a full expression of the human spirit, as are reason and sense. Perhaps this is why theatricals across the world live in various states of agitation. They seem to struggle with a form of consciousness both afflicted and perfecting in order to empower their humanity. There are occasionally unfortunate repercussions to this deeply metaphysical process, however. Some humourless performers, for example, effect a dour attitude towards their audiences in the mistaken belief that they have discovered the "virtue" of sobriety. Others, having sensed the absurdity behind this (usually Christian) mask, simply become offensive in the hope of distancing themselves from their neighbour's merriment. There are even those who disassemble their mirth to uphold a dramatic gravitas towards the general public. Yet, none of these religious weaklings will ever really achieve true strength, since such gifts are only found through joy. Once this perspective is achieved, our muscular English irony becomes observably akin to sturdy French pasquinade and wiry Azerbaijani satire. Suggesting, in creative terms, that each of these poetic traditions embraced the grim realities of—specific—human inadequacies, as well as their comedic consequences! Every indiscretion, shedding a revealing light on the possibilities of personal Meaning: facts well known to both wandering troubadours in ages past, as well as unveiled Ashik singers, to this day.

5. *Judging Covers:*

Existential reflections of this kind also show us limitations within the Academy itself. A realisation first made by the exponents of DaDa in the last century, when these revolutionaries sliced into the substance of revered cultural structures. Indeed, as mental terrorists, they delighted in reminding us Europeans that the greatest insights our world can offer occur outside the confines of a Common Room. This is why DaDa placed comedic routines on the same level as Roman *vomitoria*,[1] and advanced mathematics, while admitting the latter lacked in genuine burlesque. Sarcasm aside, such views joked at the expense of a rampant hubris increasingly embodied by present day patricians. A merchant caste proving on a yearly basis their bewildering belief that they, in themselves, form living social tapestries with implicit value! To the extent that ironic confession has now become a mode of self-justification for the educated West. Perhaps this is why DaDaism, from its exquisite inception as a counter-cultural movement in Switzerland, around 1916, proved so difficult to categorise. After all, our European middle classes continually legitimise their reflexive self-assessments by frequenting venues involved in the production of Art. No matter how uncomfortable the habitat! Posturings like these, of course, merely propelled exponents of DaDa to reject prevailing aesthetic standards more rapidly. Usual responses, on their part, ranging from open ridicule towards our modern technologically obsessed society to a deliberate cultivation of the ridiculous! Hence, DaDaism held tiny, but influential, political demonstrations, musical gatherings and theatrical performances to promote its deconstructive activities: at the same time publishing a plethora of small-scale, hyper-lucid, literary journals. In other words, direct multi-media attacks on what they felt to be a redundant Classicism: as Hans Arp noted: "revolted by the slaughter of World War I, we devoted ourselves, in Zurich, to the Fine Arts. Well far away, there was artillery thunder, we sang, painted, glued together and wrote poems to our hearts' content." What is more, DaDa's critique of so-called spiritual development in the West held the hidden message that deeper modalities of experience can only be obscured for a short while longer. Evidentially, most Baby-Boomers haven't written the one (theoretical) book within them, and even the worst vulgarian in their ranks knows that random satisfactions, abetted by disordered desires, simply blaspheme the name of Art. At the end of the day, creativity is neither undertaken as an optional element of a pilgrimage into the Absolute, nor as the War Cry of a tepid few, who have already shown their inability to take decisive action when the occasion demanded.

There was, nonetheless, one visible chink in the armour of these robust researchers. Adepts of DaDa tended to assume that natural allies could never to be found among the socially niched: a prejudice, probably originating from an inherited European sense of class position. Kurt Schwitters, as an obvious case, was rejected from certain Brotherhoods because he had a "bourgeois face." However, as the saying goes, one should "never judge a book by its cover" – and in the case of Elchin this proves to be consummately true. Neither public persona nor chosen profession narrate his entire story and Elchin's literary corpus proves, beyond doubt that rebels come in all sizes; from innumerable social backgrounds, with differing sartorial tastes and in various psycho-physical shapes. In which case, it is a real honour to find a previously unsuspected colleague, not to mention an intriguing new friend, in the person of Professor Elchin Ilyas Oglu Afandiyev; a writer little known in English-speaking countries, although a talented and prolific author of global stature. Of course, the reason for this shocking omission is to be found in the sphere of recent international politics, whereby the "Iron Curtain" drawn between the Soviet sphere and Western powers proved to be an almost impenetrable block to cutting edge artistic exchange.

6. *Vocational paths:*

As the author of *Shakespeare: a comedy in ten scenes both serious and tragic* to be staged at the Horse Hospital this coming December, Gruntlers' Theatre has the privilege of introducing Elchin to the London Stage. Thus, a few biographical facts may help to set the scene, as well as familiarise British raconteurs, with his prodigious literary outpourings. Elchin was born on 13th May 1943 in Baku, the capital city of Azerbaijan, into the family of Ilyas Afandiyev, an author of immense literary renown. From early childhood, therefore, Elchin junior found himself immersed in a world of books: local folklore, with its strangely symbolic and extremely suggestive tale-telling clearly becoming an integral part of his intellectual formation; along with the masterpieces of World Literature. By the age of 16, he had published his first story in the *Azerbaijani Youth Magazine.* Unsurprisingly then, Elchin easily completed his secondary education in 1960 and went on to study at Baku State University. Once there, rumour has it that he took to his studies with gusto and graduated with a degree in philology in 1965. This period pointing to Elchin's personal interest in the scientific side of language production! A fascination fully vindicated in 1968, when Elchin completed his postgraduate studies at the Nizami Institute of the Azerbaijan National Academy of Sciences, with the writing of a gigantic 500 page dissertation. Having said that, biographical milestones of this sort only frame the story of such a remarkable writer!

As Elchin matured, a steady stream of novels, stories and critical essays began to flow from his pen, leading scholars and pundits alike to agree that Elchin's oeuvre was highly significant as a contribution to the entire field of contemporary Azerbaijani literature. Astonishingly, the decades have witnessed the composition of more or less a 100 books; the majority of which have been translated into a huge number of languages including: Mandarin, German, English, Turkish, Spanish, Bulgarian, French, Persian, Polish, Georgian, Serbian, Uzbek, Lithuanian, Kazakh and Tajik. Indeed, Elchin's works have sold about 5 million copies worldwide. One of the attractions being that Elchin's unsettling type of storytelling captivated his reader's attention through its innovative sense of Realism, coupled with avant-garde sensibilities, imaginative courage and a strikingly elative quality. In this respect, Elchin towered above his contemporaries and embodied many of the revolutionary aims of the '60s generation; albeit often unrecognised at the time. In terms of Elchin's theatre work, the playwright has constantly demonstrated his ability to delight audiences across large parts of the globe; in huge amount because of an experimental form of stagecraft known as "Elchin Theatre." A subtle methodology, blending both recognisable national traits with a broader sense of the human condition!

7. *Comedic Cavaliers:*

Unswervingly then, in a similar way to our Viking, Cavalier and DaDa ancestors, Elchin's Theatre proclaims a healthy absence of absence. Along with them, he appears to feel a compulsion to burn down lazy assumptions and pull apart bloated, pre-conceived, certainties: the strength of his characters shouting at each audience member that the rainbow flames licking such ruins will light the darkness into a Golden Sunrise. Unquestionably, his skills as a playwright have equally allowed the topography of plot to speak with the tongue of Wrestlers, Theologians and Heraldic Notaries. Maybe specifically when it comes to any analysis concerning the lascivious lives and contradictory careers of "authority figures!" On the level of fellow theatrical, it is clear to see that Elchin repudiates these tedious Roundhead tyrants because of their tacit inability to comprehend uniquely existing Subjects. For Elchin, they ride roughshod over the uncommon. Furthermore, he presents this loose group of petty thugs as slaves to a reification of the material; their constant proclamation, he implies, nothing more than a defiant allegiance to allegedly "objective" truths. To their own contrary, people who merely pave the way into dysfunctional perspectives. Lessons first taught by Henrik Ibsen in his building of meticulous and minimalist stage divisions: between emergent barriers; between the sphere of material objects (as described by the various geometries) and an infinitely transcendent human interiority expressed through relationships; between inanimate things and a necessary essence. Undeniably therefore Elchin Theatre takes Ibsenian recommendations as a means by which dramaturgical procedures may start unfolding, or begin designing, the very meaning of Meaning.

A stance like this is more than comfortable on the English boards, since dissenting poetry is as old as this nation. Far from being a postmodern phenomenon, theatrical dissent began with the enactment of oral poetry in pre-literate periods. Nearly by definition, these performances were bequeathed through the spoken word from player to player and constructed using devices such as repetition, alliteration, rhyme and kennings to facilitate recall. In a sense, the player "composed" the performance from memory, using the version he had learned as a kind of mental template; a technique allowing actors to add their own interpretation to the material and a method still used by directors like Mike Leigh to develop a script.

What happens to European ideas like these when they leave the inherited, as well as practical parameters, of our territories has never ceased to concern me; primarily because libertarian themes give rise to political tendencies similar to narcotic dependence. Indisputably, revolutionary freedoms, deprived of context, become far too strong for unprepared pallets. Put in other phrases, in-built checks and ethical balances are loudly missing. This is mainly why I have started to recognise that the political quibbles of playwrights such as James David Rudkin and Peter Shaffer cannot be understood outside the context of Anglo-Saxon Individualism, and that their literary insights can only make complete sense within the world of Nordic letters. How else may we interpret these lines in Rudkin's play *Penda's Fen* when the central character Stephen says to his classmates:

No, no ... I am nothing pure ... my race is mixed, my sex is mixed, I am woman and man, light with darkness, nothing pure ... I am mud and flame.

So stated, these thoughts are strongly reminiscent of the character "Slash 13," in Elchin's "Shakespeare" when this other misfit says:

Once again, it's impossible because it's impossible. Get out of this straightjacket of absolutism! [...] Why don't you liberate your thinking, your hopes, imagination and fantasies? Why do you build this rigid mould and squash your dreams into it, turning them into nothing? Why construct this meaningless border between (possible) and (impossible), condemning yourselves to eternal suffering? Can't you live without suffering and sorrow? Why? What's the reason?

If we Englishmen, thenceforth, are looking for previously unsuspected cousins of theatrical Soul, we have found them in the land of lyrical fire.

8. *Concluding Comments*

Like most poets and players, William Shakespeare, the man, seems to have preferred speaking through his characters. Unnerving perhaps to contemporary audiences, this is, nevertheless, one of the explanations as to why he chose the melancholy Jaques in his play *As You Like It* to mouth the immortal words, "All the world's a stage" (2/7): an opinion which should never be taken on a surface level. Theatre, when all said and done, is a qualitative and creative kind of calculation! To write and perform poetry, or explained differently, to examine our aesthetic faculty from the inside, is measure-taking in the strictest sense of the phrase, but with potentially unending parameters. It is that joyful science by which a performer first intuits the dimensions of personal self-worth and eventually recognises the shared humanity of all those in his or her audience. Ever mindful as they are that to some extent we are all players of varying degree. This is why, for Schiller, play provided such a solid foundation for our understanding of the Beautiful, True and Good. Fun, he continually mused, literally mediates between conflicting impulses in human nature and raises our consciousness to unexpected glories. A noble thought. Without this elative tenet to Schiller's argument, moreover, the truly magical potencies of performance as an active literary Form run the risk of being hopelessly confused, or reduced to undemanding entertainment. And there's the rub! Our forthcoming DaDa interpretation of Elchin's "Shakespeare" is not only a way to introduce an ingenious Azeri playwright to British audiences, but also a missile fired against entire industries determined to sacrifice poetry to ideological redundancy; a substantive sin blurring metaphysical categories and eventually denuding our imaginative powers.

SELECTED ENDNOTE

1. A vomitorium was a passage situated either behind, or below, a tier of seats in an amphitheatre or stadium, through which big crowds can exit rapidly at the end of a performance. They can also be pathways for actors to enter and leave the stage. As a point of interest, the Latin word *vomitorium* derives from the verb *vomere,* or perhaps *vomitum,* meaning "to spew forth."

Appendix III.
Pagans

Reviewing the Television Series written and presented by Richard Rudgley on Channel Four, 2004

H IPPIES ARE THE CHILDREN OF JEAN JACQUES ROUSSEAU (1712-1778). I have often thought that as a counter-cultural "current," they may be traced back way before the sixties through the early days of the New Thought Movement, to certain anxiety-related Romantic reactions against the excesses of the Enlightenment. They were obsessed with issues surrounding higher states of consciousness, organic food and a free sexuality. Their movement was, therefore, destructive, as it stretched above the "merely" rational before its appointed cultural time. With this in mind, there is a distinct danger that Channel Four's recent documentary series *Pagans* (written and presented by Richard Rudgley), will be identified as a critique of modern social fashion instead of a potential revolution in contemporary spirituality.

From the opening credits, Rudgley sidesteps accepted notions of received history to show his audience that influences from the ancient pagan world never really diminished. He explains how the endless experimentation of early Alchemists actually did pull mineral swords from stones and explores the Astro-Theology of tribal magicians in their seasonal calculations. In homage to their ecological wisdom, one episode even shows him wearing a mysterious golden hat, which seems to have been worn by one of these wizards as a sign of authority over natural processes.

Any theology that rests on reason rather than revelation is, of course, a form of natural religion. In other words, a type of esoteric astronomy, which searches the stars to find the effects and purposes of an otherwise unknowable First Cause. Theologically insightful scholars would probably claim that the foundation of all intellectual religions, ancient as well as Modern movements, have this same source. They are also likely to contend that the symbolic scriptures of sophisticated cultures were inspired by the geometrical movements of these heavenly giants. Arguably, even the Revelation of St John the Divine confirms this opinion. After all, the strange personages populating his Apocalypse are discernible in any celestial atlas; a position demonstrated by the antipodean Speculative Freemason, Henry Melville, whose fascinating book *Veritas* (1874), details the entire sacerdotal system of stellar bodies and their suggested alignments with occult "inner constellations" mentioned in Medieval Hermetic manuscripts.

Rudgley contextualises these theories, suggesting that the principles behind this psycho-organic totality were laid down by prehistoric pagan astrologers. He adds that later initiates were rarely given access to their fundamental findings, although every now and again astrological records offered tantalising hints concerning the nature of the cosmos. This is especially curious when we recall that some modern researchers say only specific planets and stars were important to our forefathers, who appear to have regarded the universe as a gigantic living organism; a vast sustaining placenta through which the Divine Self-concept incarnated. It would further imply that human beings are not simply constituent parts of the Universe, but instead the final summarising product of evolution.

These are complex concepts, which Rudgley expounds with considerable Saviour Faire. As a born communicator, he sees no necessary divide between scholarship and informed public opinion – provided the expert in question is in command of his or her field. He easily meets this criterion himself, due to an impeccable academic background, coupled with an obvious fascination with the material. Indeed, one of his skills as a presenter is to break down abstract theoretical propositions and then describe the exposed fragments with a consummate professional enthusiasm – a talent not always shared by those he interviewed.

This became increasingly evident when watching the second program in the series. Without much assistance, Rudgley guides his viewers through the legacy of Arthurian legend; a topic which unexpectedly caught my attention due to its exegesis of the relation between poetry and physical violence. As a poet myself fascinated with the perennial truths of destruction, conflict and the grotesque, I found this episode gripping. From the outset, he details the development of folk tales around tribal warriors, who constantly perfected formidable martial skills to defend their kith and kin. Enlarging his theme, Rudgley then maps their world of highly codified chivalry, where young male muscle and bone was energetically tested by each of these "knights" against the other for the sheer joy of it. Fascinatingly, such openly erotised rutting rarely degenerated into a free-for-all, because their personal honour prevented them from sinking into a brutish battery. Differences were, nevertheless, inevitable and had to be settled without repression or lasting scars, which is why their ritualised wrestling was never expressed thoughtlessly just for the sake of temporary cathartic relief, but channelled artfully; an aesthetic blend that flowered into martial Epics as well as military Sagas.

In the final analysis, Rudgley's documentary series is a provocative and extraordinarily rich philosophical assertion. Ironically, however, its very opulence may give rise to a variety of conflicting interpretations. His work could easily be seen as a reflexive academic comment, a personal vision, or even a religious prophecy trapped in the distorting lens of cultural relativism. Rudgley, that said, intends these programs to be about the present, not the past. His understated ideological challenge to so-called western religious orthodoxy is found in a tacit defence of humanity's need to participate abstractedly with the environmental realities underlying all metaphysical superstructures, which is why Rudgley seems to feel that "Christian civilisation" is both totalitarian in its ethical imperatives and consciously unreflective about its origins. A challenge demanding considerable reflection.

Appendix IV.
Oranges and Urban Lemons

P ERHAPS LIFE IN LONDON NEVER REALLY CHANGES. A perception which may explain why British kids still sing the nursery rhyme "Oranges and Lemons" about growing up in this Capital of contrasts. They are ageless lyrics, after all, which accurately describe the cultural realities behind life in our premiere city. Unlike, Paris, the "City of Light" or Rome, the "Eternal City," "Old London Town" is a place where the sweet and sour experiences of Shakespearean theatre, spiteful gossip, commerce, vested interest, poetry, world music, skulduggery, and intrusive public surveillance, mix together as commonplace. It is a global location where differing classes, as well as a multiplicity of planetary migrants, work, interact, shop, and travel, on a daily basis. Nothing new there, of course, except that in a city where everyone exists on top of each other, the affluent go home to delightful "Greater London" residences, whereas the poor congregate within lemony "Inner City" tower blocks. Reflecting, even in these modern times, the words of this rhyme when it continues, "When will you pay me, say the bells of Old Bailey?" – testifying to rampant social inequality both then and now as characteristic of this metropolis. Indeed, the bells of "Old Bailey" continue to sound around this central criminal court for broker and bankrupt alike. Nevertheless, the sweeter bells of Shoreditch, somewhat reassuringly, chime their reply that London remains a place where fortunes can be made, dreams realised, and high-fashion toffs rub shoulders with ladies clad in department store remainders.

Visiting this city as a tourist, therefore, is never a predictable experience. Although, anyone arriving here for the first time will be overwhelmed by the art and architecture of untold centuries. Partially, collected, it must be stressed, because our burgeoning megacity was founded before England was born as a nation. Indeed, the original Roman settlement called "Londinium" only gradually housed Anglo-Saxon invaders under the new name of "Lundenwic" which, in due time, evolved into the English Port of London. Unsurprisingly then, international trade was always the real secret of its wealth. And as such, this city started to wear many masks simultaneously: as the political centre of a traditionally multi-ethnic country, a University town for young scholars, the home of liverymen and historical ghosts, not to mention the location for our Mother of Parliaments. Hence, those Princes of the Anglican Church, the Bishop of London and the Archbishop of Canterbury (who abides in Lambeth Palace on the river Thames), endlessly play an essential part in weaving these disparate threads of civic life together. Undoubtedly, by leading spectacular seasonal rituals, they reinforce a sense of shared identity among otherwise antagonistic groups. Each inherited ceremony also adding distinctive indigenous colour to our native affairs. For example, the Queen's Official Birthday Parade instantly comes to mind in this respect, along with Lord Mayors Show, as two of the best-known annual events of this kind. Without question, the latter dating back to the 16th century – and is held to this day as a celebration surrounding the annual appointment of a new Right Honourable Lord Mayor for the City of London Corporation. Certainly, travellers miss these gilded pageants at their peril.

Yet history isn't the single most important facet of living in the contemporary "smoke" as some in the provinces call our grand municipality. Truly, the glorious past is everywhere here; in royal castles, Dickensian lanes, and bronze statues guarding Big Ben. One of the most striking being that of an Iceni warrior-Queen (Boudica) whose freewheeling war chariot perpetually guards Parliament against its foes. Equal to all of this, however—as the City Fathers will quickly remind merchants—is our current pride of place in First World society. Demonstrated, they will attest, through popular tourist attractions such as the London Eye, the Tate Modern Gallery, and packed concert halls in the renowned Barbican Centre. Additionally, the treasured recipes of nearly every nation may be tasted along our streets. Pointing to the fact that more than 300 languages are spoken within London's boundaries, allowing multiculture to express its worst, as well as its best, features. So confessed, for every bewilderingly obscure protest march, or localised riot, there is an international festival, or scientific exhibition, on the South Bank. Complimentarily, the world's second largest street party, known as the Notting Hill Carnival, is held during the late August Bank Holiday each year: bringing Caribbean spice to otherwise bland, urban, streets. Assuredly, natives need to recollect that valued, international, friendships, are strengthened through remembered links with Commonwealth colleagues from the past, while we embrace new friends for our future prosperity. In this sense, the staging of "Citizens of Hell," a political satire by the Azerbaijani author Elchin Afendiyev, at the Theatro Technis in Camden during the summer of 2013, provided another bond strengthening London's ties with previously unsuspected brothers from the Land of Fire.

All of this bodes well for the foreseeable years ahead and may even prove, as far as these types of proof are possible, the well-known comment once penned by Dr Samuel Johnson that "When a man is tired of London, he is tired of life; for there is in London all that life can afford." The "Freudian" slip of "afford" being balanced by William Blake's retort "Hell is a city much like London." Either way, this is a city which coequally contains four World Heritage Sites: the Tower of London; Kew Gardens; the Palace of Westminster, and Westminster Abbey; along with the historic settlement of Greenwich (in which the Royal Observatory marks the Prime Meridian, 0° longitude, and GMT), Piccadilly Circus, St Paul's Cathedral, Tower Bridge, Trafalgar Square, and the Shard. All intermingling with museums, the British Library, the National Portrait Gallery, endless sporting events, avant-garde Fringe, and 40 West End theatres. Thus, we citizens need to be just as mindful of the pleasant "oranges" we can gift to those guests returning for a less touristic, but more enjoyable, second, third, or forth, visit, as any potential lemons.

Reduced Bibliography

Afandiyev, E., 2012. *My Favourite Madman and Other Plays*. Baku: Aspoligraf.

Aitmatov, C., 1969. *Tales of the Mountains and the Steppes*. Moscow: Progress Publishers.

Daiches, D., 1968. *A Critical History of English Literature: From the Beginnings to the Sixteenth Century*. Revised ed. London: Secker and Warburg.

Dalrymple, W., 1997. *From the Holy Mountain: A Journey Among the Christians of the Middle East*. London: HarperCollins.

Loch, S., 1957. *Athos: The Holy Mountain*. New York: Thomas Nelson & Sons.

Neville, R. C., 1992. *The Highroad Around Modernismm*. Albany: State University of New York Press.

Powys, J. C., 1996. *A Glastonbury Romance*. New York: The Overlook Press.

Robert, G., 1961. *The White Goddess: A Historical Grammar of Poetic Myth*. London: Faber and Faber.

Schuon, F., 1982. *From the Divine to the Human: Survey of Metaphsis and Epistemology*. Bloomington, IN: World Wisdom Books.

Sutherland, S., 1984. *God, Jesus and Belief*. New York: Blackwell.

Vitaliiev, V., 2008. *Passport to Enclavia, Travels in Search of a European Identity*. London: Reportage Press.